In the Name of Allah, The Most Compassionate, The Most Merciful

THE ISLAM GUIDE

An insight into the faith, history and civilisation

This book was designed and produced by
Exhibition Islam
&
Rashida Begum Alam

EXHIBITION
ISLAM

AN EXHIBITION ISLAM BOOK

Published by Exhibition Islam in 2007.
Copyright © 2007 Exhibition Islam.

ISBN 978-0-9555238-1-6

We would like to request that this book is treated with utmost care and respect due to the presence of Quranic verses in Arabic which Muslims believe to be the Word of Allah, The Most High.

Front cover images (from top left to bottom right):
The Kaaba, Makkah; Mosque of the Prophet Muhammad (ﷺ), Madinah; The Aqsa Mosque, Jerusalem; The 'Dome of the Rock', Jerusalem; The Quba Mosque, Madinah; *Al-Fatihah,* opening chapter from an 18th century Quran; Arabic calligraphy of the word 'Allah'; A 17th century brass astrolabe; A 12th century world map by Al-Idrisi; The Sun rising over the Earth; Waterfall scene, Havasupai Indian Reservation, Grand Canyon, Arizona; Globe of fine dandelion filaments; Brass screen covering the grave of the Prophet Muhammad (ﷺ); A water lily in full bloom; The Andromeda Galaxy.

Opposite Page:
Great dome of the Wilayah Persekutuan Mosque in Kuala Lumpur, Malaysia.

Back cover:
Intricate geometric design work combined with alternating dark and light stones forms the façade over one of the entrances to the Great Mosque of Cordoba, Spain. The 10th century mosque was the most magnificent of more than 1,000 mosques in the city and was at one time the second largest mosque in the Muslim world.

EXHIBITION
ISLAM
www.exhibitionislam.com

Silhouette of Masjid Putrajaya in Malaysia at sunset.

Magnificent opening page of the text of the Noble Quran
(19th century Ottoman, Exhibition Islam collection).

Contents

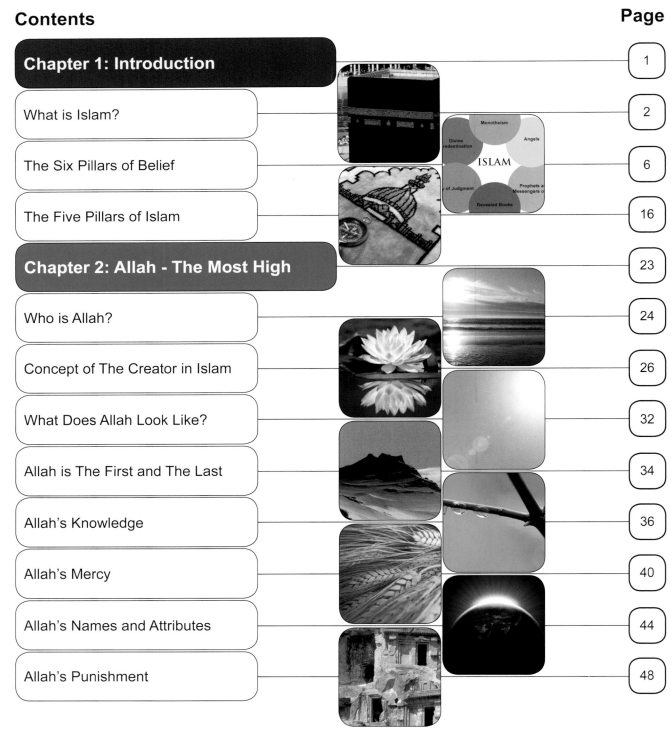

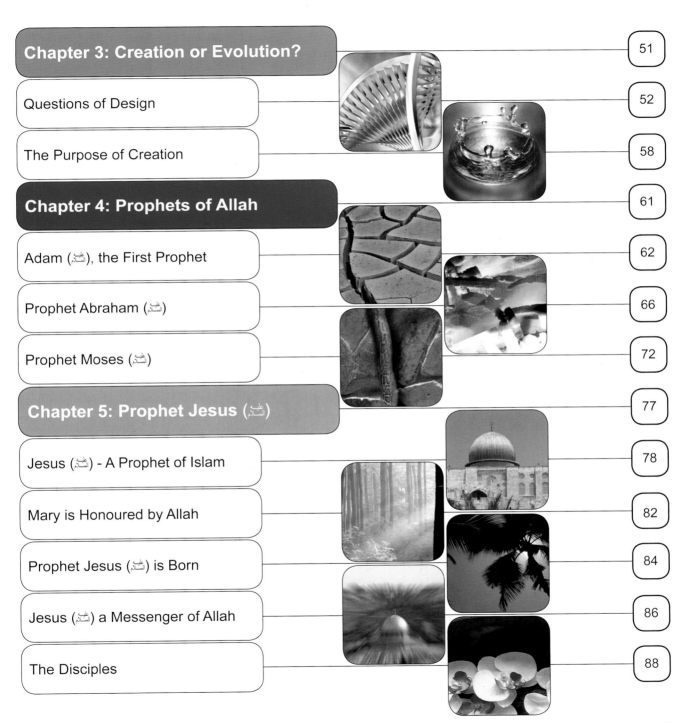

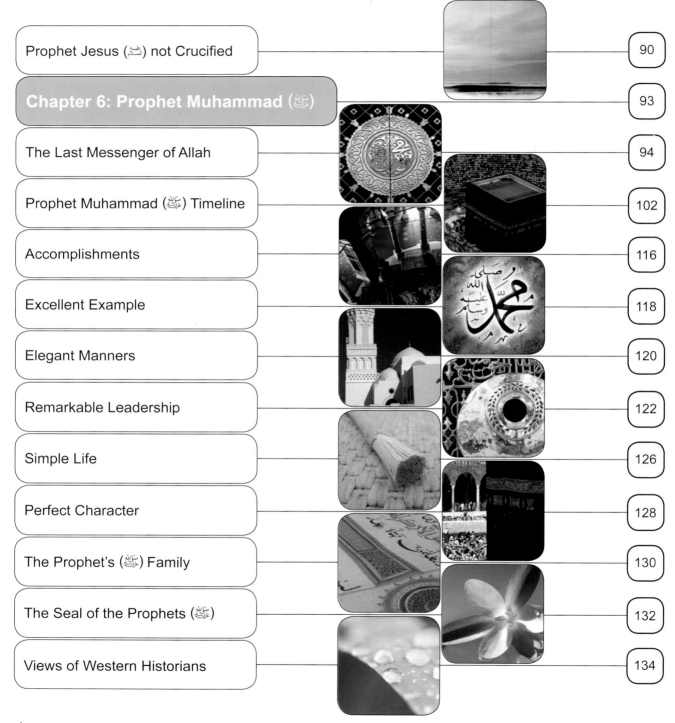

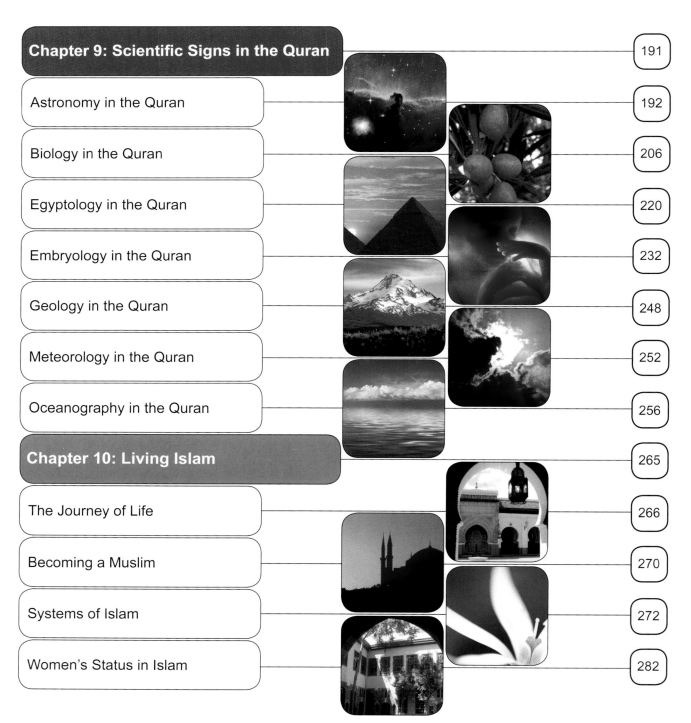

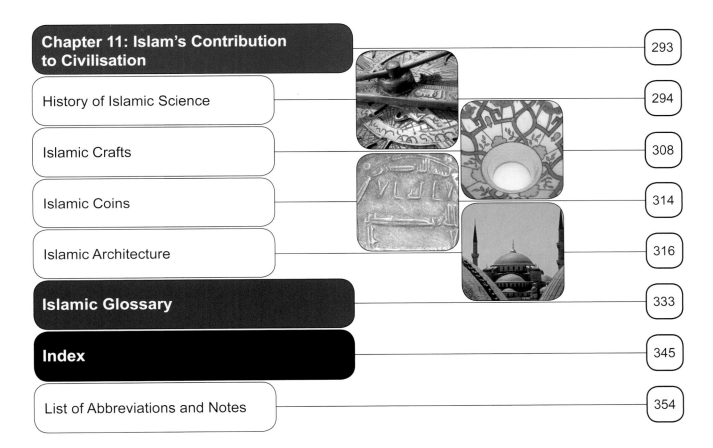
Following page: Spectacular waterfall scene, Havasupai Indian Reservation, Grand Canyon, Arizona. Preservation of the environment is very important in Islam as all of the component parts of nature are said to actively praise Allah in their continuous existence and movement. This is derived from the belief that all of creation belongs to Allah alone, and not to man.

Chapter 1
Introduction

What is Islam?

The history of Islamic civilisation stretches from the 7th century to our present day and encompasses a vast area spread over several continents from Spain to Indonesia and North Africa to China. There are over 1.3 billion Muslims in the world today, which equates to approximately a fifth of the world's population. So Islam is a truly global faith and not confined to the East or the West, or a particular nation, colour, race or tribe.

Definition of Islam

By definition 'Islam' (an Arabic word) literally means 'surrender' or 'submission'. Islam is not named after a tribe of people or an individual nor is it a name chosen by a human being. The followers of Islam, called 'Muslims', believe that it was divinely revealed by God (in Arabic, Allah).

A Complete Way of Life

Islam is regarded as more than just a religion, rather it is a total system of life. From the purification of the soul and the spirituality of personal worship to the establishment of governance and implementation of state politics, Islam provides guidance to the follower at every level. Because of its comprehensive nature, it is not surprising that Islam has become the fastest growing religion in the world.

In accordance with the principles of Islam, Muslims are directed to work towards the establishment of a just social order that totally reflects the guidance of Allah. It is not permitted for Muslims to worship anyone or anything else besides Almighty Allah, in terms of belief, speech and actions. By completely accepting and submitting to the teachings and guidance of Allah, Muslims are expected to live in peace and harmony amongst themselves, with other people and with the environment. Life is regarded as a temporary state and all Muslims throughout their lives aim to live by the commandments of Allah, with the eventual hope of entering Paradise in the next life.

The *Kaaba* (also known as *al-Kaaba al-Musharafah, al-Bait ul Ateeq* and *al-Bait ul Haram*) is the most sacred site in Islam and is located inside the mosque known as the Sacred Mosque (*Masjid-al-Haram*) in Makkah, Arabia. The *Kaaba* (literally meaning 'cube' in Arabic) is at the very heart of the Islamic world and represents the physical axis and the focal point toward which, Muslims all over the world pray five times a day. According to Islamic tradition, the *Kaaba* was first built by Prophet Adam (ﷺ). Generations later it was rebuilt by Prophet Abraham (ﷺ) and his son Prophet Ishmael (ﷺ).

Following pages: Spectacular view from one of the minarets of the Sacred Mosque in Makkah as nearly a million worshippers stand for the night-time prayer.

The Six Pillars of Belief

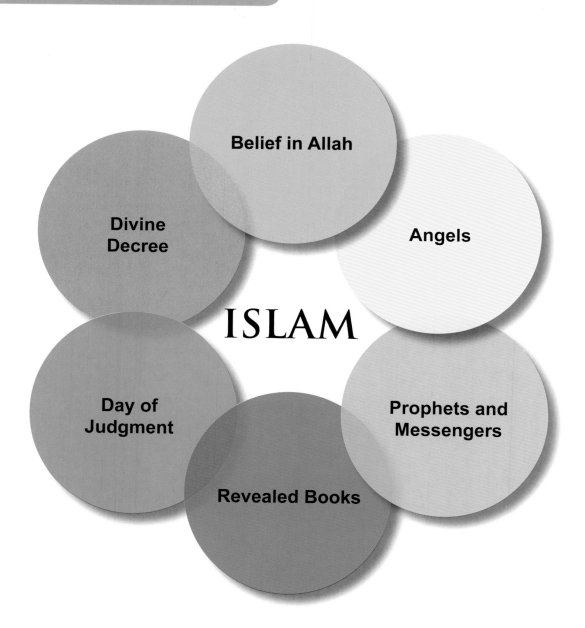

Belief in Allah

Angels

Divine Decree

ISLAM

Day of Judgment

Prophets and Messengers

Revealed Books

Monotheism (known as *Tawheed* in Arabic) is the belief in a single, universal and all-knowing supreme being, namely Allah. Muslims believe that man has been created for a noble and great purpose; so that he may worship Allah alone without any partner. This forms the first pillar of Islamic belief (*Eemaan*) and is the single most important concept in Islam. For Muslims, no act of worship or devotion has any meaning or value if the concept of monotheism is in any way compromised.

Monotheism is central to all of the Abrahamic religions and it is the first of the Ten Commandments. It is sometimes believed that Muslims worship a different Creator to the Jews and Christians. However, the pure monotheism of Islam calls all people to the worship of the Creator of Noah, Abraham, Moses, Jesus and all of the other Prophets (peace be upon them all).

Belief in Allah

The second pillar of belief is the firm conviction that Allah has created an unseen realm that includes angels and *Jinn*. Angels are beings of a different nature from human beings. Man is described in the Quran as being created from clay or earth, whereas the angels have been created from light. *Jinn*, on the other hand, are said to have been created from 'smokeless fire' and like humans they have free will and can submit to or openly defy Allah. Angels, however, are created in such a way that they always obey their Lord and never go against Divine Commands. They are not considered intermediaries between Allah and humans.

Angels carry out Allah's commandments in nature and the universe. What we usually call the 'forces of nature' become active because of the presence of angels behind them. Muslims also believe that angels watch over mankind and that every individual has them as constant companions. They keep a record of everyone's good and bad deeds and not a word is uttered without it being registered by them. Gabriel (or *Jibra'il* in Arabic) is the Archangel responsible for communicating Allah's messages to His chosen Prophets.

The Angels

The third pillar is the belief in Prophets and Messengers who were sent by Allah to humanity in order to return people to monotheism. A Messenger is a man sent by Allah with a new message, whereas a Prophet of Allah is a man who was sent to call to a message that was previously given to a Messenger. Hence, every Messenger was a Prophet but not every Prophet was a Messenger.

Muslims hold that the first of the Prophets of Allah, was Adam, who was followed by a long line of Prophets including Noah, Abraham, Ishmael, Isaac, Jacob, David, Moses and Jesus (peace be upon them all). Prophet Muhammad (may the peace and blessings of Allah be upon him, ﷺ) is regarded as the last of the Prophets and Messengers sent by Allah, hence his title *Seal of the Prophets*.

All of the Prophets and Messengers led righteous lives and served as practical examples of how to submit to Allah's Will and guided people to the path of salvation. They were all created human beings and none share in any part of Allah's divinity.

Prophets & Messengers

The fourth cornerstone of Islamic belief is that Allah revealed books to some of His Prophets. The Quran is Allah's final message to all of mankind and was revealed to Prophet Muhammad (ﷺ) by the Archangel Gabriel. The Quran is regarded as the direct word of Allah and is protected by Him from any corruption or distortion.

The Quran mentions a number of other scriptures that were revealed to the previous Prophets, namely:

The original *Scrolls* as revealed to Prophet Abraham (peace be upon him, ﷺ).

The original *Torah* as revealed to Prophet Moses (ﷺ).

The original *Psalms* as revealed to Prophet David (ﷺ).

The original *Gospel* as revealed to Prophet Jesus (ﷺ).

Muslims do not consider the scriptures revealed before the Quran, presently in circulation, as being accurate representations of their original revealed forms.

Revealed Books

Muslims regard the present life of this world as a test and preparation for the next realm of existence. On the *Day of Judgment*, this world will come to an end and all of mankind from the first to the last will be resurrected and gathered together before Allah for judgment. The *Day of Judgment* is also known by a variety of other names: the *Day of Accounting*, the *Day of Resurrection*, the *Day of Gathering* and the *Final Standing*.

Muslims consider that all human beings will ultimately be judged by Allah according to their beliefs and actions. In judging human beings, Almighty Allah will be both Merciful and Just and people will only be judged according to their capabilities. Islam teaches that life is a test wherein a sincere belief in the life of the Hereafter is the key to leading a well-balanced and moral life.

The *Day of Judgment* will mark the beginning of a life that will never end. Those people who died as believers and acted upon their belief will be rewarded on that day and will be admitted to Paradise forever.

Day of Judgment

The belief in divine decree is the sixth pillar of faith and includes belief in four things:

1) Allah knows everything that has happened in the past and what will happen in the future.

2) Allah has recorded all that has happened and all that will ever happen.

3) Whatever Allah wills to happen, happens and whatever He does not decree to happen, can never happen.

4) Allah is the Creator of everything and there is no Creator besides Him.

Belief in divine decree does not mean that human beings do not have free will. Rather, Muslims believe that Allah has given human beings the ability to choose between right and wrong. We have been given this gift, but it comes with a heavy responsibility. On the Day of Judgment, we will be held accountable for our use of this gift.

Divine Decree

The city of Madinah in Arabia was home to the first Islamic state and is the second most sacred city of Islam, after Makkah. Its importance as a religious site derives from the presence there of *Masjid al-Nabawi* or the Mosque of the Blessed Prophet Muhammad (ﷺ). The grave of Prophet Muhammad (ﷺ) lies adjacent to the mosque under the green dome pictured above. The first mosque of Islam (*Masjid Quba*) is also located near Madinah. The city of Madinah served as the capital of the Islamic world until the year 661, after which the capital was moved to Damascus.

A masterpiece of architecture, the magnificent Umayyad mosque in Damascus. Built in the 8th century, it remains to this day one of the great symbols of Islamic civilisation.

The Five Pillars of Islam

The five pillars of Islam provide the framework for the Muslim way of life. These are, the declaration of faith, five daily prayers, giving charity, fasting during the month of Ramadan and the pilgrimage to Makkah once in a lifetime.

The Declaration of Faith (*Shahaadah*)

The first pillar is the declaration of faith in Islamic Monotheism that is, to bear witness to the following, 'There is none worthy of worship except Allah and Muhammad is the messenger of Allah'. In Arabic this simple formula is referred to as the *Shahaadah*.

For Muslims, the only purpose in life is to serve and obey Allah and to do this believers must firstly announce the *Shahaadah*. This statement contains a negation followed by an affirmation. In order to believe in and worship Allah, a Muslim is first required to reject the actions and beliefs that contradict or transgress the Rights of Allah. This is achieved through following the teachings and practices of the Last Prophet Muhammad (ﷺ). Hence, the *Shahaadah* forms the most important pillar of Islam and needs to be said with conviction and understanding in order for someone to become a Muslim.

"Laa ilaaha illal-lah Muhammad-ur Rasoolullah"

"There is none worthy of worship except Allah and Muhammad is the messenger of Allah"

Prayer (*Salah*)

Salah is the name for the prayers that are performed five times a day and are a direct link between the worshipper and Allah. There are no intermediaries between Allah and the worshipper. There is no hierarchical authority in Islam such as priests. Prayers are led by a learned person who knows the Quran and is generally chosen by the congregation.

The *Adhaan* is the Islamic call to prayer and is recited aloud by a person called the *Muedhin*. The call is usually made from a minaret of a mosque five times a day summoning the faithful to mandatory (*Fard*) prayers. There is also a second call known as *Iqaama* that summons Muslims to line up for the beginning of the congregational prayers.

Prayers are performed at dawn (*Fajr*), midday (*Dhuhr*), late afternoon (*Asr*), sunset (*Maghrib*) and nightfall (*Ishaa*) and thus determine the rhythm of the entire day. In fact, visitors to the Muslim world are quite often struck by the centrality of prayers in daily life. The five prescribed prayers contain verses from the Quran and are recited in Arabic. However, personal supplications can be offered in one's own language and at any time. Although it is preferable to worship together in a mosque, a Muslim may pray almost anywhere.

Above right: Muslims must perform the obligatory prayers facing towards the direction of the *Kaaba* in Makkah. A compass usually helps to locate the direction.

Middle: Worshippers bow during the afternoon prayer in the grounds of the *al-Aqsa* Mosque in Jerusalem. The 'Dome of the Rock' can be seen in the background.

Below: The *Kaaba* is located at the centre of the multi-level Sacred Mosque in Makkah. Worshippers stand in concentric circles facing the *Kaaba* during prayer times.

Charity (Zakah)

An important principle of Islam is that everything belongs to Allah and wealth is held by human beings in trust. The word *Zakah* means both 'purification' and 'growth' and forms the third pillar of Islam. Possessions are purified by setting aside a proportion for those in need and for society in general. Like the pruning of plants, this cutting back balances and encourages new growth. Each Muslim must calculate his or her own *Zakah* individually. This involves the annual payment of a fortieth of one's capital, excluding such items as primary residence and transport.

An individual may also give as much as he or she pleases as *Sadaqah*. Although this word can be translated as 'voluntary charity' it has a wider meaning as shown by the following sayings. Prophet Muhammad (ﷺ) said: "*Charity is a necessity for every Muslim.*" He was asked: "What if a person has nothing?" Prophet Muhammad (ﷺ) replied: "*He should work with his own hands for his benefit and then give something out of such earnings in charity.*" The Companions of Prophet Muhammad (ﷺ) asked: "What if he is not able to work?" The Prophet Muhammad (ﷺ) said: "*He should help the poor and needy.*" The Companions further asked: "What if he cannot do even that?" The Prophet Muhammad (ﷺ) said: "*He should urge others to do good.*" The Companions said: "What if he lacks that also?" Prophet Muhammad (ﷺ) said: "*He should check himself from doing evil. That is also an act of charity.*" In another narration, a man asked Prophet Muhammad (ﷺ): "What (deeds) of Islam is good?" Prophet Muhammad (ﷺ) replied, '*To feed (the poor) and greet those whom you know and those whom you do not know.*" (Recorded in Saheeh Bukhari).

Fasting (*Saum*)

Every year during the 9th month of the Islamic lunar calendar (*Ramadan*), all Muslims must fast from dawn until sundown, abstaining from food, drink and sexual relations. Those who are sick, elderly, or on a journey and women who are menstruating, pregnant or nursing, are permitted to break the fast and make up an equal number of days later in the year if they are healthy and able. Children begin to fast (and to observe prayers) from puberty although many start earlier. The end of *Ramadan* is marked by the great *Eid al Fitr* celebration. Although fasting is beneficial to health, it is mainly a method of self-purification and self-restraint. By cutting oneself off from worldly comforts, even for a short time, a fasting person focuses on his or her purpose in life by constantly worshipping and being aware of the presence of the Creator, Allah.

"The month of Ramadan in which was revealed the Quran, a guidance for mankind, and clear proofs of the guidance, and the Criterion (of right and wrong). And whoever sights (the moon), let him fast the month"

(Quran, The Heifer 2:185)

Above right: As the Sun begins to set it creates a spectacular display. Muslims must break their fast immediately after sundown.

Middle: Following the practice (*Sunnah*) of Prophet Muhammad (ﷺ), Muslims break the fast with an odd number of dates. Dates have been a staple food of the Middle East for thousands of years. They are believed to have originated around the Persian Gulf and have been cultivated in ancient times from Mesopotamia to prehistoric Egypt, possibly as early as 6000 BCE.

Below: The Islamic calendar is based on lunar months which means that, celebrations, festivals and important occasions such as Ramadan do not remain fixed in a particular season, but travel through the seasons.

Pilgrimage (*Hajj*)

The annual pilgrimage to Makkah (*Hajj*) represents the fifth pillar of Islam. It is an obligation only for those who are physically and financially able to do so. In a show of true 'multi-culturalism' over two million people travel to Makkah each year from every corner of the globe providing, a unique opportunity for people of different nations, languages, colour and race to meet one another. The annual *Hajj* begins in the twelfth month (*Dhul Hijjah*) of the Islamic year. Pilgrims wear simple garments that strip away distinctions of class and culture, so that all stand equal before Allah. The rites of the *Hajj* which are of Abrahamic origin include, going around the *Kaaba* seven times and walking seven times between the hills of *Safa* and *Marwa*. The pilgrims will also stand together on the wide plains of *Arafat* outside Makkah and join in prayer for Allah's forgiveness in what is regarded as a prelude to the Day of Judgment. The close of the *Hajj* is marked by a festival, *Eid al Adha*, which is celebrated in Muslim communities everywhere with prayers and giving to the poor and needy.

Above right: Satellite image of the sacred land in which Makkah and Madinah are located. Known as the *Hijaz*, it is a narrow tract of land about 875 miles long in the western region of the Arabian peninsula, east of the Red Sea. Makkah is located in the Sirat Mountains of central Arabia and 45 miles inland from the Red Sea port of Jeddah. The Sirat Mountains consist of volcanic peaks and natural depressions creating a stark and rugged environment dominated by intense sunlight and little rain fall.

Middle: Close up view of the door of the *Kaaba*. The entire *Kaaba* is draped with a black silk cloth called the *Kiswah*, upon which passages from the Noble Quran are embroidered in gold.

Below: Entering the Sacred Mosque in Makkah, pilgrims walk seven times around the *Kaaba* in an anti-clockwise direction; this ritual is called *Tawaaf*.

Masjid al-Aqsa or the 'farthest mosque' (also known as *al-Masjid al-Aqsa, Baitul Maqdis* or *Haram-al-Sharif* - The Noble Sanctuary) in Jerusalem represents Islam's third most holiest site. It stands south of the 'Dome of the Rock' with which it forms an inseparable part. As well as being the first *Qibla* (the direction Muslims face during prayer) *Masjid al-Aqsa* represents one of only three mosques where Muslims are recommended to undertake a journey for the sole purpose of praying. The other two recommended places to pray are at the Sacred Mosque in Makkah with the *Kaaba* at its centre and Prophet Muhammad's (ﷺ) Mosque in Madinah. The virtues of praying in *Masjid al-Aqsa* are multiplied by one thousand times. The numerous virtues of *Masjid al-Aqsa* has made it central to Muslims all over the world. The love and affection for *Masjid al-Aqsa* transcends all national boundaries, languages and colour. Muslims all over the globe through the teachings of Islam hold it dear and venerate it.

Following page: Quranic verse with a background of wild grass silhouetted against a golden sunset.

21

"And to Allah belongs the unseen (secrets) of the heavens and the earth and to Him is the return of all affairs. So worship Him and trust in Him and your Lord is not unmindful of what you do."

(Quran, Hud 11: 123)

Chapter 2
Allah
The Most High

Who is Allah?

Allah is the Arabic name for God and is used by Arabic speakers regardless of religious inclination and can be used interchangeably with all of the names that Allah has given Himself. In Islam the most important concept is the fact that Allah is One and nothing shares His attributes. He has no partners, no parents or offspring and is the ultimate Creator of the universe. He is the One who was the beginning and will continue after the end as we know it. The same Creator that has been worshipped throughout time as the Originator of the universe.

Allah has created all things with a design and purpose. Included in this is the creation of the Heavens and the Earth and all of mankind, starting with the very first humans, namely, Prophet Adam (ﷺ) and his wife Eve (known in Arabic as *Hawa*). Throughout time, people started to deviate from the sole worship of Allah and started to create idols and worship these as partners or intercessors with Allah. To ascribe partners with Allah, is one of the most severe crimes against Allah, since He has no need for partners.

To Begin in the 'Name of Allah'

The entire religion of Islam is based upon the concept of gaining closeness to Allah. So there is an emphasis in Islamic tradition to begin everything with Allah's name by using the Arabic phrase, '*Bismillah*' which means 'In the Name of Allah'. Muslims, when referring to the name of Allah, often add the words '*Subhana-hu-wa-Ta-ala*' after it, meaning 'Glorified and Exalted is He' as a sign of reverence.

Allah is considered genderless, however there is no appropriate word to express this in the English language, so Allah is commonly referred to as a 'He'. Muslims also tend to use many other phrases in their daily lives that contain the word Allah, for example:

Allahu Akbar - Allah is the Greatest.
Bismillah - In the Name of Allah.
Insha'Allah - If Allah wills.
Ya Allah - Oh Allah.
Ma sha' Allah - Look at what Allah has willed!
Subhan Allah - Glory be to Allah.
Al-Hamdu li-llah - All praise be to Allah.
Jazak Allahu khayran - May Allah reward you well with goodness.

Opposite page: A beautiful sunset over an ocean with the translation of the powerful Quranic chapter known as '*Ikhlas*' or 'Purity' (of faith). *Ikhlas* is not merely the name of this chapter but also the title of its contents, for it deals exclusively with the fact that Allah is One and Eternal. Whereas other chapters of the Quran have generally been named after a word occurring in them, the word '*Ikhlas*' does not occur in this chapter. It has been given this name in view of its meaning and subject matter. For it states the foremost and fundamental doctrine of Islam in four such brief sentences that leave an immediate impression on human memory. Whoever understands it and believes in its teaching, will be free of polytheism completely.

Prophet Muhammad (ﷺ) held this chapter in great esteem and he emphasised its importance in many different ways. He would recite it frequently and disseminate it among the people. There are a great number of his sayings which speak about this chapter being equivalent to one third of the Quran.

In the Name of Allah, The Most Compassionate, The Most Merciful.

"Say, "He is Allah, (who is) One, Allah, the Eternal Refuge. He neither begets nor is He born, Nor is there to Him any equivalent."

(Quran, Purity (of faith) 112: 1 - 4)

Concept of The Creator in Islam

The concept of the Creator is very simple and easily understood in Islam. Allah is regarded as Unique and the One true Lord. He is the Sole Creator of everything and His power of creation is infinite. He created the vast expanse of the universe with countless galaxies containing billions of stars and planets of all sizes. It is Allah who created people, animals, plants, trees and all that is on the Earth. Allah also created microscopic life, atoms and sub atomic particles and many other things of which we have no knowledge. Not a leaf falls from a tree or a drop of rain from the sky except by His permission.

Allah is the Most High, the Most Loving, the Most Merciful. He has no son nor partner and none has the right to be worshipped but Him alone. He is the true Deity and every other deity is false. He is the Creator of all beings and thus is considered to be the Lord for the atheists, the Buddhists, the Christians, the Hindus, the Jews, the Muslims, the Sikhs, and all others. Muslims worship and put their trust in Him alone and they seek His help and His guidance only.

Allah is characterised with attributes of perfection and described with qualities of magnificence. He is free from defects and deficiencies. He is Ever-Living and will not die. He is Self-Sustaining, supports everything in this world and does not sleep. He is Fully-Aware; not a single atom in the Heavens or the Earth escapes Him. He is the All-Seer; He views the crawling of a black ant upon a small rock in a pitch-black cave. He is the All-Hearer; He hears the cries of the voices with the diversity of languages concerning their various needs.

Allah's words are complete and perfect in truthfulness and justice. His attributes are too majestic to be likened or equated to the attributes of His creation. His essence is highly exalted above any likeness to other essences outright. His creatures are all-embraced by His actions of justice, wisdom and mercy.

To Allah belongs the creation and command. To Him belong all-blessings and favour, the whole dominion and all-praise and commendation and glory. He is the first, there being nothing before Him and He is the last, there being nothing after Him. There is nothing above Him and there is nothing closer than Him. All of His names encompass commendation, praise and glory, this is why they are termed the 'most beautiful'. His attributes signify perfection, His characteristics glorify His splendour and His actions are all wise, merciful, of benefit and just.

There is also a strong emphasis in Islam for people to understand why they were created, how and why they live and where they go after they die. Muslims believe that Allah created the universe and all that it contains for a purpose and that He did not leave mankind neglected and void of any purpose. Rather He created human beings in order for them to worship Him alone. He showered them with blessings and favours, so that they can employ the expression of gratitude of these bounties to attain even more of His generosity.

Opposite page: A beautiful water lily in full bloom. The immense diversity of biological life on Earth represents one of the many signs pointing to the existence of an all powerful Creator.

"He is Allah, besides Whom there is no god;
the Sovereign, the Holy One, the Source of Peace
(and Perfection), the Guardian of Faith,
the Preserver of Safety, the Exalted in Might,
the Irresistible, the Supreme:
Glory to Allah! (High is He) above the partners
they ascribe to Him."

(Quran, The Gathering 59: 23)

"Allah. There is no deity except Him, the Ever-Living, the Sustainer of (all) existence. Neither drowsiness overtakes Him nor sleep. To Him belongs whatever is in the heavens and whatever is on the earth. Who is it that can intercede with Him except by His permission? He knows what is (presently) before them and what will be after them and they encompass not a thing of His knowledge except for what He wills.
His *Kursi* extends over the heavens and the earth and their preservation tires Him not. And He is the Most High, the Most Great."

(Quran, The Heifer 2: 255)

Above: The translation of the Quranic verse known as '*Ayatul Kursi*' (The verse of the chair or footstool). This verse describes the Creator in all His Magnificence and Glory. It is regarded as the most powerful verse of the entire Quran.

Left: Computer generated image of a star rising over a distant world in the outer rim of our galaxy. Muslims regard the countless stars and planets in the universe as one of the greatest signs pointing to the existence of the Creator, Allah.

Allah is regarded as perfect in every way and has no restrictions and is able to do everything that He pleases. He is as He describes Himself in His Book (the Quran) and He is over and above how His creation has depicted Him.

It is impossible to state that Allah is anything other than perfect when one considers that it is Allah who created all of the heavens, the universe, all of the plants, animals and mankind. It is not logical to conclude that Allah, Who has the power to create all this and much more, is imperfect.

The decrees of the kingdoms are under His disposal and order, they descend from Him and rise back up to Him. His angels are at His service, they execute His orders across the regions of His kingdoms, though He has no need of them.

Hence, He completed His ample favours upon all of His creations, established His perfect proof upon them, poured His bounties upon them, wrote upon Himself mercy and insured in His Book, which He wrote, that His mercy overpowers His wrath.

"Surely Allah's is the Kingdom of the heavens and the earth. He gives life and He causes death; and for you there is besides Allah no patron nor any helper."

(Quran, Repentance 9: 116)

Opposite page: Images depicting the diversity of the materials present in Allah's creation.

Above right: Water droplets hang delicately from a leaf. The presence of the green photosynthetic pigment, chlorophyll, gives the leaf its green colour.

Above left: Lava is molten rock expelled by a volcano during an eruption. Below the earth's surface, molten rock is termed magma instead of lava. When first expelled from a volcanic vent, lava is a liquid at temperatures typically from 700°C to 1,200°C (1,300°F to 2,200°F). Although lava is quite viscous, about 100,000 times the viscosity of water, it can flow many miles before eventually cooling and solidifying.

Below right: A microscopic virus particle. It is still a matter of debate whether viruses are living organisms. The majority of virologists consider them to be non-living, as they do not meet all the criteria of the generally accepted definition of life.

Below Left: Agate (a quartz like material) with beautiful patterns formed due to the presence of manganese and iron ions. Minerals range in composition from pure elements and simple salts to very complex silicates with thousands of known forms.

What Does Allah Look Like?

A fundamental belief of Muslims is that Allah does not look like His creation and we are not created in the form of Allah, nor do we make forms with our own hands and worship them claiming them to be Allah. Allah gives us certain information in the Quran about Himself, but rather than spend months and years debating the exact description of His form, this information is only given to us in an attempt for us to have an understanding – the exact details however, are known to Allah alone. Allah is Perfect and His Image is Majestic and beyond what we can comprehend. In a very simple and comprehensive verse of the Quran, Allah tells us about Himself (opposite page).

"...There is nothing like unto Him and He is the One that hears and sees (all things)."

(Quran, Consultation 42:11)

Allah is the First and the Last

In Islam, Allah is regarded as 'Ever Living' and 'Eternal'. He was 'The First', even before time was created, nothing was before Him. After everything in the creation is destroyed, Allah will be there as 'The Last' and He will remain Ever Existent and will never die, even after the end of time. Allah tells us He is 'The First' and 'The Last' in the following verses of the Quran.

"Whatsoever is in the heavens and the earth glorifies Allah and He is All-Mighty, All-Wise. His is the kingdom of the heaven and the earth. It is He who gives life and causes death; and He is able to do all things. He is the First (nothing is before Him) and the Last (nothing is after Him)..."

(Quran, Iron 57:1-3)

Opposite: A beautiful sunset over a desolate windswept landscape. Allah creates whatever He wills. He is the All-Powerful, the Giver of life and death.

In the Name of Allah, The Most Compassionate, The Most Merciful.

"Glorify the name of thy Guardian-Lord
Most High
Who has created and further given order and proportion; Who has ordained laws.
And granted guidance;"

(Quran, The Most High 87: 1-3)

Allah's Knowledge

Islamic belief is that Allah has complete knowledge of everything. Allah's Knowledge is perfect and all-encompassing. No action takes place in the whole universe except by His Knowledge and Will. He has power over all things and He is able to do everything. He is the Most Gracious, the Most Merciful, the Most Kind and the Most Beneficent. We learn of Allah's total knowledge of everything in many verses in the Quran. One of Allah's names is 'The All-Knowing' as mentioned in the following verse of the Quran:

"Verily, your Lord is the All-Knowing Creator."

(Quran, The Rocky Tract 15:86)

When Muslims say that Allah is "with us", they do not mean He is with us in person. In fact Allah is not inside nor subject to His creation, Allah is with us by His knowledge, sight and hearing. He knows everything that we do and He watches all of us extremely closely.

"It is Allah Who has created seven heavens and of the earth the like thereof (i.e. seven). His Command descends between them (heavens and earth), that you may know that Allah has power over all things and that Allah surrounds all things in (His) Knowledge."

(Quran, Divorce 65:12)

"And if all the trees on the earth were pens and the sea (were ink with which to write), with the seven seas behind it to add to its (supply), yet the words of Allah would not be exhausted. Verily Allah is All-Mighty, All-Wise."

(Quran, Luqman 31:27)

Opposite page: Deep in a lush forest, drops of water hang from a tree stem. Islamic belief is that the Creator's knowledge is unlimited. Allah knows the hidden secrets of nature and the fine mysteries of life. A drop of water does not fall, without Allah knowing about it with full measure.

> "Therefore remember Me (Allah) and I will remember you. Give thanks to Me and never deny Me."

(Quran, The Heifer 2:152)

Knowledge of the Unseen

Allah alone has knowledge of the unseen. Indeed none in the creation has this knowledge except Allah alone. We have no need of this knowledge and should not speculate to learn about the unseen by using horoscopes, fortune-tellers and so forth. Allah tells us in the Quran:

> "And with Him are the keys of the unseen (all that is hidden), none knows them but He. And He knows whatever there is in (or on) the earth and in the sea; not a leaf falls, but He knows it. There is not a grain in the darkness of the earth nor anything fresh or dry, but is written in a clear record."

(Quran, Cattle 6:59)

Only Allah alone has knowledge of the hour of reckoning when every soul will be held to account for the life they spent on earth. This knowledge has been kept with Allah alone and no-one else knows the time of the hour. Allah in His mercy has given certain signs as part of the revelation to show that the time is near but the specifics of the actual time are with Allah alone.

> "Indeed, Allah (alone) has knowledge of the Hour and sends down the rain and knows what is in the wombs. And no soul perceives what it will earn tomorrow and no soul perceives in what land it will die. Indeed, Allah is Knowing and Acquainted."

(Quran, Luqman 31:34)

Opposite page: Arabic calligraphy of the phrase 'Bismillah' set against a beautiful evening lake scene. From a young age Muslims are taught to start every action by saying *Bismillah*, which means 'In the Name of Allah'. In Islam every action carried out with the correct intention is regarded as an act of worship. Even planting trees, digging wells and looking after the environment in general can be considered as acts of worship in Islam.

Allah's Mercy

Islam asserts that Allah alone is the Most Merciful to all of His creation. Many verses of the Quran relate specifically to Allah's mercy. Muslims begin recitation of the Quran by declaring that Allah is the Most Merciful. Allah's name, Ar-Rahmaan – The Most Merciful, is mentioned in the first verse of the opening chapter of the Quran.

"In the Name of Allah, the Most Compassionate, the Most Merciful."

(Quran, The Opening 1:1)

Such is Allah's love and mercy that even those who fall short of living according to His guidance, may have their sins forgiven even by an act of kindness, coupled of course with correct belief in Allah. Prophet Muhammad (ﷺ) narrated a story about a prostitute who was forgiven her sins by Allah for providing water to a thirsty dog.

Allah's Messenger (ﷺ) said, "A prostitute was forgiven by Allah, because, passing by a panting dog near a well and seeing that the dog was about to die of thirst, she took off her shoe and tying it with her head-cover she drew out some water for it. So, Allah forgave her because of that."

(Recorded in Saheeh Bukhari)

Opposite: Muslims regard food as a blessing and mercy from Allah. Wheat (*Triticum spp.*) is a grass that is cultivated worldwide. Globally, it is the most important human food grain and ranks second in total production as a cereal crop behind maize; the third being rice.

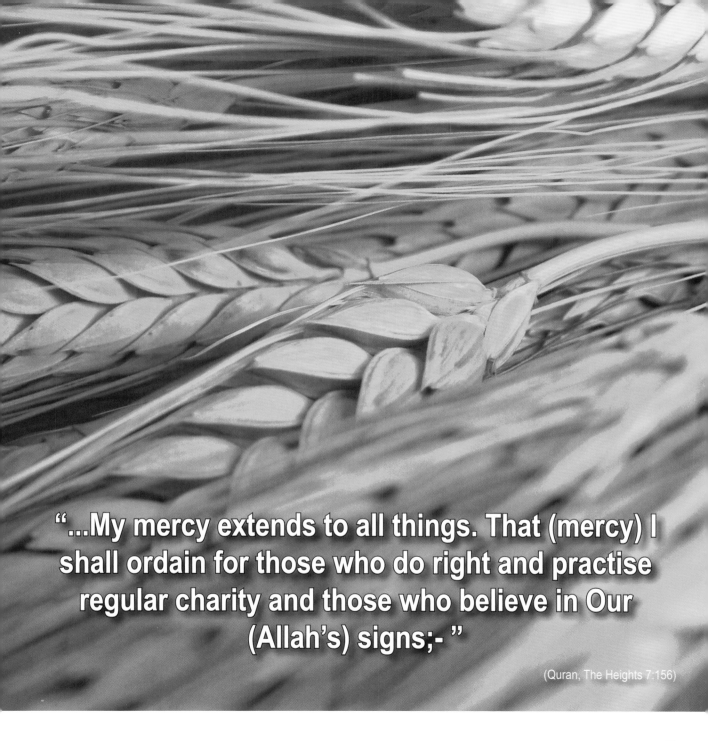

"...My mercy extends to all things. That (mercy) I shall ordain for those who do right and practise regular charity and those who believe in Our (Allah's) signs;- "

(Quran, The Heights 7:156)

Allah's Generosity

Such is Allah's generosity that not only is a person rewarded many times over for doing a good deed but even has one good deed recorded just for having the intention of doing the good deed. Moreover, if someone intended to do a bad deed but did not actually carry it out, then Allah will reward them with a full good deed in their account. Allah is so generous that if someone intended a bad deed and then carried it out, then only one bad deed is written into their account.

Opposite page: Dramatic reflection on Mirror Lake, Yosemite National Park. Islam places great emphasis on preserving natural environments as the creation of the universe is considered an open book, a guide inviting observation which increases the faith of the observer and takes them to the point of unshakeable faith in the Almighty Creator. Hence planting trees under which people seek shade or shelter from the sun is deemed to be a rewardable act. On the other hand the cutting down of trees without strong and legitimate reasons is encroaching on the bounties of Allah and destroying the beauty of the environment which Allah has created.

Say: "O People of the Scripture (the Jews and Christians), come to a word that is equitable between us and you; that we shall worship none but Allah and not associate anything with Him and not take one another as lords instead of Allah." But if they turn away, then say, "Bear witness that we are Muslims (submitting to Him)."

(Quran, The Family of Imran 3:64)

Allah's Names and Attributes

Allah has the most magnificent names and perfect attributes such as: The Gracious, The Merciful, The Beneficent, The All-Wise, The All-Knowing and The Lord of the Universe.

No one shares His Divinity, His Names or Attributes. Nothing is like Him. He is the Creator. He is neither created, nor is He a part of His creation. He is All-Powerful and absolutely Just. There is no other entity in the entire universe worthy of worship other than Him. He is The First and The Last and Everlasting. He was present when there was nothing in existence and will be present when nothing else remains. He is The Supreme, The Sovereign and The Law Giver. It is only He Who is capable of granting life and death.

We know from the Quran that Allah has many excellent and exceptional names. Allah tells Muslims to supplicate to Him, choosing the most suitable name when praying to Him. In doing so Muslims glorify and praise Allah.

"Allah has the Most Excellent Names, so supplicate Him with them..."

(Quran, The Heights 7:180)

"He is Allah, the Creator of all, the Maker of all, the Fashioner of all, His are the most beautiful names, Whatever is in the heavens and earth is exalting Him. And He is the Exalted in Might, the Wise."

(Quran, The Gathering 59: 24)

Opposite page: A list of some of the Names and Attributes of Allah. It is important to note that Muslims do not believe that Allah exists in parts where each name is incarnated as a separate deity.

The Triumphant. The One who knows all that is hidden from us. The Mighty One in His power, gravity, and eminence. The One who forgives and pardons. The One who is all-knowing about His creation. The One who is High above everyone in His power and status. The Mighty, Invincible, and Impenetrable One. The Guardian and Protector. The One who is extremely gracious and responsive to His creation. The Ruler or Sovereign, and the Judge. The One who is forbearing, mild, and gentle. He is patient, and He does not rush to punish His servants for their sins. The Praise-worthy in all respects. The Truth. The Reckoner; that is, the One who will take account of all people's deeds, and who will reward or punish them accordingly. The Ever-Living One who has no beginning and no end, He lives and does not die. The Most High One who is above all others. The Last. The Most Noble hearted. The First. The Origi-nator and Innovator who brings new things into existence after He decrees them. The Perspicacious. The One who is generous, kind, and beneficent. It has also been said that it refers to Him being true to His promise (in the context of reward). The All-Seeing One who is a witness to all ac-tions and events. He is completely familiar with the details of all that happens. The Judge who, on the day of Judge-ment, will judge with truth. He will support those who were guided, and punish those who were in error. The One who conceals and overlooks the sins of His creation. He turns in forgiveness to whoever repents, even to someone who has committed shirk (association of any type of partner with Allah). The One who forgives the sins and mistakes of his servants. The One who is categorically without any needs whatsoever. The only One deserving of worship. The Om-nipotent, All-Powerful One who is absolutely free of any weaknesses whatsoever. He can compel others, and His power cannot be resisted. The Great One; all others are less than Him. The One who is noble, generous, and gra-cious. The One who decrees the existence or creation of new things. The One who is knowledgeable and well-ac-quainted with His creation and all that they do. The One who creates everything in the creation. He is not weakened or affected by this. The One who is to His creation gra-cious and kind, friendly and gentle. The Glorified, Exalted One who is extolled and lauded by His creation. The King and Owner of all things. The Firm and Strong One. The Benefactor and Supporter who provides victory and protec-tion to those who do what He has commanded and avoid what He has forbidden. The One who encompasses or sur-rounds everything, such that nothing can escape from Him or elude Him. The One who watches over and protects His creation. The One who answers and accepts the worship and supplications of His servants. The Master who is ca-pable of anything He wishes, without weakness, without fatigue. He cannot be resisted. The Shaper and Fashioner of the new things He creates.

The Exalted, High One who is above His creation, irre-sistible in power and might, and who is above whatever lies the disbelievers may say about Him. The One who is proud, and for Allah this is not a negative trait as it is for His creation. The One who is capable of doing anything He wills. The Irresistible, Over-Powering One. The Om-nipotent, All-Powerful Master of all things. The Irresistible Subjugator who overpowers and defeats all things. Nothing can stand in front of Him except as His weak slave. The One who is Close to His servants, in the sense that He rewards obedience, and answers their supplications. He is close to whoever is sincere in worship and who repents for his or her sins. The Strong One who is capable of doing what He wills. There is nothing capable of defeating Him or of thwarting His decree. The Caretaker who manages and regulates His creation. The Pure One who is free of all de-fects. The One, meaning He who is the only one deserving of worship. He has no partner, and He has no equal. The Inheritor who inherits the earth and all that is on it because all created life shall cease, leaving only Him, the Crea-tor. The One who is Generous or Magnanimous towards His Servants. The One who loves whoever turns to Him in repentance from his or her sins. The One who bestows mercy and success on His creation. The Disposer of affairs to whom all matters are entrusted. The Ruler who supports and guards His believing servants. The Helper and Sup-porter who backs and strengthens the believers. The One who is Merciful and Compassionate. The Merciful One. The One who closely watches over His creation. The Only Pro-vider and Sustainer of His creation. The One who is free of defects, in Him, His attributes, His actions, and His speech. The Everlasting, Persistent One who does not beget and is not begotten. The One whose dominion is complete. The One who does not eat or drink. The One who listens and responds to our supplications and requests. The One who recognizes the obedience and worship of His believing servants by rewarding them. The Witness over everyone and their actions, for which He will either reward or punish them. The One who rewards the believing servants for their good deeds. The One who accepts the sincere repentance of His believing servants, and this means He forgives them. The true Judge. The One who is modest. The Giver and Provider who lavishly extends sustenance and wealth to His creation. The One who is beautiful and graceful. The One who is generous and magnanimous. The Benefactor, the Generous. The Giver of wealth and knowledge. The One who delays or slows whatever He wills. The One who hastens or speeds whatever He wills. The One who takes and constricts the sustenance and wealth of His creation. The One. The Lord. The One who is kind. The Master. The Exalted One who is praised and glorified extensively. The Healer, the One who cures. The One who is pure and good.

It is interesting that the usage of the word Allah is not exclusive to the Islamic faith; Arab Christians and various Arabic-speaking Jews (including the Teimanim and some Sephardim communities) also use it to refer to the monotheist deity. Arabic translations of the Bible also employ it, as do Roman Catholics in Malta (who pronounce it as Alla'). Christians in the Middle East who speak Aramaic (a Semitic language related to Arabic) use the word 'Allaha'. This is hardly surprising as Muslims believe that the name of Allah had existed before the time of Prophet Adam (صلى الله عليه وسلم). And it is the same Deity worshipped by Adam, Noah, Abraham, Moses, Jesus and Muhammad (peace be upon them all).

Background picture: The Sun rising over the planet Earth as seen from space. All of Allah's creation glorifies Him, yet mankind pays little heed to the many wondrous signs in

"Praise be unto Allah, Who created the heavens and the earth and made the darkness and the light. Yet those who reject faith hold (others) as equal, with their Guardian-Lord."

(Quran, Cattle 6:1)

Allah's Punishment

The true balance of an Islamic life is established by having a healthy fear of Allah as well as a sincere belief in His infinite forgiveness and mercy. Islam views that a life without fear of Allah leads to sin and disobedience. On the other hand believing that one has sinned so much that Allah will not possibly forgive you, can lead to feelings of despair. In light of this, Islam teaches that only misguided people despair of their Lord's Mercy.

Allah created the universe, bestowed human beings with a privileged position within it and left the world to function under the laws that He has decreed for it. Allah constantly observes to what level people appreciate the life He has given them and how they behave in the environment He has placed them in. Allah allows the universe to exist for a certain length of time. At the end of this time, following portents of the end of the world as we know it, mankind will be brought in front of Allah for Judgment and man will be rewarded or punished according to his good or bad deeds.

Human beings have also been created weak and regularly fall into sin. This is the nature of the human being as created by Allah in His wisdom. In Islam though, the avenue of repentance is always open to every human being. So much so that Almighty Allah loves the repentant sinner as He alone is the All-Forgiving Most Merciful. For those individuals and nations who consistently rebel against Allah's divine law, Islamic belief holds that inevitably there will be consequences.

Throughout the Quran, Allah describes numerous past nations who rejected Divine guidance and were subsequently destroyed. These stories serve as warnings to humanity of the consequences of rebellion against the commandments of Allah. The punishment may come in a variety of different ways. It could take the form of a flood or earthquake or perhaps in the form of new diseases that have never been seen before.

"And how many a city which was unjust have We shattered and produced after it another people. And when its inhabitants perceived Our punishment, at once they fled from it."

(Quran, The Prophets 21: 11-12)

Opposite page: Throughout the Quran, Allah describes numerous past nations who rejected Divine guidance and were subsequently destroyed.
Far right: The ancient ruins at Petra in Jordan are famous for having many stone structures carved into the rock.
Above right: Hathor temple of the ancient Egyptian Queen Neferatri near Awan, Egypt.
Middle: Ancient ruined dwellings built into the mountain side at Demre, Turkey.
Below: A victim of the catastrophic volcanic eruption that destroyed the Roman city of Pompeii during the 1st century CE.
Following page: A Quranic verse in the shade of a blue flower.

"...Truly, in the remembrance of Allah do hearts find rest"

(Quran, The Thunder 13: 28)

Chapter 3

Creation or
Evolution?

Questions of Design

Was the universe created? Or did it come into being by itself? The Islamic viewpoint is that the variety and complexity of the many intricate systems which constitute the fabric of both human beings and the world in which they exist, indicate that there must be a Supreme Being who created them. Uniquely, in the following Quranic verse Allah asks mankind to ponder on the cause of their coming into existence.

"Or were they created by nothing, or were they the creators (of themselves)? Or did they create the heavens and the earth? Rather, they are not certain. Or are the Treasures of your Lord with them, or are they the managers (of affairs)?"

(Quran, The Mount 52: 35-37)

An important principle to consider is that of 'cause and effect'. It follows that, if there is any evidence of design this itself would indicate the existence of a designer, in which case all other theories would be immediately nullified. So, when human beings come across footprints on a beach, they immediately conclude that they were made by another human. No one imagines that the waves from the sea settled in the sand and by chance produced a depression looking exactly like a human footprint. Similarly, we must recognise all around us the footprints of intelligent design made by a Supreme Creator.

Let's think about any purpose built product in life for a moment, a car for instance. The components that make up the car; steel, plastic, rubber etc., are assembled in such a way that they demonstrate meticulous forethought and planning.

It is obvious that cars do not appear due to random chance events and that manufacturers put considerable effort into producing them. If cars could appear by chance, then car manufacturers would never have existed at all. In fact the reality is that every product that we see around us, from the very simple to the most complex, has been made to a certain design. Briefly, 'design' means a harmonious assembly of various parts into an orderly form towards a common goal. Going by this definition, one would have no difficulty in asserting that a car is designed. This is because there is a certain goal, which is to transport people and cargo. In realisation of this goal various parts such as the engine, tyres and body are planned and assembled in a manufacturing plant.

However, what about a living creature? Can the mechanism of flight in birds for instance, be designed as well? Before giving an answer, let us repeat the evaluation we did for the example of a car. The goal at hand, in this case, is to fly. For this purpose, hollow bones and strong muscles that move these bones are utilized together with feathers capable of suspending the bird in the air. Wings are shaped aerodynamically to allow efficient flight. Lungs and metabolism are in tune with the need for high levels of energy. The presence of multiple, unique and specialised systems that all function simultaneously shows that the mechanism of flight in birds is the product of a certain design. If one examines any other creature besides a bird, we find that they are all examples of meticulous design. If one continues further on this quest, one would discover that humans are also designed.

Computer generated image of a DNA double helix. The structure of DNA was unravelled in 1953 at the MRC unit in Cambridge, UK. The origin of DNA along with many other complex molecules of life, remains one of the miracles of creation that evolution has yet to explain.

The study of our natural environment leads to an important conclusion; all creatures in nature, including humans are of a design. This, in turn, shows the existence of a particular Creator who designs all creatures at will, sustains the entire natural universe and holds absolute power and wisdom.

In recent times some scientists have sought to deny the existence of a Creator. Matter, in their opinion, is eternal and mankind is merely a chance product, an accident of nature. According to them, there is no purpose to existence and life has evolved by itself over hundreds of millions of years starting from simple inorganic molecules and gaining in complexity and order. However, the arguments in favour of evolution with blind chance as the driving force for our existence are both desperate and illogical as the following examples will demonstrate.

Imagine a chimpanzee with a typewriter trying to type out the whole history of humanity. How long do you think it would need, given that the chimpanzee pressed the keys at random? One year? One thousand years? One Million years? One Billion years? Or perhaps never. The reality is that the probability of the chimpanzee accomplishing this task is zero. For arguments sake lets increase the chances of success by having billions of chimps each with a typewriter. However, the probability for each individual chimpanzee will still tend towards zero, even after four and a half billion years of effort. Yet in the same time inorganic matter is supposed to have evolved into man by blind chance and random mutation.

"To Him (Allah) is due the primal origin of the heavens and the earth; when He decrees a matter He says to it: "Be"; and it is."

(Quran, The Heifer 2: 117)

Opposite page: Highly magnified coloured scanning electron micrograph (SEM) of nerve fibres (axons, purple) in a nerve cell (neurone). The neurone is composed of numerous fibres separated by layers of connective tissue (endoneurium, orange). The fibres carry electrical nerve impulses away from the neurone cell body, towards other nerve cells, the muscles or organs. Each fibre is surrounded by a fatty insulating layer known as a myelin sheath (pink in cross-section), which increases the transmission speed of the nerve signals. Nerves in the body serve to collect, interpret and relay information.

In the brain neurons makes on average 1000 synaptic connections with other neurons, which means that a brain can contain between one hundred trillion and one quadrillion synaptic connections. This is one of the wonders of Allah's creation that sets humans apart from all other creatures. The brain is involved in everything we do. How we think, how we feel, how we act and even how we interact with others.

IMAGE CREDIT: SCIENCE PHOTO LIBRARY.

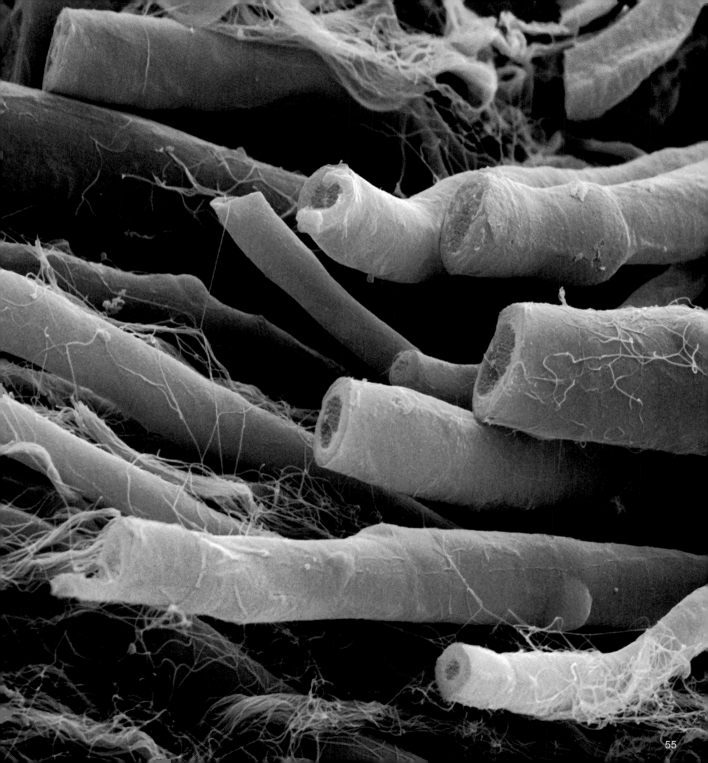

The advent of biochemistry has also started to show us how even apparently simple biological systems can be very complex. Simple living cells have hundreds of developed systems which can be compared to a city. There are power stations producing energy, factories manufacturing enzymes and hormones, complex transportation systems, pipelines carrying raw material, advanced laboratories breaking down substances, and a vast data bank in the form of DNA. For example, light sensitive cells in tiny creatures, microscopic rotors found in bacteria or microscopic cilia found in the human throat, are all examples of extremely complex systems with numerous interconnected and vital pieces that have been precisely designed to function with each other. Fossils tell us nothing about the ability of evolution to develop a complex system 'from scratch'. Evolutionists spend much time and effort in uncovering new fossils but they have little to say about the biochemistry of vision or so many other intelligently designed complex molecular systems.

Hence, the greatest evidence of The Creator is His creation. Nature and our study of nature, both proclaim the fact that there is One God who, in His Wisdom, has created and continues to sustain the universe. The very existence of the universe, with its superb organisation is inexplicable except as having been brought into existence by a Creator - a Being with an infinite intelligence - rather than a blind force.

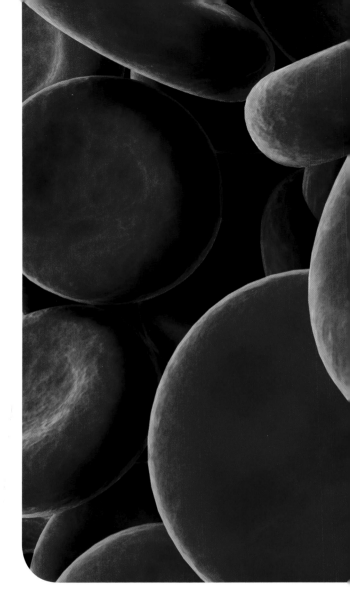

Opposite: Highly magnified image of red blood cells. Red blood cells are the most common type of blood cell and are the vertebrate bodies principal means of delivering oxygen from the lungs to the body tissues via the blood. A single drop of blood contains millions of red blood cells which are constantly travelling through the body. Red blood cells also play an important role in the coagulation cascade, which represents another highly complex and finely tuned biological system that has been intricately designed rather than evolved by chance.

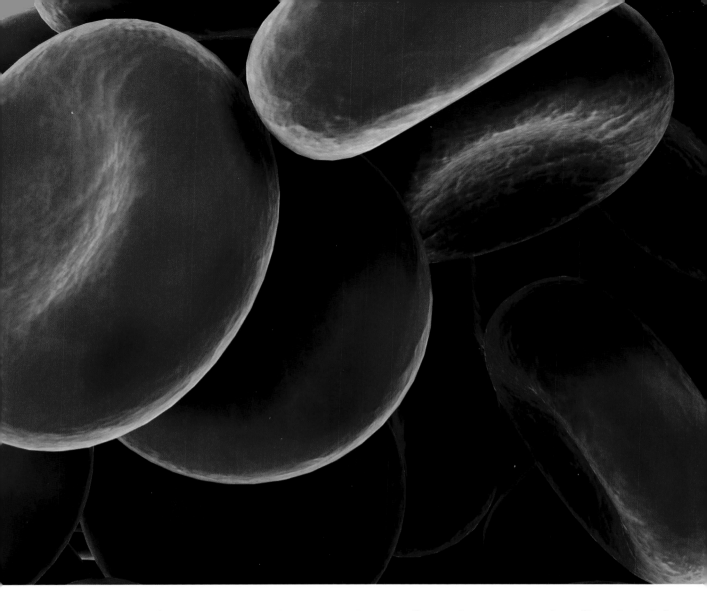

"On the earth are signs for the certain (in faith)
As also in your own selves. Then will you not see?"

(Quran, The Winnowing Winds 51: 20-21)

The Purpose of Creation

As we have discussed previously, the reality rationally points to the decisive fact that there must have been an intelligence behind the origin of life. Once we have established the fact that there is a Creator, then a series of questions arise: Why did the Creator create us? What does He want us to do? What does He look like? Has He left mankind any instructions? How can we know Him? Does the Creator communicate with mankind? The question: For what purpose did Allah create us, is the next most important and fundamental question that needs to be addressed. Islam teaches the principle that if we know our aim in life then we will be able to work towards it and reach it.

The science of human physiology totally refutes the idea that man was created for no purpose. It is universally agreed that every part of the human body was created for a purpose, i.e. the hands touch, the eyes see, the nose smells and so forth. The natural conclusion is that whatever is true for the part must also apply to the whole. In other words the purpose of the creation of the whole must be closely linked with the creation of every part of it. Hence, the creation of man as a whole must have a wisdom and purpose behind it. Islam teaches us that man's sole purpose in life is simply to worship Allah the Creator.

Background: High speed photography captures a splash crown formed by a drop of water. Regarded as one of the miracles of nature, formed by the combination of two gases (hydrogen and oxygen), water is a tasteless, odourless and nearly colourless substance in its pure form. It is essential to all known forms of life and is also known as the most universal solvent. Water is one of the most abundant substances on Earth, existing in many places and forms.

However, Allah Almighty is not in need of human worship, so He did not create human beings to fulfil some need on his part. If not a single human being worshipped Allah it would not diminish His glory in any way. Allah is perfect, He alone exists without any needs. All created beings have needs, consequently it is mankind that needs to worship Allah alone.

Concept of Worship

The concept of worship in Islam is misunderstood by many people, including some Muslims. Worship is commonly taken to mean performing ritualistic acts such as prayers, fasting, charity etc. This limited understanding of worship is only one part of the meaning of worship in Islam. That is why the traditional definition of worship in Islam is a comprehensive definition that includes almost everything in any individual's activities. In other words, worship is everything one says or does for the pleasure of Allah. For Muslims this includes rituals as well as beliefs, social activities, obeying, legislating and ruling by Allah's laws alone as well as personal contributions to the welfare of one's fellow human beings.

"And Allah has created every animal from water; Of them there are some that creep on their bellies; Some that walk on two legs; and some that walk on four; Allah creates whatever He wills For verily Allah has power over all things."

(Quran, The Light 24: 45)

"And I (Allah) created not the Jinn and mankind except that they should worship Me (Allah Alone)."

(Quran, The Winds that Scatter 51: 56)

Chapter 4

The Prophets
of Allah

Adam (ﷺ), the First Prophet

One of the central Islamic beliefs is that Islam started with the very first human beings on Earth, namely, Prophet Adam (ﷺ) and his wife Eve. In fact the history of the Prophets that followed could be considered as the history of mankind. After Prophet Adam (ﷺ), Allah sent many Prophets to teach mankind. They each offered teachings relevant to the lives of people at the time, however the central message was the same: that is to worship the One true God, Allah, and live according to His laws.

Muslims believe that throughout time the Creator has sent us 124,000 Prophets, starting from Prophet Adam (ﷺ) and ending with the last Prophet, Muhammad (ﷺ). Each Prophet carried the same message of Divine guidance to his people, namely the worship of the One Deity, Allah. Some of the Prophets were also Messengers in that they were given revealed scripture. In the case of the Final Prophet, Muhammad (ﷺ), the message was intended for the whole of mankind and not just his people at the time.

The struggle that some of the Prophets faced when they tried to convey the message is detailed in many places in the Quran. The problems they encountered, the solutions they brought and their exemplary and noble behaviour is uniquely highlighted. Moreover, their example and good character is still applicable and very relevant to the lives of people today.

Miracles

In order to show people that they spoke the truth, Prophets were given supporting proof by Allah in the form of miracles (defined as 'actions or events which do not follow the known laws of nature' - Oxford English Dictionary). The Prophets were usually given miracles in those fields that were popular amongst the people of that age. For example in the time of the Prophet Moses (in Arabic *Musa*, ﷺ) the art of sorcery and magic was common practice. When Prophet Moses (ﷺ) transformed his *staff* into a living serpent, the Pharaoh's sorcerers knew that what they had witnessed was no sorcerer's trick and they accepted Moses (ﷺ) as being the Prophet of Allah.

Similarly, during the time of Prophet Jesus (in Arabic *Eesa*, ﷺ) the practice of healing and medicine was commonplace and people placed great faith in healers. When the people saw Prophet Jesus (ﷺ) healing the blind and giving life to the dead with Allah's permission they instantly knew that such things were beyond human capability and believed that it could be nothing but a miracle sent by Allah.

The miracles of the Prophets that came before Prophet Muhammad (ﷺ) are no longer with us today. However, The Merciful Creator gave Prophet Muhammad (ﷺ) a miracle for all of mankind and for all time, i.e. an everlasting miracle, namely the Quran. This would remain the source of truth and guidance long after Prophet Muhammad (ﷺ) had left this world.

The Prophets of Allah mentioned in the Quran (peace be upon them all). English versions of the names are given with the Quranic name in brackets where applicable. However, it is clearly stated in the Quran that this list is not comprehensive: "And certainly We sent messengers before you: there are some of them that We have mentioned to you and there are others whom We have not mentioned to you..." (Quran, The Forgiver 40:78).

MUHAMMAD
(ﷺ)

JESUS
(EESA)

JOHN
(YAHYA)

ZACHARIAS
(ZAKARIYA)

ELIJAH
(ELIAS)

ELISHA
(AL-YASA)

JONAH
(YUNUS)

SOLOMON
(SULAYMAN)

AARON
(HARUN)

MOSES
(MUSA)

EZEKIEL
(DUL-KIFL)

DAVID
(DAWUD)

JOSEPH
(YUSUF)

JOB
(AYUB)

JACOB
(YAQUB)

ADAM

ISAAC
(ISHAAQ)

SHOAIB

LOT
(LUT)

ENOCH
(IDRIS)

SALIH

HUD

NOAH
(NUH)

ABRAHAM
(IBRAHIM)

ISMAIL
(ISHMAEL)

63

ADAM

The Father of Mankind

عليه السلام

And (mention, O Muhammad), when your Lord said to the angels, "Indeed, I will make upon the earth a vicegerent." They said, "Will You place upon it one who causes corruption therein and sheds blood, while we declare Your praise and sanctify You?" Allah said, "Indeed, I know that which you do not know."
And He taught Adam all the names. Then He showed them to the angels and said, "Inform Me of the names of these, if you are truthful."
They said, "Exalted are You; we have no knowledge except what You have taught us. Indeed, it is You who is the Knowing, the Wise."

(Quran, The Heifer 2: 30-32)

Background: Mossaic-like pattern formed as a clay surface dries under a baking sun. A notion repeated many times in the Quran is that man has been created from clay or soil. In fact the basic elements making up the human body can all be found in our natural environment.

NOAH

The Perservering

عليه
السلام

We had certainly sent Noah to his people
and he said, "O my people, worship Allah;
you have no deity other than Him.
Indeed, I fear for you the punishment
of a tremendous Day.

Said the eminent among his people,
"Indeed, we see you in clear error."
(Noah) said,
"O my people, there is not error in me, but
I am a messenger from the
Lord of the worlds.

I convey to you the messages of my Lord
and advise you;
and I know from Allah what you
do not know."

(Quran, The Heights 7: 59-62)

Background: A flash of lightning reflected on water. In
the Quranic narration we learn that Prophet Noah (ﷺ) was
instructed by Allah to build an 'ark' to protect himself from the
deluge that was about to drown his people.

Prophet Abraham (﷽)

Prophet Abraham (in Arabic *Ibrahim*, ﷽) is regarded as one of the greatest Prophets in history and is held in high esteem by Muslims, Jews and Christians alike. In Islamic teaching he is honourably referred to as the 'Friend of Allah'. He was born in the Babylonian city of Ur in present day Iraq, where he began his mission. During his lifetime he visited many different places and went through many struggles to convince the people of the world that they should worship Allah alone. He travelled to Haran and then went to Palestine, where he established centres of his mission at Bethel, Hebron and Beir-Sheba. He appointed his nephew, Prophet Lut (﷽), with the purpose of continuing his mission. From Palestine he went to Egypt which was second only to Iraq in terms of developed civilisation and culture at the time. From there he travelled to Arabia, where he was commanded by Allah to build the *Kaaba*. He appointed his eldest son, Prophet Ishmael (﷽) as its guardian. He returned to Hebron, where his second son, Prophet Isaac (﷽), continued his mission after his death. From the two sons of Prophet Abraham (﷽) sprang two nations, the Ishmaelites from Prophet Ishmael (﷽) and the Israelites from Prophet Isaac (﷽).

Abraham (﷽) was born during a period when the Babylonians had forgotten about worshipping Allah alone. Paganism had become rampant; they worshipped the sun, the moon and the stars as gods. They also prayed to wooden and stone idols that were housed in grand temples. Many elaborate rituals would be performed daily with rich offerings of food made to the idols and the powerful temple priests.

According to Islamic tradition, Prophet Abraham (﷽) was endowed with spiritual understanding from an early age, as Allah had enlightened his heart and mind by giving him wisdom from childhood. Remarkably, his father was an idol maker by profession which led to much debate and conflict with the young Abraham (﷽). From his early childhood Abraham (﷽) was well aware that his father made strange statues, since he had often played with them; sometimes sitting on their backs, just as people ride donkeys and mules. One day he innocently asked why it was that his father made these statues. His father replied that these statues were gods that people worshipped. Abraham (﷽) was astonished, the concept of worshipping an idol that could neither see, nor hear, nor speak, seemed totally illogical to Abraham (﷽).

As the years passed, Abraham's (﷽) heart had become full of hatred for the idols that his father made for people to worship. As a young intelligent man he could not understand how a sane person could carve a statue and then worship what he had made. The idols did not eat, drink, or talk and they could not even turn themselves right-side-up if someone turned them up-side down. How could people believe that such statues could harm or benefit them? It was during this time that he realised that there was only One God despite what the people said. Allah chose Abraham (﷽) as a Prophet through divine revelation in order to teach and guide mankind to worship the true Lord and Creator of the Universe.

ABRAHAM

The Friend of Allah

عليه
السلام

"Indeed, Abraham was a
(comprehensive) leader, devoutly
obedient to Allah, inclining toward
truth and he was
not of those who associate others
with Allah.

(He was) grateful for His favours.
Allah chose him and
guided him
to a straight path.

And We gave him good
in this world and indeed,
in the Hereafter he will be among
the righteous."

(Quran, The Bee 16: 120-122)

Background: The desert is an inhospitable environment and
a stern challenge to any traveller. Prophet Abraham (ﷺ) spent
most of his life travelling throughout the Middle East across
this type of landscape.

"O fire! Be you coolness and safety for Abraham."

(Quran, The Prophets 21: 69)

After attaining prophethood, Abraham (ﷺ) was commanded by Allah to start teaching his people. He was a strong willed young man who worked very hard. He would debate with his father and the public with great vigour regarding the folly of worshipping idols. In turn, his father and the people around him, would ridicule him and treat him harshly. Society in general though paid no heed to Prophet Abraham's (ﷺ) teachings. The priests in particular had become very powerful figures in society, so they were fiercely opposed to his message. If people were to abandon their pagan ways, then they would be deprived of their power and position in society.

There came a point in time when Prophet Abraham (ﷺ) decided that some practical examples were necessary to prove his point once and for all. So Prophet Abraham (ﷺ) came up with a plan to show the absurdity of idol worship. He knew that there was going to be a great celebration on the bank of the river which would be attended by all the towns folk. He waited until the city was empty, then went cautiously towards the temple. He proceeded to smash all of the idols with an axe except one of the larger ones, on whose neck he hung the axe before leaving. When the people returned, they were shocked to see their 'gods' smashed to pieces, lying scattered all over the temple. They suspected Abraham (ﷺ) immediately and furiously demanded his capture and punishment. Prophet Abraham (ﷺ) did not resist and was brought before the people.

Prophet Abraham (ﷺ) was asked if he was responsible for breaking the idols. He told them to ask the biggest idol, as it was still standing whole and was holding an axe. They replied that he knew very well that idols could not speak or move. This gave Prophet Abraham (ﷺ) the chance to prove the foolishness of worshipping these lifeless objects. Although they realised

the power of his arguments, their sheer anger and arrogance would not allow them to admit their foolishness. It was decided that Prophet Abraham (ﷺ) would be burnt alive. Prophet Abraham (ﷺ) had complete faith in Allah and remained patient throughout the ordeal.

In Islamic tradition Prophet Abraham (ﷺ) was cast into a fire, but his descent into the blaze was like the descent into a cool garden. The flames were still there, but they did not burn for Almighty Allah had issued His command. The fire submitted to the will of Allah, becoming cool and safe for Prophet Abraham (ﷺ). When the fire eventually had burnt itself out, people were completely amazed to find that Prophet Abraham (ﷺ) was untouched. Shocked by the whole incident they let him go. After this event, a small number of people did accept him as a Prophet and began to follow his teachings. Sadly, they were compelled to keep their belief a secret out for fear of harm or death at the hands of the rulers.

The ruler of the land at the time was a king called Nimrod and when he heard of Prophet Abraham's (ﷺ) safe exit from the fire he became very angry. He feared that the status of godhead he had proclaimed for himself was now challenged by an ordinary human being. He summoned Prophet Abraham (ﷺ) to the palace and held a debate with him. Unfortunately for Nimrod, Prophet Abraham (ﷺ) won the debate. He explained to Nimrod the beauty of Allah's creation, His power and wisdom and the fact that idol worship was detested by Allah, for He is the Only Lord of the universe and disposer of its affairs.

Despite the fact that there were only a few people who accepted Prophet Abraham's (ﷺ) teachings, he went on preaching and underwent a chain of tests and trials to prove his obedience and sincerity to Allah. When people started to persecute him, he was commanded by Allah to leave that area and go to Palestine. In compliance with the commandment of Almighty Allah, Prophet Abraham (ﷺ) did not lose a moment's rest. He continued calling out to the masses and teach them about the worship of Allah alone.

Islam teaches that Allah ordered Prophet Abraham (ﷺ) to take his second wife *Hajira* and their baby son Ishmael (ﷺ) and leave them in the valley of *Bakka* (the original name of Makkah). In accordance with this Divine Commandment he set out on a long and troublesome journey. It was during this time that the spring of *Zamzam* emerged in the valley during *Hajira's* search for water for her baby son Ishmael (ﷺ). Prophet Abraham's (ﷺ) family settled in the valley and many people from far and wide came to settle in the same area. Gradually this locality grew in size and was named Makkah.

Prophet Abraham (ﷺ) himself had travelled back to Palestine to join his first wife, Sarah. While he was in the valley of Makkah he had displayed his unstinted submission to the orders of Allah by being willing to sacrifice his beloved son Ishmael (ﷺ). It was around this time that he was informed of glad tidings regarding the birth of a baby from Sarah, his first wife. His second son was named *Isaac* (ﷺ) and would also become a Prophet of Allah and the father of the Israelite nation.

Another one of the many great achievements that marks Prophet Abraham's (ﷺ) life was, the rebuilding of the *Kaaba* in Makkah.

Muslims regard the *Kaaba* as the very first place of worship on Earth. Allah had commanded Prophet Adam (ﷺ) to build it in the valley of Makkah. However, it was Prophet Abraham (ﷺ) who reconstructed the *Kaaba* with the help of his son, Prophet Ishmael (ﷺ).

In summary Prophet Abraham's (ﷺ) life was full of many great tests and trials, however he always had firm faith in Allah and never missed a moment's rest in calling for the worship of Allah. He gained thousands upon thousands of followers during his lifetime. When he passed away, he was buried in Hebron, twenty miles south-west of Jerusalem.

Opposite page: Image of the well of *Zamzam* as it may have looked thousands of years ago during the time of Prophet Abraham (ﷺ). Muslims believe that the well was revealed to *Hajira*, the second wife of Prophet Abraham (ﷺ), when she was desperately seeking water for her infant son Ishmael (ﷺ). The well is located within the present day Sacred Mosque (*Masjid al Haram*) in Makkah, near the *Kaaba*, the holiest place in Islam. Makkah is located in a hot dry valley with few other sources of water. Muslim tradition holds that *Hajira* ran seven times back and forth in the scorching heat between the two hills of *Safa* and *Marwa*, looking for water. Ishmael is said to have scraped the ground with his heel and the *Zamzam* spring appeared. The grandfather of the Prophet Muhammad (ﷺ), Abdul Muttalib, is said to have rediscovered the well after it had been neglected and had filled with sand. He became the guardian of the well, charged with maintaining it and serving the Arabs who came to Makkah on pilgrimage (as was done even in pre-Islamic times).

Nowadays the *Zamzam* well is 30 metres deep and there are some springs contributing to the well at approximately 13 metres below the surface. Hundreds of millions of litres of *Zamzam* water are distributed to the millions of visitors to Makkah every year. Pumping tests reveal that removal of Zamzam water at 8000 litres per second for more than a 24 hour period shows that the water level drops by up to 13 metres, after which the water level stops receding. The water level recovers just 11 minutes after pumping has been stopped indicating that the aquifer feeding the well seems to recharge from rock fractures in neighbouring mountains around Makkah (Source: Zamzam studies and Research Centre).

Prophet Moses (ﷺ)

In the Quran, the Prophet that is most often employed by Allah as an example for future generations is the Prophet Moses (in Arabic Musa, ﷺ). For Muslims the events of Prophet Moses (ﷺ) and the other Prophets' lives are taken not as a history lesson of the ancient past but as examples relevant to people today. Many centuries before the birth of Prophet Moses (ﷺ), Prophet Joseph (in Arabic Yusuf, ﷺ) and his family had settled in Egypt. They were called the children of Israel, or the Israelites. Generations later they would become known as the 'Jews'. At that time ancient Egypt was one of the greatest centres of world civilisation. The Israelites that had settled there gradually increased in number and gained considerable power. The Israelites did not tend to intermingle with the native people, so they remained isolated and were considered as foreigners in Egypt. As the generations passed, the Israelites lost their position and status and became enslaved by the Egyptians.

Before the birth of Prophet Moses (ﷺ) Egypt came under the rule of a tyrannical Pharaoh. Racial discrimination, depravity, torture and cruelty were the norms in Egyptian society at the time. The Pharaoh also considered himself to be a god and expected complete obedience from his people. To make matters worse, without any justification, Pharaoh had decreed that all male children born to the Israelite subjects should be killed. The Israelite nation suffered immensely under the tyrannical Pharaoh and longed to be free again. It was under these conditions that by His Mercy, Allah sent Prophet Moses (ﷺ) to bring about an end to the persecution and remind the people about the worship of Allah.

When Prophet Moses (ﷺ) was born, his mother was very concerned about his safety, but Allah commanded her to put him in a basket and place it on the river Nile. She then sent her daughter to follow the little 'boat' to see where it went. The basket floated towards Pharaoh's palace, where his men fished it out and brought the baby to him. He wanted to kill the child immediately, but his wife *Aasiya*, who was a pious woman, stopped him. They did not have children of their own, so she asked him to adopt the child. Pharaoh agreed to his wife's request and then called a group of women to breast feed the crying child. However, the baby refused milk from all, except from his real mother who was amongst the group. So Allah reunited mother and child in the very palace of Pharaoh.

The years passed and Prophet Moses (ﷺ) grew up in the household of Pharaoh to be a fine Egyptian nobleman. However, a series of events occurred that would change his life forever. Following an incident in which an Egyptian man was killed, Prophet Moses (ﷺ) was exiled and had to leave Egypt. He found himself in the land of Madyan where he married Safura, daughter of the Prophet Shoaib (ﷺ). After staying in Madyan for many years, he left to return to Egypt. On their way to Egypt, during a severe winter night Prophet Moses (ﷺ) and his wife had lost their way. They saw a fire in the distance, so Prophet Moses (ﷺ) told his wife to stay where she was while he went to the fire, to bring some of it back or even find someone who could help them. When he reached the fire he saw that the flames were coming from a green tree but there was no one present.

MOSES
The Spoken to

"And has the story of Moses reached
you? When he saw a fire and said to
his family, Stay here; indeed, I have
perceived a fire; perhaps I can bring you
a torch or find at the fire some guidance.

And when he came to it, he was called,
O Moses, Indeed, I am your Lord, so
remove your sandals. Indeed, you are in
the sacred valley of Tuwa.

And I have chosen you, so listen to what
is revealed (to you).

Indeed, I am Allah. There is no deity
except Me, so worship Me and establish
prayer for My remembrance.

Indeed, the Hour is coming,
My design is to keep it hidden so
that every soul may be recompensed
according to that for which it strives.

(Quran, Ta-Ha 20: 9-15)

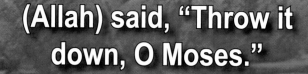

(Allah) said, "Throw it down, O Moses."

So he threw it down and thereupon it was a snake, moving swiftly.

(Allah) said, "Seize it and fear not; We will return it to its former condition..."

(Quran, Ta Ha 20: 19-21)

Background: Prophet Moses (☸) staff transforms into a snake.

Following page: Situated at an immense distance of 1,500 light years from Earth, the Great Nebula of Orion bears testimony to the unimaginable power of the Creator of the Universe, Allah. It is perhaps the most beautiful and brightest object in the night sky. It is also one of the most scrutinized and photographed. The nebula is estimated to be 30 light years across and includes neutral clouds of gas and dust and associations of stars. It is visible using binoculars as a fuzzy patch of light surrounding the sword stars below Orions belt. A telescope reveals a wealth of detail and a hint of green colour. Long exposure photographs show the red colour caused by the glow of hydrogen gas.

IMAGE CREDIT: HUBBLE TELESCOPE/NASA/ESA/STSCI.

Whilst Prophet Moses (ﷺ) looked around in surprise, he suddenly heard a voice saying, "O Moses, I am your Lord!". The voice then asked him to throw his walking staff onto the ground. At once it changed into a snake. Moses (ﷺ) was then commanded to lift the snake without fear and as he did so, it changed back into a stick. Next he was told to put his hand under his arm. When he drew it out again, his hand glowed with a bright light, like the Sun.

After having seen these great signs, Prophet Moses (ﷺ) was commanded by Allah to return to Egypt and together with his brother Prophet Aaron (ﷺ), invite people to worship the One true God. So Prophet Moses (ﷺ) returned to Egypt and informed Pharaoh that he was a Messenger of Allah and that he had brought clear proofs to show that he was speaking the truth. He threw his stick on the ground and it changed into a snake. The miracle frightened Pharaoh and he turned to his ministers for advice. They assured him that Prophet Moses (ﷺ) was just a good sorcerer and that their own sorcerers could easily perform such tricks. On hearing this advice Pharaoh arrogantly announced a great public gathering in his court, where his magicians would challenge Prophet Moses (ﷺ). People travelled from afar to attend the unique spectacle. However, the event itself backfired on Pharaoh; his sorcerers performed their usual conjurers tricks by throwing pieces of rope on the ground which began to wriggle like snakes. Prophet Moses (ﷺ) then threw his staff down which again transformed into a snake. Pharaoh and his sorcerers watched in horror as the snake began to eat all the pieces of rope. The bewildered sorcerers realised immediately that this was not magic but a miracle and threw themselves in prostration saying, "We believe in the Lord of Aaron and Moses" (Quran, 20: 70).

Pharaoh was furious, but the magicians would not change their minds, so he had their hands and feet cut off and then had them killed.

Allah told Prophet Moses (ﷺ) to warn Pharaoh that He would punish him and his people if they continued with their wicked ways. As Pharaoh considered himself a god he was too proud to listen to the warning. Soon the country was hit by famine. Swarms of locusts ate away the crops. The river Nile flooded its banks causing great destruction. The people were afflicted with disease. When all of this happened the people rushed to Prophet Moses (ﷺ) asking him to pray for their relief and promised to follow his religion. However, when they were cured they soon returned to their idol worship.

Prophet Moses (ﷺ) gathered his people and left for Palestine. Pharaoh learnt of their escape and followed them with a huge army. When the Israelites reached the Red Sea they saw Pharaoh approaching and were sure they were going to be killed. However, it was here that Prophet Moses (ﷺ) performed one of his greatest miracles; he struck the waters of the sea with his walking stick and the waters parted, making a dry path. The people rushed through the crossing, reaching the other side safely. When Pharaoh saw the path he followed in haste, but Allah caused him to be drowned. So fell the curtain on Pharaoh's tyranny and the waves threw his corpse up to the western seashore. The Egyptians saw him and knew that their 'god' whom they worshipped and obeyed was a mere slave who could not keep death away. Prophet Moses (ﷺ) led his people safely out from Egypt and after wandering in the desert for some years, he led his people to the 'Holy Land'. After Prophet Moses (ﷺ) had passed away, the Israelites prospered and ruled over the 'Holy Land' for as long as they obeyed the commandments of Allah.

Say: "We believe in Allah and in what has been revealed to us and what was revealed to Abraham, Ishmael, Isaac, Jacob and the Tribes and in (Books) given to Moses, Jesus and the Prophets from their Lord; we make no distinction between one and another among them and to Allah do we bow our will (in Islam)."

(Quran, The Family of Imran 3: 84)

Chapter 5
Prophet Jesus
(peace be upon him)

Jesus (ﷺ) - A Prophet of Islam

Known in the Quran as *Eesa bin Maryam* (Jesus, son of Mary), Muslims have immense love and respect for this Messenger of Allah. He is regarded as a Prophet, a reformist, the 'anointed one' (Messiah) and the 'Spirit of Allah' who was elevated to heaven. His name is never mentioned without invoking Allah's peace upon him. He was born miraculously: he spoke from the cradle as a baby, cured leprosy and those born deaf and blind, raised the dead and blew life into inanimate objects - all by the Will of Allah. Muslims do not believe that he was Allah or part of a trinity or that he was crucified or that he was the 'son of God'.

The Quran contains many verses regarding the life of Prophet Jesus (ﷺ). His high status to Muslims is highlighted by the fact that the Quran mentions him by name 25 times. In comparison Prophet Muhammad (ﷺ) is only mentioned by name five times. The fact that he is mentioned more than Prophet Muhammad (ﷺ), is not surprising for Muslims as the Quran is regarded as the word of Allah. As Prophet Muhammad (ﷺ) did not author the Quran himself, he did not have any control over its contents. It is also revealing that Mary, the mother of Jesus (ﷺ), is mentioned in the Quran and a chapter is named after her rather than any members of Prophet Muhammad's (ﷺ) family. Muslims also believe that anyone who disbelieves in Jesus (ﷺ) is not a Muslim, because a person who disbelieves in any one of the Prophets disbelieves in all of them. So Muslims firmly believe in Prophet Jesus (ﷺ) and in his message, which was the same message given to all of the other messengers, namely to worship Allah alone.

One of the most poignant and telling mother-son relationships in the Quran is that of Jesus, son of Mary. Prophet Jesus (ﷺ) was sent at a time when the Romans had conquered Palestine and the Israelites lived under subjugation once more. The remarkable story of Prophet Jesus (ﷺ) begins with his grandparents, Hannah and Imran and the birth of his mother Mary. Allah also reveals the parallel story of Prophet Zacharias (ﷺ) and his son the Prophet John (ﷺ).

Opposite page: The term the 'farthest mosque' is considered in Islamic tradition as the general name for the precinct of *al-Haram al-Sharif* (The Noble Sanctuary) in Jerusalem, as well as the specific name for the *al-Aqsa* mosque located at its southern edge. The original *al-Aqsa* mosque is regarded as the second 'house of Allah' to be built by the Prophet Adam (ﷺ) on Earth after the *Kaaba* in Makkah. Since that time, it has been destroyed and rebuilt several times. Around 1000 BCE, Prophet Solomon (ﷺ) is believed to have rebuilt a grand House of Worship at the site. However, it was burnt to the ground by the Babylonians in 586 BCE. It was consecrated again in 515 BCE, rebuilt by Herod in 20 BCE and destroyed by Titus in the year 70.

The Byzantine Christians used the area as a dump and it was in this state that the second Caliph of Islam, Umar Ibn al-Khattab (ﷺ), found it. In 638 he ordered the place cleaned and built a House of Prayer at the southern end of the sanctuary, the *Masjid al-Aqsa*. For centuries the Jews had been banned by Christian rulers from worshipping at the site, when Jerusalem passed into Islamic rule, in line with the justice and tolerance of Islam, the Caliph Umar Ibn al-Khattab (ﷺ) allowed the Jews to worship freely at the site once more. The *al-Aqsa* mosque was completed by Caliph Abd al-Malik in 647 where it stands to this day.

The Quranic narrative continues with the miraculous birth of Jesus (ﷺ). In Islamic tradition the mother of Jesus (ﷺ) was unique, in that she gave birth to a son by a miracle without the intervention of any physical means. The Prophethood of Jesus (ﷺ) is described with an emphasis on the miracles performed by him. This chapter contains an account of Prophet Jesus' (ﷺ) life taken from the Quran.

> (Mention, O Muhammad) when the wife of Imran said, "My Lord, indeed I have pledged to You what is in my womb, consecrated (for Your service), so accept this from me. Indeed, You are the Hearing, the Knowing." But when she delivered her, she said, "My Lord, I have delivered a female." And Allah was most knowing of what she delivered, "And the male is not like the female. And I have named her Mary and I seek refuge for her in You and (for) her descendants from Satan, the expelled (from the mercy of Allah)." So her Lord accepted her with good acceptance and caused her to grow in a good manner and put her in the care of Zacharias.
>
> (Quran, The Family of Imran 3: 35-37)

Opposite: The spectacular 'Dome of the Rock' stands on the sacred site in Jerusalem opposite the *al-Aqsa* Mosque. It was built by the ninth Caliph of Islam, Abd al-Malik between 687 and 691. The domed structure is the earliest Islamic monument to have survived in its original form to the present day. It is lavishly decorated with tiles bearing verses from the Quran.

Mary is Honoured by Allah

The story of Prophet Jesus (ﷺ) continues in chapter three of the Quran, with the news from Allah that Mary was to conceive a child with the aid of a special miracle.

Behold! The angels said: "O Mary! Allah has chosen you and purified you; chosen you above the women of all nations. "O Mary! worship your Lord devoutly; prostrate yourself and bow down (in prayer) with those who bow down."

This is part of the tidings of the things unseen which We reveal unto you (O Prophet Muhammad!) by inspiration; you were not with them when they cast lots with arrows as to which of them should be charged with the care of Mary; nor were you with them when they disputed (the point).

Behold! The angels said "O Mary! Allah gives you glad tidings of a Word from Him: his name will be Messiah Jesus the son of Mary held in honour in this world and the Hereafter and of (the company of) those nearest to Allah.

"He shall speak to the people in childhood and in maturity and he shall be (of the company) of the righteous." She said: "O my Lord! How shall I have a son when no man has touched me?" He said: "Even so: Allah creates what He wills; when He has decreed a plan He but says to it `Be' and it is! "And Allah will teach him the Book and Wisdom the Law and the Gospel.

(Quran, The Family of Imran 3: 42-48)

"Messiah the son of Mary was no more than a Messenger; many were the Messenger that passed away before him. His mother was a woman of truth. They had both to eat their (daily) food.

See how Allah does makes His Signs clear to them; yet see in what ways they are deluded away from the truth!"

(Quran, The Table Spread 5: 75)

Opposite page: A glorious morning in Allah's creation as rays of sunshine break through tall trees in a forest. For Muslims the Creator is Beautiful and loves beauty, all things in creation point to His Magnificence. He creates out of nothing whatever He wills and has power over all things in creation.

Prophet Jesus (�™) is Born

Such is the respect and honour that is given to Mary by Allah that the chapter called *Maryam* in the Quran is named after her. No other woman in the history of mankind is honoured in this way.

**And mention, (O Muhammad), in the Book (the story of) Mary, when she withdrew from her family to a place toward the east.
And she took, in seclusion from them, a screen. Then We sent to her Our Angel and he represented himself to her as a well-proportioned man.**

**She said, "Indeed, I seek refuge in the Most Merciful from you, (so leave me), if you should be fearing of Allah."
He said, "I am only the messenger of your Lord to give you (news of) a pure boy."**

She said, "How can I have a boy while no man has touched me and I have not been unchaste?" He said, "Thus (it will be); your Lord says, 'It is easy for Me and We will make him a sign to the people and a mercy from Us. And it is a matter (already) decreed.' "

So she conceived him and she withdrew with him to a remote place. And the pains of childbirth drove her to the trunk of a palm tree. She said, "Oh, I wish I had died before this and was in oblivion, forgotten."

But he called her from below her, "Do not grieve; your Lord has provided beneath you a stream. And shake toward you the trunk of the palm tree; it will drop upon you ripe, fresh dates.

So eat and drink and be contented. And if you see from among humanity anyone, say, 'Indeed, I have vowed to the Most Merciful abstention, so I will not speak today to (any) man."

(Quran, Mary 19: 16-26)

After Mary had given birth, people were suspicious and started to accuse her of sin. The Quran reveals how the baby Jesus (�™) miraculously spoke from the cradle in defence of his pious mother.

**"Then she brought him to her people, carrying him. They said, "O Mary, you have certainly done a thing unprecedented.
O sister of Aaron, your father was not a man of evil, nor was your mother unchaste."
So she pointed to him. They said, "How can we speak to one who is in the cradle a child?"**

(Jesus) said, "Indeed, I am the servant of Allah. He has given me the Scripture and made me a Prophet. And He has made me blessed wherever I am and has enjoined upon me prayer and charity as long as I remain alive. And (made me) dutiful to my mother and He has not made me a wretched tyrant."

And peace is on me the day I was born and the day I will die and the day I am raised alive." That is Jesus, the son of Mary, the word of truth about which they are in dispute.

(Quran, Mary 19: 27-34)

"...Do not grieve; your Lord has provided beneath you a stream. And shake toward you the trunk of the palm tree; it will drop upon you ripe, fresh dates."

(Quran, Mary 19: 24-25)

Jesus (ﷺ) a Messenger of Allah

The narrative continues with the Quran revealing some of the miracles that were performed by Prophet Jesus (ﷺ). The miracles tended to centre around healing and curing, as people at the time placed great faith in healers. They were performed by Allah's permission as a sign to the people that Prophet Jesus (ﷺ) was a true Messenger of Allah.

"(Be warned of) the Day when Allah will assemble the Messengers and say, "What was the response you received?" They will say, We have no knowledge. Indeed, it is You who is Knower of the unseen."

(The Day) when Allah will say, "O Jesus, Son of Mary, remember My favour upon you and upon your mother when I supported you with the Pure Spirit and you spoke to the people in the cradle and in maturity; and (remember) when I taught you writing and wisdom and the Torah and the Gospel; and when you designed from clay (what was) like the form of a bird with My permission, then you breathed into it and it became a bird with My permission; and you healed the blind and the leper with My permission; and when you brought forth the dead with My permission; and when I restrained the Children of Israel from (killing) you when you came to them with clear proofs and those who disbelieved among them said, "This is not but obvious magic."

(Quran, The Table Spread 5: 109-110)

"And He will teach him writing and wisdom and the Torah and the Gospel, And (make him) a Messenger to the Children of Israel, (who will say), 'Indeed I have come to you with a sign from your Lord in that I design for you from clay (that which is) like the form of a bird, then I breathe into it and it becomes a bird by permission of Allah. And I cure the blind and the leper and I give life to the dead by permission of Allah. And I inform you of what you eat and what you store in your houses. Indeed in that is a sign for you, if you are believers.

And (I have come) confirming what was before me of the Torah and to make lawful for you some of what was forbidden to you. And I have come to you with a sign from your Lord, so fear Allah and obey me.

Indeed, Allah is my Lord and your Lord, so worship Him. That is the straight path."

(Quran, The Family of Imran 3: 48-51)

Opposite page: High speed descent to the 'Dome of the Rock'. The structure stands on the sacred site known to Muslims as 'The Noble Sanctuary' (al-Haram al-Sharif) in Jerusalem.

"Both in this world and in the hereafter, I am the nearest of all the people to Jesus, the son of Maryam. The Prophets are paternal brothers, their mothers are different but their religion is one."

(Saying of Prophet Muhammad (ﷺ), recorded in Bukhari)

The Disciples

The disciples of Prophet Jesus (ﷺ) declared that they were Muslims who believed in his message and would obey their Lord. However, they wanted some more proof in the form of food sent from heaven, so they could satisfy themselves that they were on the right path. So Prophet Jesus (ﷺ) prayed for 'a table spread with food'.

"And (remember) when I inspired to the disciples, "Believe in Me and in My Messenger Jesus." They said, "We have believed, so bear witness that indeed we are Muslims (in submission to Allah)."

(And remember) when the disciples said, "O Jesus, Son of Mary, can your Lord send down to us a table (spread with food) from the heaven? (Jesus) said," Fear Allah, if you should be believers."

They said, "We wish to eat from it and let our hearts be reassured and know that you have been truthful to us and be among its witnesses."

Said Jesus, the son of Mary, "O Allah, our Lord, send down to us a table (spread with food) from the heaven to be for us a festival for the first of us and the last of us and a sign from You. And provide for us and You are the best of providers."

(Quran, The Table Spread 5: 111-114)

"O you who believe! Be Allah's helpers, even as Jesus son of Mary said unto the disciples: Who are my helpers for Allah? They said: We are Allah's helpers. And a party of the Children of Israel believed, while a party disbelieved..."

(Quran, The Ranks 61: 14)

Prophet Jesus (ﷺ) Not Crucified

Islam holds that Prophet Jesus (ﷺ) was not crucified but was raised to heaven by Allah. The sayings of Prophet Muhammad (ﷺ) reveal that Jesus (ﷺ) will return before the end of time to lead the battle against the forces of evil. Allah refers in the Quran to the Israelites and their boasting about the crucifixion as follows:

"And (for) their saying, "Indeed, we have killed the Messiah, Jesus, son of Mary, the Messenger of Allah." And they did not kill him, nor did they crucify him; but (another) was made to resemble him to them. And indeed, those who differ over it are in doubt about it. They have no knowledge of it except the following of assumption. And they did not kill him, for certain.

Rather, Allah raised him to Himself. And ever is Allah Exalted in Might and Wise.

And there is none from the People of the Scripture but that he will surely believe in Jesus before his death. And on the Day of Resurrection he will be a witness against them."

(Quran, Women 4:157-159)

And (beware the Day) when Allah will say, "O Jesus, Son of Mary, did you say to the people, 'Take me and my mother as deities besides Allah?'" He will say, "Exalted are You! It was not for me to say that to which I have no right. If I had said it, You would have known it. You know what is within myself and I do not know what is within Yourself. Indeed, it is You who is Knower of the unseen.

I said not to them except what You commanded me: to worship Allah, my Lord and your Lord. And I was a witness over them as long as I was among them; but when You took me up, You were the Observer over them and You are, over all things, Witness.

If You should punish them indeed they are Your servants; but if You forgive them indeed it is You who is the Exalted in Might, the Wise.

Allah will say, "This is the Day when the truthful will benefit from their truthfulness." For them are gardens (in Paradise) beneath which rivers flow, wherein they will abide forever, Allah being pleased with them and they with Him. That is the great attainment.

To Allah belongs the dominion of the heavens and the earth and whatever is within them. And He is competent over all things.

(Quran, The Table Spread 5:116-120)

Opposite page: Quranic verse explaining the similitude between Prophets Adam (ﷺ) and Jesus (ﷺ), against a beautiful sunset over a beach. The photograph has been taken using a slow shutter speed.

Following page: Exquisite water garden in the grounds of probably the most famous example of 12th century Muslim architecture in Spain, the Al-Hambra (Red Castle).

JESUS

The Spirit of Allah

عليه
السلام

"Indeed, the example of Jesus to Allah is like that of Adam. He created Him from dust; then He said to him, "Be," and he was. The truth is from your Lord, so do not be among the doubters.

Then whoever argues with you about it after (this) knowledge has come to you say, "Come, let us call our sons and your sons, our women and your women, ourselves and yourselves, then supplicate earnestly (together) and invoke the curse of Allah upon the liars (among us)."

Indeed, this is the true narration. And there is no deity except Allah. And indeed, Allah is the Exalted in Might, the Wise. But if they turn away, then indeed Allah is Knowing of the corrupters.

(Quran, The Family of Imran 3: 59-63)

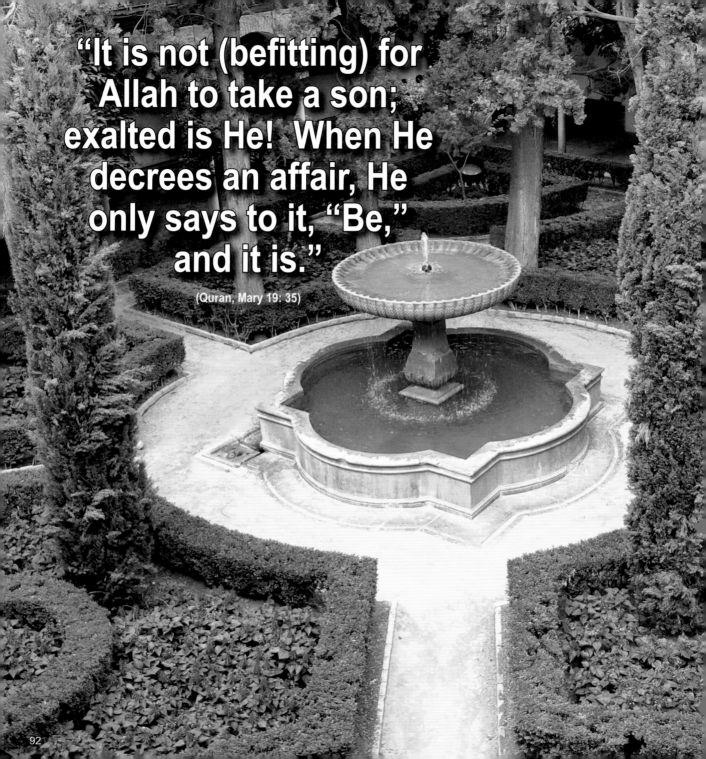

"It is not (befitting) for Allah to take a son; exalted is He! When He decrees an affair, He only says to it, "Be," and it is."

(Quran, Mary 19: 35)

Chapter 6
Prophet
Muhammad

(may the peace and blessings of Allah be upon him)

The Last Messenger of Allah

Arabian society before Islam

Prophet Abraham (ﷺ) had two sons, Ishmael (ﷺ) and Isaac (ﷺ), both of whom were appointed as Prophets by Allah. The Prophet Isaac (ﷺ) was the father of the Israelite nation, otherwise known as the 'Jews'. For many centuries, Allah had favoured the Israelites and sent them many Prophets even though they broke His covenant. Before the Blessed Prophet Muhammad (ﷺ) was born, the Israelites had been sent Prophet Jesus (ﷺ) some six hundred years earlier to remind them of Allah's commandments once more. However, the message of Prophet Jesus (ﷺ) was rejected by most people at the time. It would be many centuries later before Prophet Muhammad (ﷺ) would appear as had been chronicled in their scriptures. Guided by certain signs in their scriptures, many Jewish tribes had travelled from Palestine and settled in Arabia in and around the city of Yathrib in anticipation.

The Ishmaelite or Arab nation had settled widely in Arabia. They were descendants of Prophet Abraham (ﷺ) through his son Prophet Ishmael (ﷺ). The *Kaaba* in the very centre of Makkah, which had been built by the Prophets Abraham (ﷺ) and Ishmael (ﷺ) for the worship of Allah, was still a central place of worship for the Arab tribes. The people of the tribe of Quraysh in particular, commanded the highest level of respect due to their position as caretakers of the sanctuary. Although it was called the 'House of Allah', over the centuries the Ishmaelite nation had largely forgotten the pure monotheism as taught by their forefathers, Prophets Abraham and Ishmael (ﷺ) and had fallen into paganism.

Idols had become the chief objects of worship because they were believed to be intercessors with Allah. Whilst paganism had become widespread in society, some individuals rejected pagan worship and all the practices associated with it. They longed to seek out the true religion of their forefathers.

Prostitution, indecency, drunken orgies and adultery were rampant among pre-Islamic Arab society at the time. Superstition, senseless blood feuds, tribal disputes, slavery and oppression of the helpless had become the norm. Idol worship had replaced the pure teachings of the Prophet Abraham (ﷺ). Pre-Islamic Arab men had no limit to the number of wives they could marry. In fact women were a marketable commodity regarded as a piece of property. Whilst some held their children dear, many others buried their female children alive because of an illusory fear of poverty and shame weighed heavily on them. Trade was the most common way to earn a living. However, poverty and hunger were the prevailing features in Arabia.

Although pre-Islamic Arabia had a large number of evils, it also had some praiseworthy virtues. For example it was famous for its hospitality, keeping a covenant, sense of honour, perseverance and leading a simple bedouin life.

Opposite page: One of the great doors to the Mosque of the Prophet Muhammad (ﷺ) in Madinah, bearing the Arabic inscription 'Muhammad is the Messenger of Allah'.

Following pages: Present day domes and minarets of the first mosque of Islam built in Quba just outside Madinah. Its foundation stones were positioned by the Prophet Muhammad (ﷺ) himself upon his emigration from the city of Makkah to Madinah in the year 622.

Birth and Early Life of Muhammad (ﷺ)

Prophet Muhammad (ﷺ) was born of noble lineage, in Makkah in the year 570 into one of the most powerful Arabian tribes, the Quraysh. His Father, Abdullah, passed away before his birth and he was brought up by his mother Aaminah bint Wahab until she passed away in 576. He was then cared for by his grandfather until he too passed away two years later. His kind uncle, Abu Talib, then took over his care.

As a young man Prophet Muhammad (ﷺ) was valiant, handsome, strong yet gentle. He displayed exceptional virtues as a very trustworthy individual. Members of various tribes would invite him to act as an arbitrator in their disputes. His reputation for being truthful, honest, trustworthy, generous and sincere, became so well known that people nicknamed him *Al-Amin* (The Trustworthy).

Muhammad (ﷺ) never partook in the customs of the Quraysh at that time. He would withdraw to the mountains for days at a time to remove himself from the drunken rampages of the people. He never worshipped the idols placed in the *Kaaba* and never engaged in the immoral practices of the people. At the age of 25, he married Lady Khadija (may Allah be well pleased with her, ﷺ) a noble widow 15 years his senior. They remained married for the next 25 years until her death.

The Beginning of Prophethood

During one of the spiritual retreats which he made habitually in a cave on top of a mountain outside Makkah, Prophet Muhammad (ﷺ) had an amazing encounter with Angel Gabriel. The angel started to reveal Allah's Word to him, namely the Quran. The angel also announced that "Muhammad is the Messenger of Allah".

Prophet Muhammad (ﷺ) was forty years old when he received his first revelation. For the next thirteen years he preached the Word of Allah to the Makkans, inviting them to abandon idolatry and accept the religion of the One God. A few accepted his call but most Makkans, especially those of his own tribe, opposed him violently, seeing in the new religion a grave danger to their economic as well as social domination based upon their control of the *Kaaba*.

Prophet Muhammad (ﷺ) continued to call the people to Islam and gradually a number of men and women began to accept the faith and submit themselves to its teachings. As a result, persecution of Muslims increased until the Blessed Prophet (ﷺ) was forced to send some of his companions to Abyssinia (Ethiopia) where they were protected by the Christian king, Negus.

The period of time that the Blessed Prophet Muhammad (ﷺ) spent in Makkah was also one of very intense spiritual experience for him as well as his companions. These early Muslims formed the nucleus of the new religious community that was soon to spread worldwide. It was during this period of Islam that Allah ordered the direction of prayers to be changed from Jerusalem to Makkah. Today Jerusalem still remains one of the most sacred cities of Islam, along with Makkah and Madinah.

Opposite page: The first mosque in Madinah was built by Prophet Muhammad (ﷺ) himself. Subsequent Islamic rulers greatly expanded and decorated the mosque. An important feature of the site is the green dome adjacent to the mosque, under which the grave of Prophet Muhammad (ﷺ) is located.

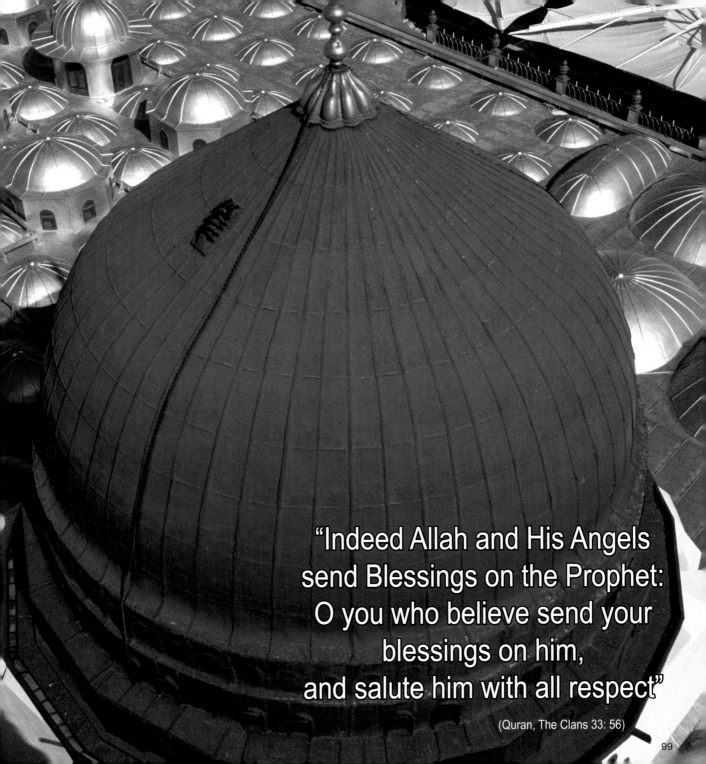

"Indeed Allah and His Angels
send Blessings on the Prophet:
O you who believe send your
blessings on him,
and salute him with all respect"

(Quran, The Clans 33: 56)

99

Migration to Madinah

In the year 622, Prophet Muhammad (ﷺ) was ordered by Allah to migrate to Yathrib, a city north of Makkah. He followed the Divine Command and left with his followers for that city which henceforth was known as 'The City of the Prophet' (*Madinat al-Nabi*) or simply Madinah. This event in history was so momentous that the Islamic calendar begins from the date of the migration (*Hijrah* in Arabic). In Madinah, the Prophet of Allah established the first Islamic society which has served as the model for all later Islamic societies.

Victory at Makkah

After the establishment of the Islamic state in Madinah, several battles took place against the invading Makkans which, the Muslims won against great odds. Soon, more tribes began to join Islam and within a few years most of Arabia had embraced the religion of Islam. After many trials and eventually successive victories, the Prophet of Allah, Muhammad (ﷺ), returned triumphantly to Makkah where the people embraced Islam at last. He forgave all his former enemies and marched to the *Kaaba*, where he ordered his cousin Ali (may Allah be well pleased with him, ﷠) to join him in destroying all of the idols. He reconstituted the rite of pilgrimage as founded by Prophet Abraham (ﷻ). He then returned to Madinah and later made another pilgrimage to Makkah.

It was during this last pilgrimage that he delivered his farewell address. Upon his return to Madinah he fell ill and after a few days, he passed away in the year 632. To this day, he lies buried in the chamber of his house next to his mosque, *Masjid Al Nabawi*.

In a few short years after his passing away, Islamic civilisation spread to most of the known world at the time. It would dominate world affairs for the next thousand years.

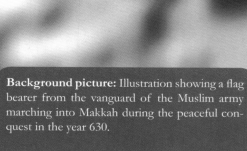

Background picture: Illustration showing a flag bearer from the vanguard of the Muslim army marching into Makkah during the peaceful conquest in the year 630.

Following pages: Worshippers perform evening prayers at the Sacred Mosque in Makkah.

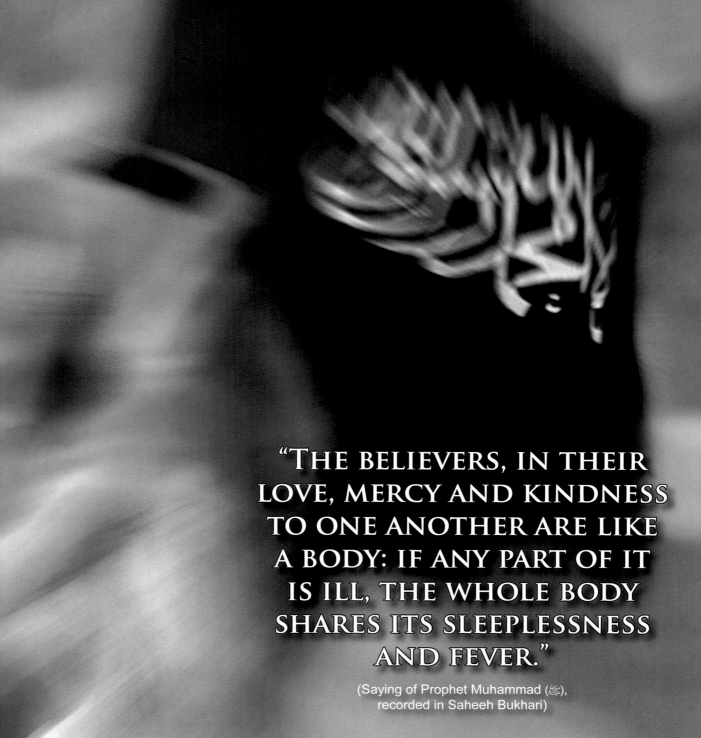

"THE BELIEVERS, IN THEIR LOVE, MERCY AND KINDNESS TO ONE ANOTHER ARE LIKE A BODY: IF ANY PART OF IT IS ILL, THE WHOLE BODY SHARES ITS SLEEPLESSNESS AND FEVER."

(Saying of Prophet Muhammad (ﷺ), recorded in Saheeh Bukhari)

Prophet Muhammad (ﷺ) - Timeline

The Orphan Child

The birth of Muhammad (ﷺ).

Muhammad (ﷺ) is entrusted to the tribe of Bani Sa'ad for his early upbringing.

Muhammad (ﷺ) passes into the custody of his kind uncle, Abu Talib.

The Trustworthy Youth

Muhammad (ﷺ) is renowned for his reputation of honesty and good manners.

CE — **570** — **576** — **578** — **583** — **586** — **595**

Muhammad's (ﷺ) mother, Aaminah bint Wahab, passes away.

Whilst on a journey to Syria with his uncle, Muhammad (ﷺ) is recognised by Bahira, a Christian monk, as a future prophet.

The Righteous Husband & Loving Father

In Makkah, aged 25 Prophet Muhammad (ﷺ) marries his first wife Lady Khadija (ﷺ), a wealthy widow aged 40. They would stay together for the next 25 years.

The Seeker of Truth

Muhammad (ﷺ) helps to rebuild the *Kaaba*.

As Muhammad (ﷺ) never worshipped any idols and always felt an aversion to them, he is restless about the idolatry and other social and moral ills that exist in his society. He starts to find peace in solitude outside of *Makkah*.

The secret call to Islam continues as the Prophet Muhammad (ﷺ) teaches the first Muslims patience, kindness to parents, modesty and remembrance of Allah.

Prophet Muhammad (ﷺ) preaches to his kinsfolk and warns them about the Day of Judgement.

The pagan Makkans now start to oppose Prophet Muhammad (ﷺ).

605 — **610** — **611** — **612** — **613** — **614**

The Receiver of Divine Revelation

Around the age of 40, Muhammad (ﷺ) visits Mount Nur to contemplate on the wider aspects of creation. On Mount Nur, he finds privacy in the cave of Hira. Muhammad's (ﷺ) Prophethood begins with the first revelation of the Quran. His wife, close friends and family accept Islam.

The first phase of the Islamic call to worship Allah alone begins in secret.

The Patient Warner

The Messenger of Allah, Muhammad (ﷺ) receives the first revelation regarding publicly preaching Islam.

He starts to warn the Makkans about the evils of idol worship, killing, stealing, infanticide and about many other vices prevalent in Makkan society.

Prophet Muhammad (ﷺ) speaks out against injustice and oppression.

The Makkans offer Prophet Muhammad (ﷺ) worldly gains if he stops speaking against their beliefs and customs.

Prophet Muhammad (ﷺ) stands firm as harassment of the weaker Muslims turns into persecution and torture.

103

Arabian Peninsula Circa 600

Byzantine Empire

Mediterranean Sea

Egypt

Arabia

Red Sea

Yemen

Abyssinia

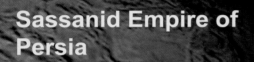

Sassanid Empire of Persia

Persian Gulf

Arabian Sea

Key:

Jerusalem ●

Tabuk ●

Madinah ●

Makkah ●

Aden ●

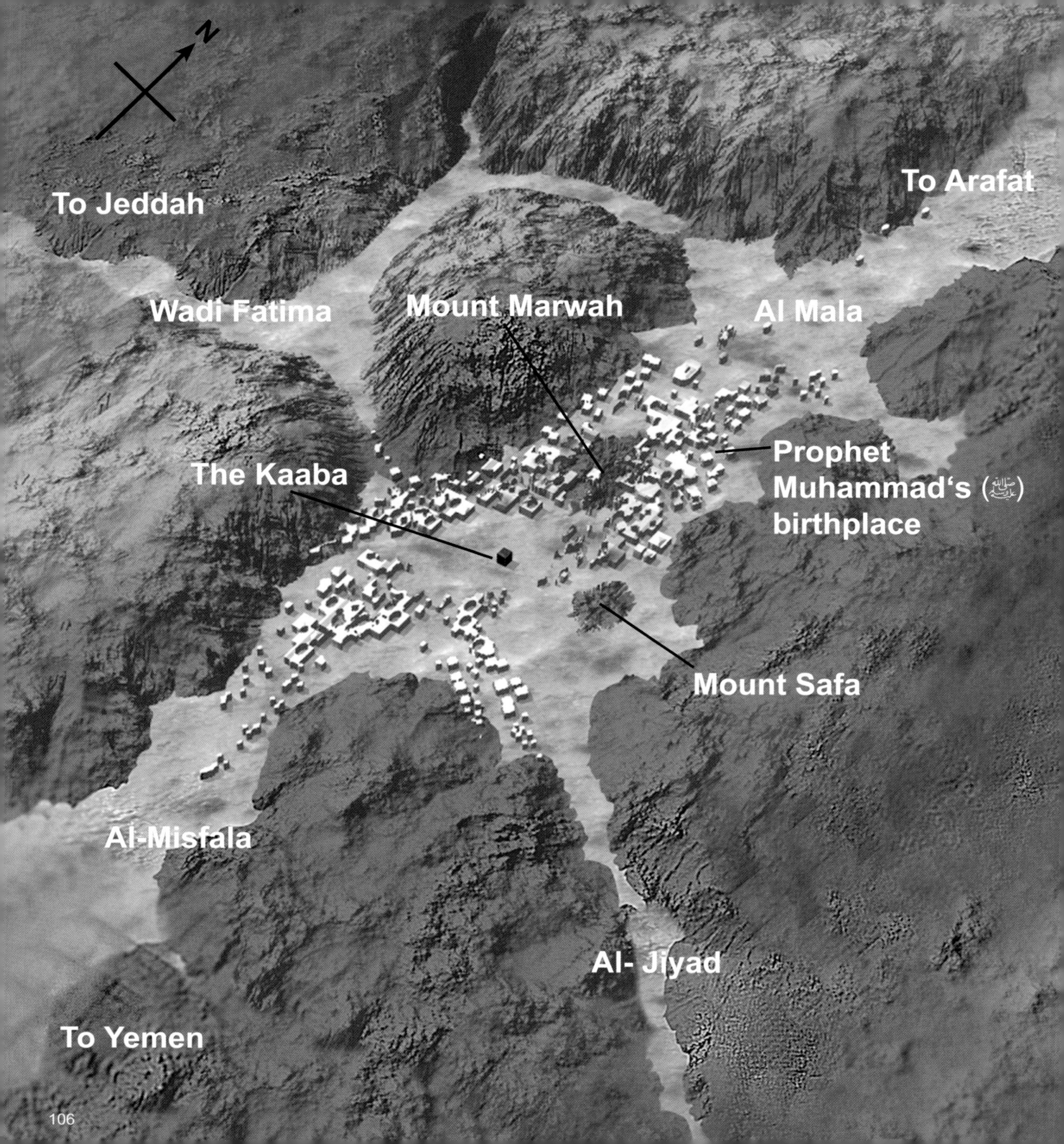

To Jeddah

To Arafat

Wadi Fatima

Mount Marwah

Al Mala

The Kaaba

Prophet Muhammad's (ﷺ) birthplace

Mount Safa

Al-Misfala

Al- Jiyad

To Yemen

106

"It is He (Allah) Who has sent amongst the unlettered a Messenger (Muhammad) from among themselves to rehearse to them His Signs, to sanctify them and to instruct them in scripture and wisdom although they had been before in manifest error."

(Quran, Friday 62: 2)

Right: Surrounded by eight towering minarets, the *Kaaba* lies at the heart of the Sacred Mosque in Makkah. In the distance the steep and craggy rock mountain range containing Mount Nur can be seen. It was in a cave on top of this mountain that Prophet Muhammad (ﷺ) received the first revelation of the Quran.

Opposite page: Map of Makkah, circa 600.

Prophet Muhammad (ﷺ) - Timeline

The House of Al-Arqam is established where Prophet Muhammad (ﷺ) secretly teaches the Muslims. He emphasises charity, education and literacy.

In the face of intense persecution some Muslims migrate to Abyssinia (Ethiopia).

In spite of the boycott Prophet Muhammad (ﷺ) continues to speak out against idolatry, infanticide, the oppression of women and slavery.

The boycott is eventually broken. Prophet Muhammad (ﷺ) remains steadfast upon the worship of Allah. This is the Prophet's *Year of Grief* as his wife, Lady Khadija (ﺭ) and his Uncle Abu Talib both pass away shortly after the boycott has ended.

The Prophet of Allah visits Taif in order to gather support for the Islamic call. The mission ends in failure. Prophet Muhammad (ﷺ) marries a widow, Lady Sawdah (ﺭ).

CE   615   616   617   618   619   620

Muslim spirits lift as Prophet Muhammad's (ﷺ) uncle, Hamzah (ﺭ) and a Makkan noble, Umar ibn al-Khattab (ﺭ) accept Islam.

The Makkans try to tempt Prophet Muhammad (ﷺ) with offers of wealth and power. The Prophet Muhammad (ﷺ) refuses.

In response the Makkans impose a harsh social boycott on Prophet Muhammad (ﷺ) and his family.

As the boycott continues Prophet Muhammad (ﷺ) remains determined to preach the message of peace, justice, tolerance and equality.

Prophet Muhammad (ﷺ) secretly meets some men from Madinah who accept Islam.

Al-Miraj takes place. This is the miraculous journey of Prophet Muhammad (ﷺ) from Makkah to Jerusalem and then to the Heavens.

Prophet Muhammad (ﷺ) marries Lady Ayesha (ﺭ).

Five daily prayers are prescribed by Allah.

Route of the Hijra

Traditional trade route

Madinah

Makkah

Jeddah

The first pledge of Aqabah takes place by a group of people from Madinah.

The Prophet of Allah commands them not to slander or steal and not to commit adultery or kill their children.

621 **622**

The second 'Aqabah pledge occurs. In June 622, the pagan Makkans learn of the pledge.

Prophet Muhammad (ﷺ) commands his followers to migrate to Madinah.

The pagan Makkans remain defiant and attempt to kill Prophet Muhammad (ﷺ).

Prophet Muhammad (ﷺ) migrates to Madinah.

The route taken by Prophet Muhammad (ﷺ) and his companion Abu Bakr As-Siddeeq (ﺭ) during their migration or *Hijra* to Madinah in the year 622. The city of Madinah lies some 400 km north of Makkah. The pair first travelled in the opposite direction and hid in a cave to avoid the pagan Makkans who had sent out search parties. Then they secretly travelled avoiding the traditional caravan routes between Makkah and Madinah. They arrived in Madinah one month later and were met by a huge number of the jubilant men, women and children who had been eagerly anticipating their arrival.

109

Map of Madinah (formerly known as Yathrib) circa 622.

N

Aqiq valley

Harratul Wabarah

Palm garden

Sil mountains

1.

9.

Ranona valley

2.

7.

At-Tahan valley

10.

5.

4.

Asir Mountains

Palm garden

To Makkah

6.

3.

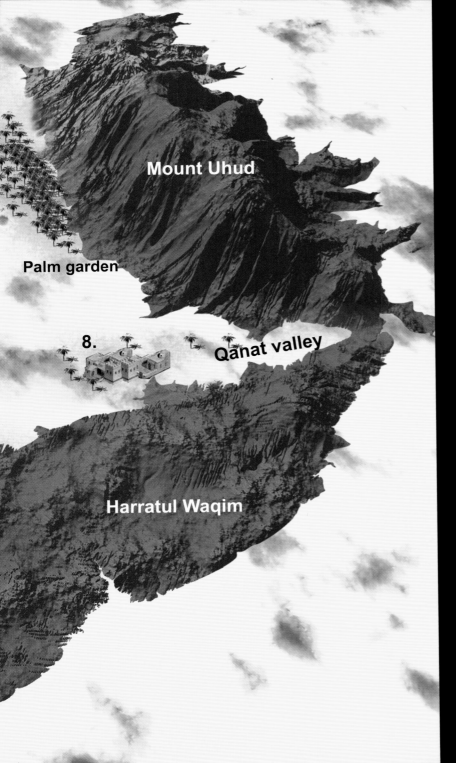

A simplified map showing the city of Madinah and the various tribes (*Banu*) living around the city.

Key:
1. Madinah.
2. Prophet Muhammad's (ﷺ) mosque.
3. Houses of Banu Quraiza.
4. Houses of Banu Zafar.
5. Houses of Banu Qainuqa.
6. Citadel of Ka'b bin Al-Ashraf.
7. Al-Bakia cemetery
8. Houses of Banu Haritha.
9. Houses of Banu Abd al-Ash-hal.
10. Quba.

Mount Uhud

Palm garden

8.

Qanat valley

Harratul Waqim

Prophet Muhammad (ﷺ) - Timeline

A New Beginning in Madinah.

Prophet Muhammad (ﷺ) establishes a just Islamic society based on the worship of Allah.

The Muslims build the Prophet's Mosque in Madinah.

The pagan Makkans are intent on starting hostilities with the Muslims in Madinah.

Allah gives permission to the Muslims to fight in self defence.

In defence of Madinah Prophet Muhammad (ﷺ) leads the Muslim battalions into battle at Mount Uhud. The expedition to Bani Nadeer takes place after the battle of Uhud.

New laws and guidance continue to be revealed as alcohol, interest and gambling are prohibited.

Prophet Muhammad (ﷺ) explains womens' rights, the rights of orphans and the Laws of inheritance.

CE — **622** — **623** — **624** — **624** — **625** — **626**

Prophet Muhammad (ﷺ) signs an alliance treaty with the Arab and Jewish tribes living in and around Madinah.

Muslims and Jews are to support each other and both can freely practice their own religion.

Women are given high and honourable status. Giving charity and the freeing of slaves is encouraged.

The Courageous Leader

Prophet Muhammad (ﷺ) teaches honesty, trustworthiness and humility.

The public call to prayer is established. Quranic revelations continue as fasting and charity are made compulsory.

Outnumbered 3 to 1. the Muslims show great courage during the Battle of Badr.

The Muslims gather a force of 1,500 men to meet the Makkans at the wells of Badr for the second time. However, the pagans turn back without a fight.

Later in the same year the Messenger of Allah sets out with a force of 1000 to head off an invasion at Dumatul-Jandal.

The Muslims are forced to defend Madinah again at the Battle of Khandaq (The Trench). The pagan Makkans lay siege to Madinah for one month, but are unable to capture it.

The Prophet Muhammad (ﷺ) sends military expeditions to many rebellious areas including Bani Lihyan, Al-Ghamir, Bani Tha`labah, Al-Jumun, Al-`Ais, Wadi Al-Qura, Bani Al-Mustaliq, Bani Kalb & Bani Sa'd.

Prophet Muhammad (ﷺ) proceeds to Makkah with 2000 men, women and children. They perform the Umrah without hindrance from the Makkan pagans.

The Muslims fight courageously against a huge Roman army. The battle of Mu'tah proved to be the most significant and fiercest battle during the lifetime of the Messenger of Allah.

The Blessed Prophet Muhammad (ﷺ) dispatches his friend Abu Bakr (ؓ), to lead the Muslims in performing the pilgrimage.

627 **628** **629** **630** **631** **632**

The Noble Statesman

The Messenger of Allah leads a lesser pilgrimage (*Umrah*) to Makkah. Prophet Muhammad (ﷺ) signs a ten year peace treaty with the pagan Makkans at Al-Hudaibiyah.

Now the Muslims intensify their peaceful efforts in propagating Islam to the tribes of Arabia. Prophet Muhammad (ﷺ) also sends letters to the kings beyond Arabia inviting them to embrace Islam.

The pagan Makkans break the peace treaty. The Muslims muster an army of 10,000 and march to Makkah. They enter Makkah peacefully on the 1st of January 630. The pagan Makkans offer no resistance. Prophet Muhammad (ﷺ) orders that all of the idols be removed from the *Kaaba*. He also forgives the Makkans and their leaders for all their years of hostility and persecution by declaring a general amnesty.

The Last Messenger of Allah

The Arab people race towards embracing Islam. Many delegations arrive in Madinah from various parts of Arabia. The Messenger of Allah announces his intention to go on pilgrimage to Makkah. Thousands of people come to Madinah to join him on the journey.

The Blessed Prophet Muhammad (ﷺ) passes away on the 12th of Rabi`al Awwal in the 11th year after Migration. He was 63 years old.

113

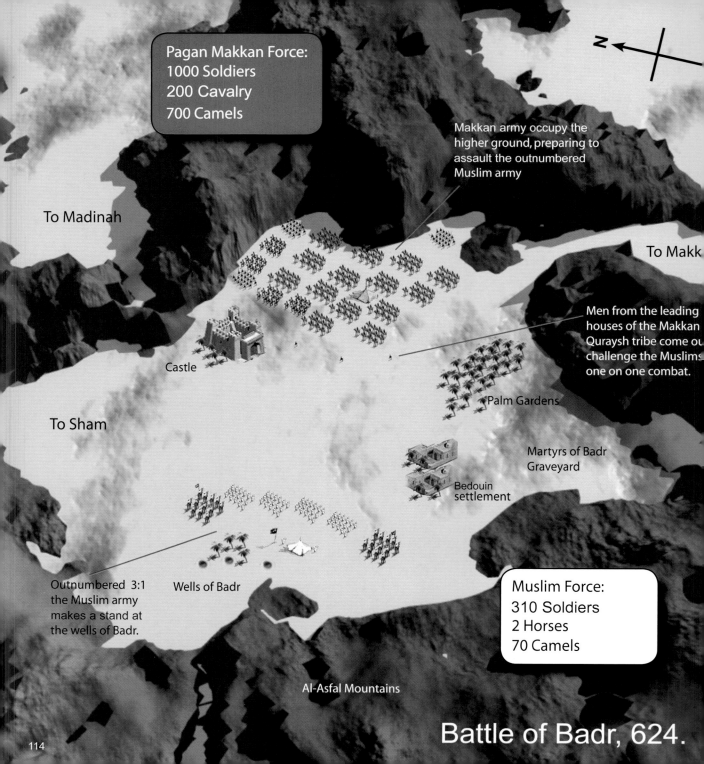

Pagan Makkan Force:
1000 Soldiers
200 Cavalry
700 Camels

N

To Madinah

Makkan army occupy the higher ground, preparing to assault the outnumbered Muslim army

To Makk

Men from the leading houses of the Makkan Quraysh tribe come ou challenge the Muslims one on one combat.

Castle

Palm Gardens

To Sham

Martyrs of Badr Graveyard

Bedouin settlement

Outnumbered 3:1 the Muslim army makes a stand at the wells of Badr.

Wells of Badr

Muslim Force:
310 Soldiers
2 Horses
70 Camels

Al-Asfal Mountains

Battle of Badr, 624.

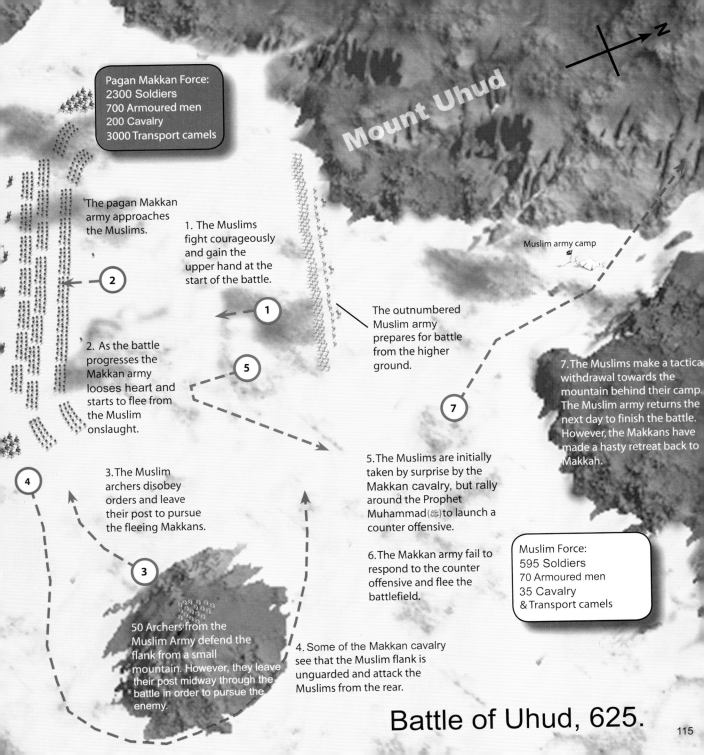

Pagan Makkan Force:
2300 Soldiers
700 Armoured men
200 Cavalry
3000 Transport camels

Mount Uhud

The pagan Makkan army approaches the Muslims.

Muslim army camp

1. The Muslims fight courageously and gain the upper hand at the start of the battle.

The outnumbered Muslim army prepares for battle from the higher ground.

2. As the battle progresses the Makkan army looses heart and starts to flee from the Muslim onslaught.

7. The Muslims make a tactical withdrawal towards the mountain behind their camp. The Muslim army returns the next day to finish the battle. However, the Makkans have made a hasty retreat back to Makkah.

3. The Muslim archers disobey orders and leave their post to pursue the fleeing Makkans.

5. The Muslims are initially taken by surprise by the Makkan cavalry, but rally around the Prophet Muhammad(ﷺ)to launch a counter offensive.

6. The Makkan army fail to respond to the counter offensive and flee the battlefield.

Muslim Force:
595 Soldiers
70 Armoured men
35 Cavalry
& Transport camels

50 Archers from the Muslim Army defend the flank from a small mountain. However, they leave their post midway through the battle in order to pursue the enemy.

4. Some of the Makkan cavalry see that the Muslim flank is unguarded and attack the Muslims from the rear.

Battle of Uhud, 625.

115

Accomplishments

Muslims regard Prophet Muhammad (ﷺ) as the final Messenger sent by Allah and as a mercy and blessing for all of mankind. History testifies that he accomplished his mission to convey Allah's prescribed way of life to the people during and after his lifetime.

Prophet Muhammad (ﷺ) taught the concept of the Unity of Allah and the rejection of all false deities. He showed how the Unity of Allah opened the way for the existence of a good and just system where everyone's rights were protected. This brought a complete change of society which in his time was rife with killing and tribal wars. The new faith demanded absolute equality of all members in the sight of Allah, without distinction of colour, race, tribe or sex. The rule of *Shariah* law was established and everyone was equal before the law. Women were raised in status and given honourable rights and slaves were given equal status with other people.

Prophet Muhammad's (ﷺ) universal message was meant for the whole of mankind. In Madinah he created a society that was truly united under the Islamic way of life. It included people of different countries, nations, natures, and characters. This example is still applicable today and Muslims believe that it provides a foundation for the idea of a world community living in harmony, unity and peace, by obeying the Law of The Almighty Creator, Allah.

Prophet Muhammad (ﷺ) also showed mankind its real position in relation to the universe. By observing and investigating the physical world, one can see the signs of the Creator's presence in everything. Discovering the secrets of nature makes it possible for mankind to exert some control over the physical world for the benefit of all. In fact this particular teaching of Prophet Muhammad (ﷺ) has inspired generations of Muslim scientists over the centuries.

Prophet Muhammad (ﷺ) also led men and women to a path of knowledge in place of ignorance, to reason in place of superstition and tradition, and to freedom of thought and research in place of blind acceptance of the opinions of ancestors and political leaders. History shows that it was Prophet Muhammad (ﷺ) who brought people out of slavery, both to other men and to their own egos and offered them the true mastery of their own lives in obedience to the laws of Allah.

Opposite page: Internal view of the Dome of the Rock in Jerusalem.

"You (Muhammad) indeed stand on an exalted standard of character."

(Quran, The Pen 68: 4)

Excellent Example

Prophet Muhammad (ﷺ) was human and created from flesh and blood like any other human being. Muslims, however, regard him as a perfect human in every sense and set a code of conduct by his words and actions. His life is unique and unparalleled in human history and will remain a guide for other men and women in every aspect of life.

Prophet Muhammad (ﷺ) was indeed the living example for the whole of humanity, not only on a personal and spiritual level, but also how to conduct one's affairs within society. He showed us through his example how to worship Allah, live a moral life, relate to the world around us and keep ourselves clean as well as how to behave as a statesman and a military leader. With his family he was a caring husband and a loving father. He provided a beautiful example as a patient teacher and a trustworthy friend with his close companions.

His example is still relevant and alive through-out the Islamic world today because of the comprehensive way in which his life has been recorded. Every aspect of his life, his actions, sayings, his consent and silence in response to issues put to him, have been recorded in an elaborate chain of narration called the 'Sunnah'. This has enabled the scholars and jurists of Islam to define Muslim life in detail through the way in which Prophet Muhammad (ﷺ) behaved.

His Mercy

Prophet Muhammad (ﷺ) was a very forgiving and merciful person. In the Quran Allah says;

"And We (Allah) have sent you (Muhammad) not but as a mercy to all the worlds."

(Quran, The Prophets 21: 107)

An excellent example of his mercy was when he conquered Makkah in the year 630 at the head of a huge army. Rather than taking revenge and retaliation on those who had persecuted him, he forgave the Makkans and their leaders by declaring a general amnesty.

Another example of his mercy is his love of the poor and needy. He would distribute everything that he received by way of charity. He once told his wife Lady Ayesha (ﷺ);

"O Ayesha, love the poor and let them come to you and Allah will draw you near to Himself."

(Recorded in Saheeh Bukhari)

Opposite page: Artwork of the word 'Muhammad', Allah bless him and give him peace (Exhibition Islam collection). Arabic calligraphy is a primary form of art for Islamic visual expression and creativity. Throughout the vast geography of the Islamic world, Arabic calligraphy is a symbol representing unity, beauty and power.

119

Elegant Manners

Prophet Muhammad (ﷺ) was an embodiment of excellent morals and character. His graceful conduct and charming manners demonstrated the perfection of his noble character. He was indeed an excellent example to all mankind and himself practised what he preached. It is reported by many eminent companions of Prophet Muhammad (ﷺ) that he was the most polite, courteous and gentle in manners. He talked with grace and dignity and he never hurt anyone's feelings. He would often say, "*The best among you are the best in character*." (Recorded in Saheeh Bukhari). His servant, Anas (ﷺ), said that, "I served the Prophet (ﷺ) for ten years and he never said to me, "Uff" (a minor harsh word denoting impatience) and never blamed me by saying, "Why did you do so or why didn't you do so?" (Recorded in Saheeh Bukhari). Many of Prophet Muhammad's (ﷺ) companions also reported that they had not seen anyone more given to smiling than Allah's Messenger. It was his practice to greet and shake hands with people when first meeting them. Wherever he went he greeted everyone who came along his path.

If undesirable incidents occurred at gatherings, he would be tolerant and forgiving. For example a bedouin once urinated in the mosque and the people ran to beat him. The Blessed Prophet Muhammad (ﷺ) stopped them saying, *"Do not interrupt his urination (i.e. let him finish)."* Then the Prophet asked for water and poured it over the area (Recorded in Saheeh Bukhari).

Above: Masjid al Qiblatain (or the Mosque with two *Qiblas*), is situated in Madinah, a few kilometres from Prophet Muhammad's (ﷺ) Mosque. During the first years of Islam, the direction of the daily prayers (or *Qibla*) was towards Jerusalem and then by Divine Command the direction was changed towards Makkah. The original version of this mosque was used during the transitional period and therefore had two Qiblas. The current structure was constructed recently at the site of the earlier mosque.

"You have indeed in the Messenger of Allah a beautiful pattern of (conduct) for anyone whose hope is in Allah and the Final Day and who engages much in the praise of Allah."

(Quran, The Clans 33: 21)

Above: External views of the present day Prophet Muhammad's (ﷺ) Mosque in Madinah.

Remarkable Leadership

The companions of Prophet Muhammad (ﷺ), had the privilege to view his conduct in person. They would have observed the way in which he conducted himself, the way he put into practice whatever he taught. The Blessed Prophet Muhammad (ﷺ) was the leader of his house and his people. When the Muslims were commanded to pray, he would pray the most. When mosques were being built, he helped to build them. He didn't stand back and ask for them to be constructed. There were never any luxuries, lavish palaces and plush residences for him.

When the Muslims were being persecuted in Makkah and the boycott commenced, Prophet Muhammad (ﷺ) kept his composure and stayed amongst the Muslims enduring the same hardship. Whenever the Muslims had to defend themselves in battle he commanded the troops from the front. By comparison it is easy to witness today how modern leaders act in a contradictory manner to their sayings – politicians who lie and cheat are commonplace and leaders of countries who engage in unnecessary wars. None of this was evident from the life of the Prophet Muhammad (ﷺ).

Opposite: Enlarged view of the brass screen covering the sacred grave of Prophet Muhammad (ﷺ). Alongside are buried his two companions, Abu Bakr Al-Siddeeq (ﷺ) and Umar ibn Al-Khattab (ﷺ), the first two Rightly Guided Caliphs in Islamic history.

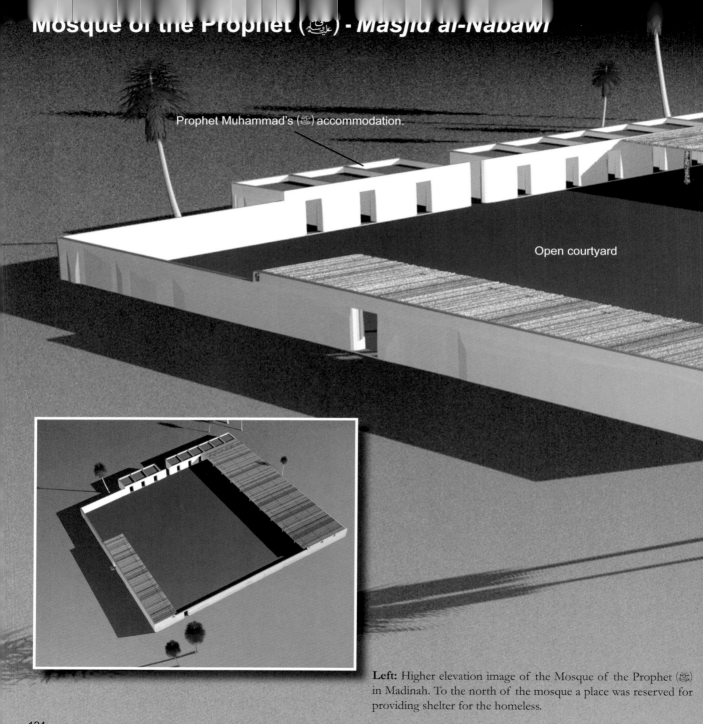

Prophet Muhammad's (ﷺ) accommodation.

Open courtyard

Left: Higher elevation image of the Mosque of the Prophet (ﷺ) in Madinah. To the north of the mosque a place was reserved for providing shelter for the homeless.

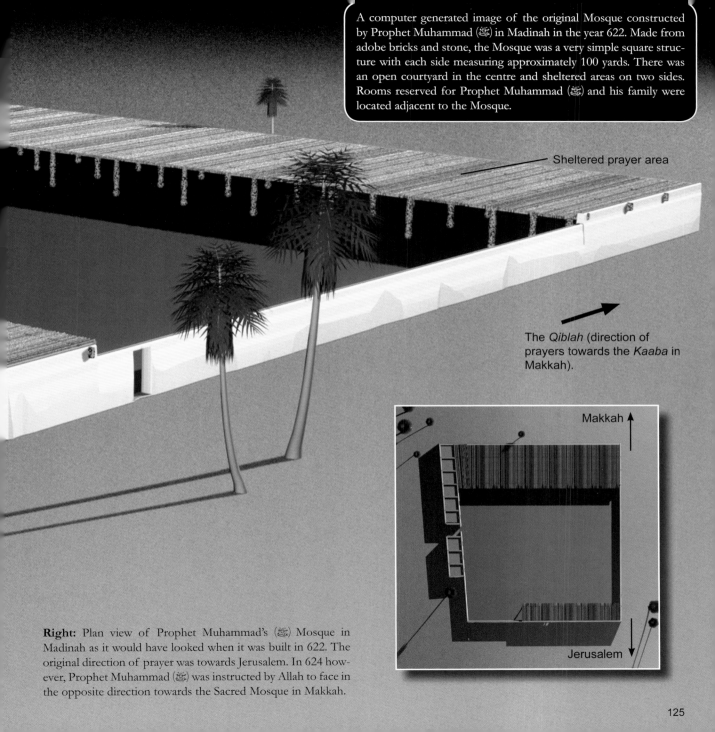

A computer generated image of the original Mosque constructed by Prophet Muhammad (ﷺ) in Madinah in the year 622. Made from adobe bricks and stone, the Mosque was a very simple square structure with each side measuring approximately 100 yards. There was an open courtyard in the centre and sheltered areas on two sides. Rooms reserved for Prophet Muhammad (ﷺ) and his family were located adjacent to the Mosque.

Sheltered prayer area

The *Qiblah* (direction of prayers towards the *Kaaba* in Makkah).

Makkah

Jerusalem

Right: Plan view of Prophet Muhammad's (ﷺ) Mosque in Madinah as it would have looked when it was built in 622. The original direction of prayer was towards Jerusalem. In 624 however, Prophet Muhammad (ﷺ) was instructed by Allah to face in the opposite direction towards the Sacred Mosque in Makkah.

Simple Life

Prophet Muhammad (ﷺ) preferred to live a very simple life. His simplicity was reflected in his dress, food and his dwelling. He emphasised hygiene, cleanliness and refinement. He preferred to dress in white or pale colours. He disliked garish colours or gaudy dresses of silk. He would mend his own shoes and even patched his own clothes.

Prophet Muhammad (ﷺ) lived in a small room with hardly any furniture in it. There was a mattress sewn with palm-tree strings and a leather pillow stuffed with palm-tree leaves. A leather bottle of water would hang on the wall. He liked to use perfumes and to comb his hair. He did not like people to leave their hair flowing around in a dishevelled state.

Conversation

The Blessed Prophet Muhammad (ﷺ) spoke in a soft voice and his manner was friendly and endearing. He was easily understood and people remembered what he said to them. His wife, Lady Ayesha (ﷺ) said, "Allah's Messenger did not go on talking rapidly as you do, but would talk in such a way that anyone who wished to count his words would be able to do so."

His Swords and Armour

Prophet Muhammad (ﷺ) had owned several swords that all had proper names. The earliest sword that he inherited from his father was named *Mathoor*. His most famous sword had the knob of its hilt made of silver and was named *Zulfiqar*. This was the sword that the Prophet Muhammad (ﷺ) carried with him during the peaceful conquest of Makkah.

Prophet Muhammad (ﷺ) also owned a helmet and a few coats of armour. His most famous coat of armour, named *Zat al Fuzool*, was pawned to a Jewish man when he died.

Night Worship

Before going to bed, Prophet Muhammad (ﷺ) would recite some chapters of the Quran and sleep in the first part of the night after the evening prayer. He would get up after midnight or when one-third of the night was left. He would clean his teeth with his tooth stick or *Miswak*, wash himself (ablution) and then engage himself in prayers in the deep silence of the night. He always slept on his right side with his right hand under his cheek.

Opposite page: Prophet Muhammad (ﷺ) emphasised dental hygiene and the use of the natural toothbrush known as *Miswak* was highly recommended prior to performing the five daily prayers. A *Miswak* is typically made from the *Salvadora Persica* tree growing in the Middle East. Other tree types that are used are the arak tree, peelo tree, olive, walnut and trees with bitter roots. In addition to strengthening the gums, eliminating odour and preventing tooth decay recent scientific research has shown that *Miswak* can also reduce bacteria in the mouth (*The immediate antimicrobial effect of a toothbrush and miswak on Cariogenic bacteria - A Clinical study*, The Journal of Contemporary Dental Practice, Volume 5, No 1, February 15, 2004). The reported benefits of using *Miswak* particularly before the daily prayers means that it is still widely used throughout the world.

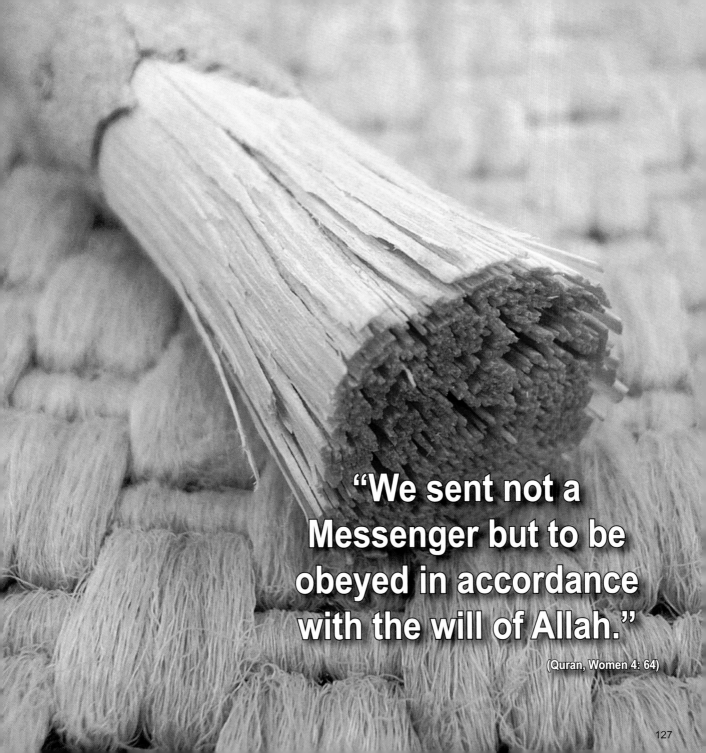

"We sent not a Messenger but to be obeyed in accordance with the will of Allah."

(Quran, Women 4: 64)

Perfect Character

It is a great virtue to regularly implement good moral conduct in our lives. Prophet Muhammad (ﷺ) lived strictly by this principle during his lifetime. He always put into practice every rule and regulation that he set in the light of divine guidance. He never deviated from his normal standard of conduct throughout his life. His wife, Lady Ayesha (ﷺ), once asked him *"Which actions are most beloved unto Allah?"* Prophet Muhammad (ﷺ) replied, *"That which are consistent, even if small."* (Saheeh Bukhari). He was also very fair and just in his business dealings with other people and there was never a complaint of any kind against him.

Love for Prophet Muhammad (ﷺ)

The love of Prophet Muhammad (ﷺ) is a key aspect of Islam. His name is never mentioned without invoking peace and blessings of Allah upon him. Prophet Muhammad (ﷺ) is not considered to be divine, but a human being. However, he was no ordinary human being. He is seen by Muslims and many non-Muslims alike, as the most perfect of all of Allah's creation, shining like a jewel among stones, a beacon of truth and justice, a light and mercy for all of mankind.

His cousin and close companion, Ali ibn Abi Talib (ﷺ), describing Prophet Muhammad (ﷺ), said, "He was the most generous of heart, truthful of tongue, softest in disposition and noble in relationship."

Ali ibn Abi Talib (ﷺ) also said, when asked: "How was your love for the Messenger of Allah?" He said: "He was, by Allah, dearer to us than our children, our wealth, our fathers, our mothers and a cold drink on a day of great thirst."

Prophet Muhammad (ﷺ) is very dear to Muslims everywhere to the extent that love for Prophet Muhammad (ﷺ) is a measure of faith and it is only completed and perfected when the love for Prophet Muhammad (ﷺ) exceeds love for everything else in this world, including life itself. Allah says in the Noble Quran:

"The Prophet is preferable for the believers even to their own selves..."

(Quran, The Clans 33:6)

To affirm this Prophet Muhammad (ﷺ) is reported to have said: *"None of you becomes a believer until I am dearer to him than his children, his parents and all mankind."* (Recorded by Saheeh Bukhari and Muslim).

For Muslims, the love for Prophet Muhammad (ﷺ) breathes life into his or her practice of religion. Without this love, religion is reduced to an empty adherence to a set of rules and rituals. So Muslims have always loved the Messenger of Allah and will continue to do so by protecting his honour and following his example.

Opposite page: Worshippers travel anti-clockwise around the *Kaaba* seven times in an act of worship known as *Tawaf*. A black cloth adorned by golden verses of the Noble Quran covers the building. The south-eastern corner of the *Kaaba* houses the Black Stone, a symbol of the original covenant between Allah and man.

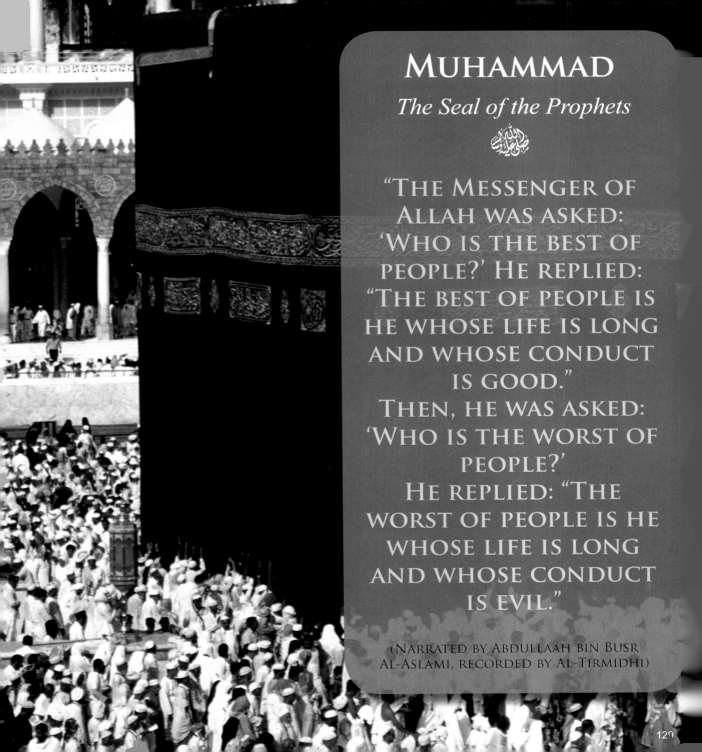

MUHAMMAD

The Seal of the Prophets
ﷺ

"THE MESSENGER OF ALLAH WAS ASKED: 'WHO IS THE BEST OF PEOPLE?' HE REPLIED: "THE BEST OF PEOPLE IS HE WHOSE LIFE IS LONG AND WHOSE CONDUCT IS GOOD."
THEN, HE WAS ASKED: 'WHO IS THE WORST OF PEOPLE?'
HE REPLIED: "THE WORST OF PEOPLE IS HE WHOSE LIFE IS LONG AND WHOSE CONDUCT IS EVIL."

(NARRATED BY ABDULLAAH BIN BUSR AL-ASLAMI, RECORDED BY AL-TIRMIDHI)

The Prophet's (ﷺ) Family

For the majority of his life Prophet Muhammad (ﷺ) had only one wife, Lady Khadija (رضي الله عنها). After she passed away he married a number of righteous wives who helped spread the message of Islam. He married for different reasons: to cement alliances or to help those who had been widowed or abandoned so that they had someone to take care of them. Muslims hold the wives of Prophet Muhammad (ﷺ) in great esteem and they are known as the 'Mothers of the Believers'. By marrying women from different tribes, Prophet Muhammad (ﷺ) also wanted to demolish the Arab tribes' enmity to Islam and extinguish their intense hatred towards each other.

Another very important point is that Prophet Muhammad's (ﷺ) wives, especially those who outlived him, played a vital role in conveying Prophetic traditions to the Muslims. Lady Ayesha (رضي الله عنها), for instance, related a large number of Prophet Muhammad's (ﷺ) actions and statements. She was far more learned than most men at the time and became a very influential and inspirational person at the time, so much so that she is regarded as one of the greatest scholars in Islamic history. Remarkably, her life, legal statements and works have been studied by students and teachers throughout Islamic history for the last 1,400 years. She played an active role in education and social reform. Her house became a school and academy for young boys and girls, including orphans, where she educated and trained them under her care and guidance. Her example in promoting education, particularly the education of Muslim women is one which has been followed to this day in the Islamic world.

Prophet Muhammad (ﷺ) treated all children with great kindness and mercy. Children were very fond of him and he always gave them attention and love. Prophet Muhammad (ﷺ) had three sons who died in their infancy. He also had four daughters who married and had children. However, it was only Fatima (رضي الله عنها), his youngest daughter, who outlived him.

> **"O Prophet! Truly We have sent you as a Witness, a Bearer of Glad Tidings, and Warner, - And as one who invites to Allah's (grace) by His leave and as a lamp spreading light. Then give the glad tidings to the Believers, that they shall have from Allah a very great Bounty."**
>
> (Quran, The Clans 33: 45-47)

Opposite: A rare example of a 15th century Quran page written in *Bihari* script from India, highly decorated using gold and other colours. The word Allah is written in gold throughout, as are the chapter headings. The image shows the beginning of chapter 39; **"The revelation of this Book is from Allah, the Exalted in Power, full of Wisdom."**

The Seal of the Prophets

The purpose of all the Messengers from Allah was the same, to remind people to leave everything except the worship of one God. Throughout history, Prophets have been sent to all people so that on the 'Day of Judgment' no one will be able to argue with Allah that they were left without guidance.

"(We sent) messengers as bringers of good tidings and warners so that mankind will have no argument against Allah after the Messengers..."

(Quran, Women 4:165)

Muslims are required to treat all of the Messengers of Allah with an equal amount of respect and love. Because of the finality of Prophet Muhammad (ﷺ) and the universal nature of his teachings, he has the highest status amongst the Messengers. He is the 'Seal of the Prophets', the final one, that was sent to the whole of mankind. There will be no other Prophets and Messengers sent after him.

And Allah tells us in the Quran:

"We (Allah) have not sent you (O Muhammad) except as a giver of glad tidings and a warner to all mankind"

(Quran, Saba 34:28)

Opposite: An example of the beauty of Allah's creation. Close-up of a purple crocus flower in full bloom floating on water.

"Muhammad is not the father of any of your men, but (he is) the Messenger of Allah and the Seal of the Prophets: and Allah has full knowledge of all things."

(Quran, The Clans 33: 40)

133

Views of Western Historians

"My choice of Muhammad to lead the list of the world's most influential persons may surprise some readers and may be questioned by others, but he was the only man in history who was supremely successful on both the secular and religious level. ...It is probable that the relative influence of Muhammad on Islam has been larger than the combined influence of Jesus Christ and St. Paul on Christianity. ...It is this unparalleled combination of secular and religious influence which I feel entitles Muhammad to be considered the most influential single figure in human history." (*The 100, A Ranking of the Most Influential Persons in History* by Michael H. Hart, New York, 1978, p. 33).

"Prophet Muhammad's mission was to propagate the worship of the One and Only God (in Arabic Allah), the Creator and Sustainer of the Universe. His mission was essentially the same as that of earlier Prophets of God. In the historical context, many such terminologies about Muhammad, Islam and Muslims were borrowed from earlier European writings of the eleventh to the nineteenth century, a time when ignorance and prejudice prevailed." (Thomas Carlyle in *Heroes and Hero Worship and the Heroic in History*, 1840).

"The lies (Western slander) which well-meaning zeal has heaped round this man (Muhammad) are disgraceful to ourselves only. A silent great soul, one of that who cannot but be earnest. He was to kindle the world, the world's Maker had ordered so." (A. S. Tritton in *Islam*, 1951).

"The good sense of Muhammad despised the pomp of royalty. The Apostle of God submitted to the menial offices of the family; he kindled the fire; swept the floor; milked the ewes; and mended with his own hands his shoes and garments. Disdaining the penance and merit of a hermit, he observed without effort or vanity the abstemious diet of an Arab." (Edward Gibbon and Simon Oakley in *History of the Saracen Empire*, London, 1870).

"I wanted to know the best of the life of one who holds today an undisputed sway over the hearts of millions of mankind.... I became more than ever convinced that it was not the sword that won a place for Islam in those days in the scheme of life. It was the rigid simplicity, the utter self-effacement of the Prophet, the scrupulous regard for pledges, his intense devotion to his friends and followers, his intrepidity, his fearlessness, his absolute trust in God and in his own mission. These and not the sword carried everything before them and surmounted every obstacle. When I closed the second volume (of the Prophet's biography), I was sorry there was not more for me to read of that great life." (Sir George Bernard Shaw in *The Genuine Islam*, Vol. 1, No. 8, 1936).

"History makes it clear, however, that the legend of fanatical Muslims sweeping through the world and forcing Islam at the point of sword upon conquered races is one of the most fantastically absurd myths that historians have ever repeated." (Edward Gibbon in *The Decline and Fall of the Roman Empire*, 1823).

Prophet Muhammad's (ﷺ) Letter to Heraclius, King of the Byzantines

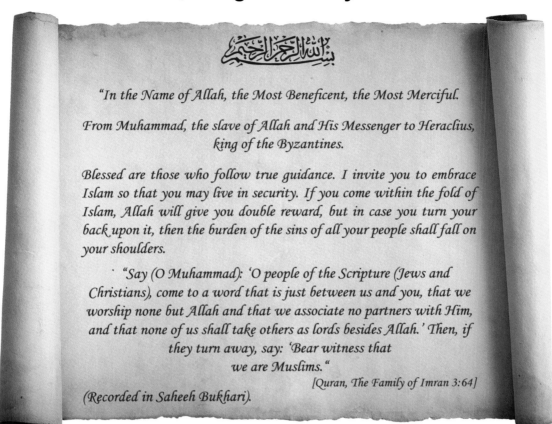

"In the Name of Allah, the Most Beneficent, the Most Merciful.

From Muhammad, the slave of Allah and His Messenger to Heraclius, king of the Byzantines.

Blessed are those who follow true guidance. I invite you to embrace Islam so that you may live in security. If you come within the fold of Islam, Allah will give you double reward, but in case you turn your back upon it, then the burden of the sins of all your people shall fall on your shoulders.

"Say (O Muhammad): 'O people of the Scripture (Jews and Christians), come to a word that is just between us and you, that we worship none but Allah and that we associate no partners with Him, and that none of us shall take others as lords besides Allah.' Then, if they turn away, say: 'Bear witness that we are Muslims."

[Quran, The Family of Imran 3:64]

(Recorded in Saheeh Bukhari).

Above: The Muslim envoy, Dihyah bin Khalifah Al-Kalbi, was ordered to hand the letter over to king of Busra, who would in turn, send it to Heraclius. Incidentally, Abu Sufyan bin Harb, who by that time had not embraced Islam, was summoned to the court and Heraclius asked him many questions about Prophet Muhammad (ﷺ) and the religion which he preached. The testimony which this avowed enemy of Prophet Muhammad (ﷺ) gave regarding the personal excellence of Prophet Muhammad's (ﷺ) character and the good that Islam was doing the human race, left Heraclius wonder-struck.

Following page: A saying of Prophet Muhammad (ﷺ) against a green background. For Muslims it is truly a blessing and a mercy from the Creator, Allah, that we have been given colour vision. A world without colour would be dull and uninspiring. Colour is a property of light that depends on wavelength. When light falls on an object, some of it is absorbed and some is reflected. The apparent colour of an opaque object depends on the wavelength of the light that it reflects; e.g. a green object observed in daylight appears green because it reflects only the waves producing green light. Black and white are not generally considered true colours; black is said to result from the absence of colour and white from the presence of all colours mixed together.

"THE MERCIFUL ARE SHOWN MERCY BY THE ALL-MERCIFUL. SHOW MERCY TO THOSE ON EARTH AND ALLAH WILL SHOW MERCY TO YOU."

(Saying of Prophet Muhammad (ﷺ), Recorded in Al-Tirmidhi)

Chapter 7

The Rightly Guided Caliphs

Caliph - What does it mean?

The word 'Caliph' is the English form of the Arabic word 'Khalifa,' which is an abbreviated form of the phrase Khalifatu Rasulillah (meaning 'Successor to the Messenger of Allah'). This title 'Khalifatu Rasulillah' was first used for Abu Bakr (رضي الله عنه), who became the elected head of the Muslim community after the death of the Prophet Muhammad (ﷺ).

Why there was a need for a Caliph.

"The Prophets governed the affairs of the 'Tribe of Israel', whenever one died another one succeeded him. However, after me there are no more Prophets, there are successors (khulafa) and they will number many."

(Saying of Prophet Muhammad (ﷺ), recorded in Bukhari)

The primary responsibility of the Caliph as the head of the Muslim community was to continue in the path of Prophet Muhammad (ﷺ). In line with the earlier messengers of Allah, the mission of Prophet Muhammad (ﷺ) was to call people to the worship of the One True God. Muslims regard that religion was perfected and the door of Divine revelation was closed at the death of the Prophet Muhammad (ﷺ). After him the Caliph was to shepherd the Muslim community in accordance with the Quran and the teachings of the Prophet Muhammad (ﷺ). The Caliph was a ruler over Muslims but not their sovereign since sovereignty belongs to Allah alone. He was to be obeyed as long as he obeyed Allah. He was responsible for creating and maintaining conditions under which it would be easy for Muslims to live according to Islamic principles and to see that justice was done to all.

The Rightly-Guided Caliphs of Islam

The first five Caliphs who truly followed in the Prophet Muhammad's (ﷺ) footsteps after his death are known as 'The Rightly Guided Caliphs' They were some of the closest companions of the Prophet Muhammad (ﷺ), namely, Abu Bakr, Umar, Uthman, Ali and Hasan (may Allah be well pleased with them all). Muslims love them dearly and hold them in great esteem, their names are never said without being followed by the invocation "may Allah be well pleased with him". They lived simple and righteous lives and strove hard for the religion of Islam. Their justice was impartial, their treatment of others was kind and merciful and they were at one with the people - the first among equals. After them, some of the later Caliphs assumed the manners of kings and emperors and the true spirit of equality of ruler and ruled was not always adhered to.

The mission of Prophet Muhammad (ﷺ) and after him that of the Rightly-Guided Caliphs, was not political, social or economic reform, although such reforms were a logical consequence of the success of this mission nor the unity of a nation and the establishment of an empire, although the Islamic nation did unite and vast areas came under one administration. Nor was is to spread a civilisation, science or culture, although many civilisations, scientific and cultural achievements were gained. Their only mission was to deliver Allah's message to all the peoples of the world and to invite them to submit to Him, while being the foremost among those who submitted.

Opposite page: 11th century Al-Hambra Palace, Cordoba, Spain.

Born in the year 573 in Makkah, Abu Bakr al-Siddeeq (ﷺ) was a prominent and wealthy figure among the Makkans. From a very early stage he became one of the greatest companions of the Prophet Muhammad (ﷺ).

Learned, noble and brave, he was the first adult male to accept Islam from Prophet Muhammad (ﷺ). Abu Bakr al-Siddeeq (ﷺ) saw many of the remarkable events during the lifetime of Prophet Muhammad (ﷺ). He fought in many battles, endured hardships and spent all his wealth freely to establish Islam.

After the death of the Prophet of Islam, he became the first of the Rightly Guided Caliphs. Parts of Syria and Palestine were added to the Islamic lands as well as much of Iraq during his rule. He died in Madinah in 634 and lies buried next to his dear friend the Messenger of Allah, Muhammad (ﷺ).

"If I were to take a friend other than my Lord, I would take Abu Bakr as a friend."

(Saying of Prophet Muhammad (ﷺ), recorded in Muslim)

ABU BAKR AL-SIDDEEQ

Born in Makkah, Umar ibn al-Khattab (ﷺ) was renowned for his tremendous personal courage, steadfastness and fairness in giving judgments. From amongst the heroes of the Makkan nobility in the pre-Islamic period of ignorance, he entered Islam five years before the emigration to Madinah when he was 35 years old. He fought in all the battles alongside Prophet Muhammad (ﷺ) and after Abu Bakr's (ﷺ) death, he became the second of the Rightly Guided Caliphs.

During his ten and a half year Caliphate, twelve thousand Mosques were built and all of Syria, Palestine, Egypt, as well as the entire Arabian peninsula were added to the Islamic lands. He became famous for his entry into Jerusalem and his pact with the Jews and Christians who were allowed to live and worship freely under the protection of the Muslims in Jerusalem. He was martyred in 644 and lies buried alongside the Messenger of Allah and Abu Bakr al-Siddeeq (ﷺ) in Madinah.

"Allah has placed truth upon Umar's tongue and heart."

(Saying of Prophet Muhammad (ﷺ), recorded in Abu Dawud)

Background: Dome of Masjid Putrajaya, Malaysia.

Opposite page: Interior view of the 10th century Great Mosque of Cordoba, Spain.

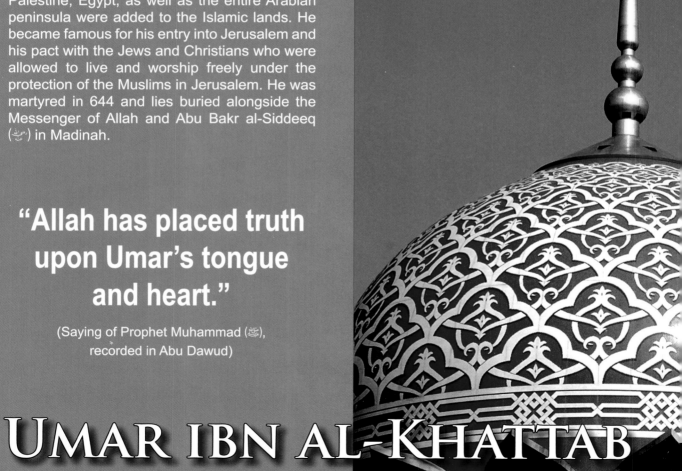

UMAR IBN AL-KHATTAB

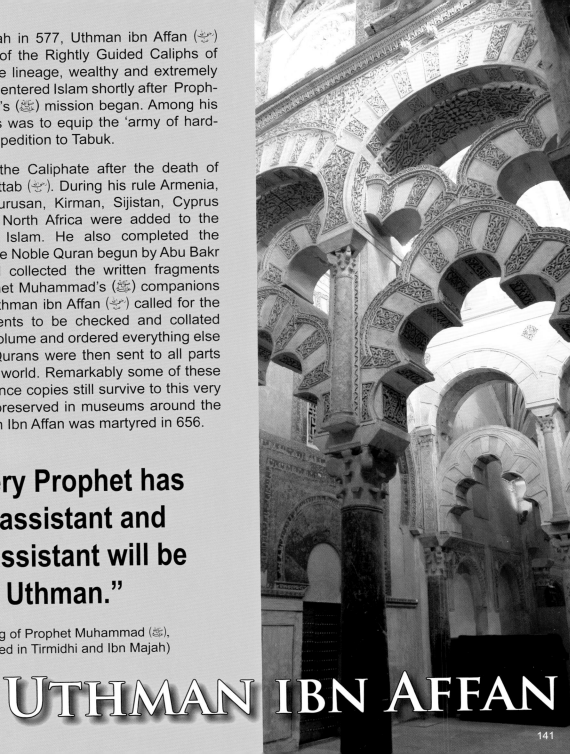

Born in Makkah in 577, Uthman ibn Affan (ﷺ) was the third of the Rightly Guided Caliphs of Islam. Of noble lineage, wealthy and extremely handsome, he entered Islam shortly after Prophet Muhammad's (ﷺ) mission began. Among his greatest works was to equip the 'army of hardship' for the expedition to Tabuk.

He accepted the Caliphate after the death of Umar ibn Khattab (ﷺ). During his rule Armenia, Caucasia, Khurusan, Kirman, Sijistan, Cyprus and much of North Africa were added to the dominions of Islam. He also completed the gathering of the Noble Quran begun by Abu Bakr (ﷺ), who had collected the written fragments that the Prophet Muhammad's (ﷺ) companions possessed. Uthman ibn Affan (ﷺ) called for the written fragments to be checked and collated into a single volume and ordered everything else to be burnt. Qurans were then sent to all parts of the Muslim world. Remarkably some of these original reference copies still survive to this very day and are preserved in museums around the world. Uthman Ibn Affan was martyred in 656.

"Every Prophet has an assistant and my assistant will be Uthman."

(Saying of Prophet Muhammad (ﷺ), recorded in Tirmidhi and Ibn Majah)

UTHMAN IBN AFFAN

Ali ibn Abi Talib (رضي الله عنه), the 'Friend' of Allah and 'Commander of the Faithful' was the fourth of the Rightly Guided Caliphs of Islam. Born of noble lineage in Makkah (circa 600) he was a cousin of Prophet Muhammad (ﷺ) who raised him from the age of five. He was the first male to accept Islam from Prophet Muhammad (ﷺ) and the first to pray behind him. When Prophet Muhammad (ﷺ) paired off the Makkan emigrants with the Madinan helpers, he told Ali, "*You are my brother*".

A renowned swordsman, strong and valiant, he carried the Muslim armies' *standard* during battle. When Ali ibn Abi Talib (رضي الله عنه) became the fourth Rightly Guided Caliph he made Kufa in Iraq his capital and patiently endured dissension and civil strife with which the Muslim nation had become afflicted by during his Caliphate. Extremely courageous, wise and a fair judge, an eloquent speaker with a sea of spiritual wisdom, he was amongst the most learned of Companions of Prophet Muhammad (ﷺ). He was martyred during 661 in Kufa.

"You (Ali) are my brother in this world and the next."

(Saying of Prophet Muhammad (ﷺ), recorded in Tirmidhi)

ALI IBN ABI TALIB

Background: 16th century Suleymaniye Mosque, Istanbul, Turkey.

Al-Hassan Ibn Ali Ibn Abi Talib (رضي الله عنه), was the grandson of Prophet Muhammad (ﷺ) and the last of the Rightly Guided Caliphs of whom Prophet Muhammad (ﷺ) attested. He was born three years after the momentous migration of Prophet Muhammad (ﷺ) from Makkah to Madinah.

Al-Hassan (رضي الله عنه) closely resembled his grandfather the Prophet Muhammad (ﷺ) in many ways and had many of his virtues. He was an extremely pious man and performed the pilgrimage (*Hajj*) by foot twenty-five times.

He was sworn into the office of Caliph after the assassination of his father, Ali Ibn Abi Talib (رضي الله عنه). However, he stood down as Caliph approximately six months later due to much turmoil and political strife. He died in Madinah in the year 671.

"O Allah! I love him, so please love him."

(Saying of Prophet Muhammad (ﷺ), recorded in Saheeh Bukhari)

Background: Dome of the Rock, Jerusalem.

AL-HASAN IBN ALI

143

Prophet Muhammad's (ﷺ) Letter to Negus, King of the Abyssinia

In the Name of Allah, the Most Beneficent, the Most Merciful.

"This letter is sent from Muhammad, the Prophet of Allah, to Negus Al-Ashama, the king of Abyssinia (Ethiopia).

Peace be upon him who follows true guidance and believes in Allah and His Messenger. I bear witness that there is no god but Allah Alone with no associate, He has taken neither a wife nor a son and that Muhammad is His slave and Messenger. I call you unto the fold of Islam; if you embrace Islam, you will find safety.

"Say (O Muhammad): 'O people of the Scripture (Jews and Christians), come to a word that is just between us and you, that we worship none but Allah and that we associate no partners with Him and that none of us shall take others as lords besides Allah.' Then, if they turn away, say:
'Bear witness that we are Muslims.' "
[Quran, The Family of Imran 3:64]

Should you reject this invitation, then you will be held responsible for all the evil of your people."

(Recorded in Saheeh Bukhari).

Chapter 8

The Noble Quran

Introduction to the Quran

It is not a book of history yet Muslims regard it as the most authentic source of history. It is not a textbook of law and politics yet it describes principles of statecraft that has guided mankind for centuries. Whilst it is also not a book of science and philosophy, it has unravelled many mysteries of philosophy and science. It has also offered exact guidelines on economics and sociology as well as numerous other subjects.

This book is written in the Arabic language and is known as the Quran. Over fourteen centuries ago it transformed the simple shepherds and wandering bedouins of Arabia into the founders of a new and vast civilisation, builders of cities and collectors of libraries.

> # "ALIF LAM RA.
> # THESE ARE
> # THE VERSES OF THE
> # BOOK OF
> # WISDOM."
>
> (Quran, Jonah 10: 1)

Opposite: Opening pages from a magnificent 250 year old Quran hand written in Kufic script from North Africa. The Quran represents the pinnacle of linguistic perfection and is regarded by Muslims as inimitable.

بسم الله الرحمن الرحيم

سورة الفاتحة

الحمد لله رب العالمين الرحمن الرحيم

مالك يوم الدين إياك نعبد وإياك نستعين

اهدنا الصراط المستقيم صراط الذين

أنعمت عليهم ولا الضالين

سورة البقرة

بسم الله الرحمن الرحيم

الم ذلك الكتاب لا ريب فيه هدى للمتقين الذين

يقيمون الصلاة ومما رزقناهم ينفقون والذين

يؤمنون بما أنزل إليك وما أنزل من قبلك وبالآ

خرة هم يوقنون أولئك على هدى من ربهم وأو

لئك هم المفلحون إن الذين كفروا سواء عليهم

Muslims regard the Quran as a unique book beyond the limits of human capability, with a supreme author and an eternal and universal message. Its contents are not confined to a particular theme or style, but contain the foundations for an entire system of life. The subject matter ranges from very specific articles of faith and commandments to more general moral teachings. It also prescribes certain rights and obligations and rules on crime and punishment, private and public law.

The Quran is rich both in its diverse subject matter and literary style. A message may be in the form of a direct stipulation, a reminder of Allah's favours on His creation, an admonition or a rebuke. Stories of past communities are narrated, followed by the lessons to be learnt from their actions and subsequent fates. The Quran contains a complete code which provides guidance in all areas of life, whether spiritual, intellectual, political, social or economic. It is a code which is not limited to time, place or nation.

Above: A magnificent Andalusian Quran page hand written in Spain, circa 13th century.

Left: A page from a beautiful Quran handwritten in elegant Maghribi style Arabic script on vellum. This Quran was copied during the 12th century in the city of Cordoba, Spain. Note the use of gold verse markers and coloured diacritic marking scheme (part of the prestigious Exhibition Islam collection).

Opposite page: The Royal Mamluk Baybars Quran, held at the British Museum, is recognised as a masterpiece of Islamic calligraphy and illumination. It was produced in Cairo around 1304 and is named after the ruler who commissioned it. The script is written entirely in gold and is illuminated with gold wire work.

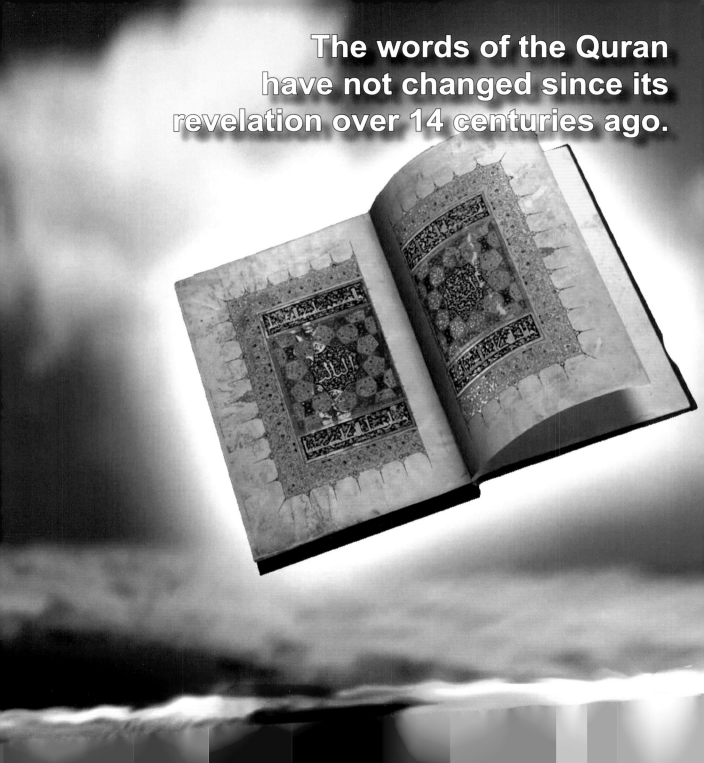

The words of the Quran have not changed since its revelation over 14 centuries ago.

"In the name of Allah, Most Gracious,
Most Merciful.

Praise be to Allah, the Cherisher and
Sustainer of the worlds;

Most Gracious, Most Merciful;
Master of the Day of Judgment.

You do we worship and
your aid we seek.

Keep us on the right path,

The path of those whom you have
favoured; Not the (path) of those who
earn Your anger nor of those
who go astray"

(Quran, The Opening 1: 1-7)

Opposite: The first chapter of the Quran called *Al-Fatihah*
(The Opening; translated above) from an 18th century Persian Quran. Richly decorated throughout using precious gold
and other colours. This Quran is beautifully hand written on
handmade polished paper (Exhibition Islam collection). This
chapter is recited by all Muslims at least 20 times a day during
daily prayers.

Who Wrote the Quran?

There are four possibilities regarding the authorship of the Quran - 1) Non-Arabs 2) Pagan Arabs 3) Prophet Muhammad (ﷺ) 4) The Almighty Creator, Allah. It is important to examine each of these possibilities in turn.

Did non-Arabs write the Quran?

The Arabic language was at its peak in expression, vocabulary, aesthetic and poetic value during the 7th century when the Quran was written. Anyone who is able to speak the classical Arabic of the Quran would argue that a non-Arab could not possibly have written such an extensive and brilliant piece of literature in the Arabic language.

Did the pagan Arabs write the Quran?

What the Quran teaches goes directly against the pagan Arab culture, religion and gods, that existed during the 6th and 7th centuries. The Quran condemns idol worship, whilst the pagan Arabs loved their idol gods. The Quran raised the status of women whilst the pagan Arabs treated women as animals. And whereas the Quran condemns and prohibits taking interest on money, the Arabs freely levied heavy interest rates on loans and businesses.

Furthermore, the Quran condemns and prohibits alcohol and gambling, whereas the Arabs indulged in gambling and consumed alcohol freely. The pagan Arabs would never write a book that contradicted their normal customs, culture and religious beliefs.

The Quran was also far superior to any of the Arabic poetry and literature of its time. It contains a unique literary style, awe-inspiring rhythm and unequalled expression. Even if the pagan Arabs had wanted to write the Quran they would never have been capable of accomplishing such a feat.

Right: An 18th century Quran from China written in a local variant of Sini script (Exhibition Islam collection).

152

Did Prophet Muhammad (ﷺ) write the Quran?

Many Western historians today still hold the view that only Prophet Muhammad (ﷺ) could have been the author of the Quran. In refutation of this assertion, firstly Prophet Muhammad (ﷺ) had no personal reason to write the Quran, causing the entire Makkan society to become his enemy. Why would he write something that vehemently opposed all of the norms of society and thereby lose his family, relatives and friends? He had to endure years of persecution, hostility and even attempts on his life in Makkah and face many invasions in Madinah in order to deliver the universal message of Islam.

It is also widely acknowledged that Prophet Muhammad (ﷺ) could not read nor write. He had received no formal education and he never went to school. In fact he had no teacher of any kind in any subject. Yet the Quran contains information on a huge range of subjects. Moreover, Prophet Muhammad (ﷺ) was not regarded as a poet, he could not possibly have produced a piece of literature so perfect which, exceeded the best styles of Arabic poetry of all time. Furthermore, the personal sayings of the Prophet Muhammad (ﷺ) are meticulously recorded in books of *hadith*. If we examine the Arabic style of the *hadith* and compare it to the style of the Quran, we can see that they are clearly distinguishable.

The Quran was also revealed over a period of 23 years. It would have been impossible for anyone to retain the exact same style of Arabic in the Quran over such a long period of time, regardless of ever-changing personal circumstances. Human authors tend to gradually change their writing style and also their views and thoughts. Yet the style and message of the Quran remains consistent from beginning to end.

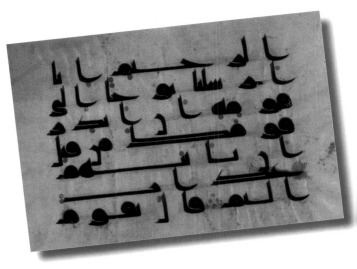

Above: An elegant Quran written in Kufic script during the 10th century. Note the use of a red dotting scheme (Bardo Museum, Tunisia).

The Quran honours Mary, the mother of Jesus (peace be upon them). In fact there is a whole chapter of the Quran named after her. However, the Quran does not contain a chapter named after the wives, mother or daughters of Prophet Muhammad (ﷺ) as might be expected by people if he had been the author of the Quran. Furthermore, there is even a verse rebuking Prophet Muhammad (ﷺ) for ignoring a blind person, whilst he was in the midst of important discussions with tribal leaders. This shows that it is nonsensical for Prophet Muhammad (ﷺ) to have been the author of the Quran.

153

Above: Words from the Quran written on parchment from the renowned Yemeni collection. In the early days of Islam, Qurans were written on parchment, which was much heavier than paper. A complete Quran could weigh several kilograms.

154

The Direct Word of Allah

A human writer is usually very knowledgeable in a specific subject, or a few related subjects. However, even a casual reader will realise that the Quran discusses a vast array of diverse subjects with equal command of the language and depth of knowledge. No human being in history has written such a comprehensive book with such absolute perfection. The only proposition remaining is that the Quran was divinely revealed by the Creator. In fact Muslims regard the Quran as the direct 'Word of Allah' alone.

"That (this) is indeed an honourable recitation.
In a Book well-guarded
Which none shall touch but the purified.
A revelation from the Lord of the Worlds."

(Quran, The Event 56: 77-81)

Previously Revealed Books

A Chain of Prophets

Islam teaches that Allah has given revelations to a selected chain of individuals, namely the Prophets and Messengers throughout history (see p. 18). All of these Prophets and Messengers called people to the same thing, namely to worship One God alone without any partners. The culmination of Allah's revelations is the Quran. Muslims regard it as the final, infallible, direct and complete record of the exact words of Allah, brought down by the Archangel Gabriel and firmly implanted in the heart of His final Prophet and Messenger, Muhammad (ﷺ).

Opposite: The Noble Sanctuary in Jerusalem forms the backdrop for this highly visual depiction of the previously revealed scriptures descending to earth.

The Miraculous Quran

Miracles of the Previous Prophets

The miracles of the Prophets that came before Prophet Muhammad (ﷺ) are no longer with us today. However, the merciful Creator gave Muhammad (ﷺ) the Quran as a miracle for all of mankind and for all time, which would remain the source of truth and guidance long after Prophet Muhammad (ﷺ) had left this world.

Looking back through history we find that Prophets of Allah were always sent with proofs in the form of miracles to show people that they spoke the truth. These miracles usually centred around a popular theme of that era or time. A miraculous demonstration would make people realise that the Prophet spoke the truth and had support from divine power.

Thus, Prophet Moses (ﷺ) was able to transform his walking staff into a real snake, baffling Pharaoh's sorcerers. He also parted the Red Sea while escaping from the Pharaoh. Prophet Jesus (ﷺ) was given the power to cure disease and give life to the dead, astonishing the practitioners who felt proud of their limited knowledge of healing and who had begun to disregard and deny the Power and Glory of Allah.

Why the Quran is Regarded as a Miracle by Muslims

The Quran was a miracle for the Arabs; it challenged and surpassed the limits of their literary expression. To this day the Quran, revealed to the Last and Final Prophet, Muhammad (ﷺ), is still as relevant to the lives of people today. Unlike the miracles of previous Prophets that were limited in time to those people who witnessed the event.

Prophet Muhammad (ﷺ) was sent to the Arabs who arrogantly claimed to be the masters of the Arabic language. They were renowned for their achievements in poetry and elocution. Having great pride in their linguistic skills they would take great pleasure in challenging each other in public speaking contests. As a constant reminder to all, the seven most acclaimed poems were hung in the 'House of Allah', namely the *Kaaba*. When the poets heard the Quran's inimitable linguistic style and matchless eloquence, it became apparent at once that this was far beyond the capability of human beings. Some accepted the Quran as the word of Allah, yet the majority of Makkans remained proud and arrogant and adamantly refused to accept Islam. They contented themselves by pouring scorn on Prophet Muhammad (ﷺ) and making false accusations against him. They would also warn people against listening to Prophet Muhammad (ﷺ).

Above: The celebrated 'blue' Qurans are regarded as the peak of Islamic calligraphy. This extremely rare Quran leaf was written on blue vellum during the 9th century in North Africa or Islamic Spain. The Kufic style of writing is very stylised and geometric, characteristic of most early Quranic manuscripts. Only a handful of Qurans written on coloured vellum are known to exist and of these the blue vellum ones are the most exquisite. During this period writing materials were extremely expensive. Dyed vellum and writing in gold ink would have been a costly process (Exhibition Islam collection).

"(This is) the revelation of the Book in which there is no doubt, from the Lord of the Worlds."

(Quran, The Prostration 32: 2)

The Three Stages of Revelation

Islamic tradition holds that the revelation of the Quran had three stages. The first stage occurred when the Quran was written on the 'preserved tablet', it was then revealed to the 'lowest heaven'; and lastly it was revealed to Prophet Muhammad (ﷺ) on earth through the Angel Gabriel. The start of revelation would change Prophet Muhammad's (ﷺ) life forever and shape the course of world history for centuries to come.

Before the start of his prophethood, Muhammad (ﷺ) was one of the few individuals in Makkah who never worshipped an idol in his entire life. He was always deeply concerned about the many vices prevalent in Makkan society. After his marriage to Lady Khadija (﵁) he regularly retreated to the hills of the desert outside Makkah for several days. There he would meditate and pray to Allah in solitude. It was there, one day, in a cave called *Hira*, that the Angel Gabriel came to him and said to him, "*Read!*" He said, "*I am not a reader*," for Prophet Muhammad (ﷺ) had not learnt to read or write in his entire life. As he explained in his own words:

"The angel caught me and pressed me so hard that I could not bear it any more. He then released me and again asked me to read and I replied, "I do not know how to read." Thereupon he caught me again and pressed me a second time till I could not bear it any more. He then released me and again asked me to read but again I replied, "I do not know how to read." Thereupon he caught me for the third time and pressed me and then released me and said, "Read in the name of your Lord, Who has created (all that exists); Has created man from a leech-like clot; Read! And your Lord is the Most Noble."

(Recorded in Saheeh Bukhari)

A Gradual Revelation

From that momentous occurrence in the cave, the Quran was revealed gradually to Prophet Muhammad (ﷺ) over the next 23 years. He could receive a few words at a time or sometimes an entire chapter (or *Surah* in Arabic). The Arabs were used to hearing long eulogies in one sitting, so they were astonished at this mode of revelation. The frequent revelations of the Quran made it easier for the early Muslims to face the persecution and tortures inflicted upon them by the pagan Makkans. Many verses of the Quran contained answers to questions posed by the people and guidance about various events that happened at different times in the growth of the Islamic community. The Quran comprises of numerous principles, commands and prohibitions. If the entire Quran was revealed all at once, it would have become obligatory to obey all of it simultaneously and this would have been a heavy burden on new Muslims.

"And those who disbelieve say, Why was the Quran not revealed to him all at once? Thus (it is) that We may strengthen thereby your heart. And We have spaced it distinctly."

(Quran, The Criterion 25: 32)

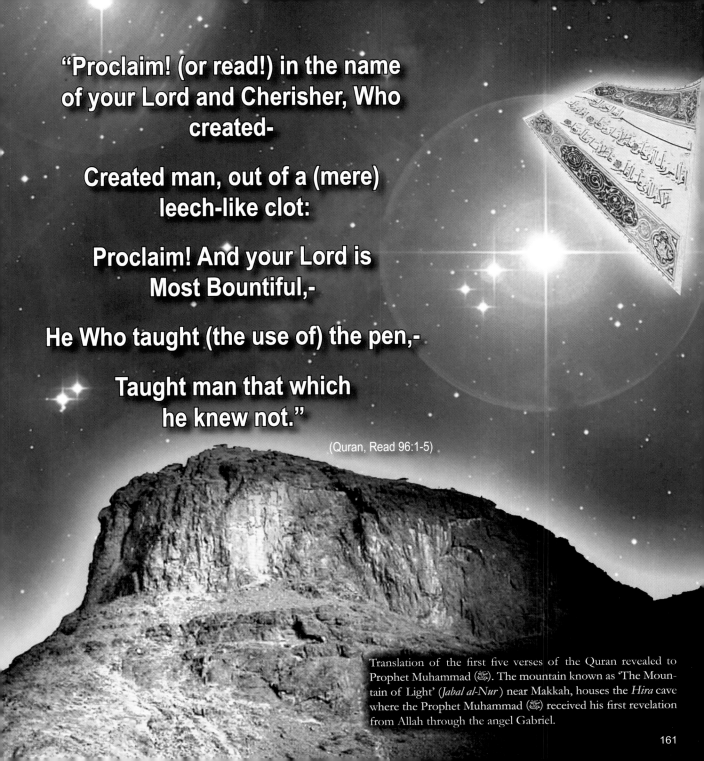

"Proclaim! (or read!) in the name of your Lord and Cherisher, Who created-

Created man, out of a (mere) leech-like clot:

Proclaim! And your Lord is Most Bountiful,-

He Who taught (the use of) the pen,-

Taught man that which he knew not."

(Quran, Read 96:1-5)

Translation of the first five verses of the Quran revealed to Prophet Muhammad (ﷺ). The mountain known as 'The Mountain of Light' (*Jabal al-Nur*) near Makkah, houses the *Hira* cave where the Prophet Muhammad (ﷺ) received his first revelation from Allah through the angel Gabriel.

161

The Three Stages of Revelation of the Quran

The First Stage

The Quran existed before the creation of the heavens and Earth, as the speech of Allah and was written by the order of Allah into the book known as the 'Preserved Tablet' (*al-Lauh al-Mahfuz*). Muslims believe that the entire Quran, along with everything else that has happened, is happening or is waiting to happen until the Day of Judgement is written in the 'Preserved Tablet'. The precise nature of how and when it was written is knowledge that is with Allah alone.

Allah says in the Quran:

"Nay! This is a Glorious Quran, (Inscribed) in al-Lauh al-Mahfuz (The Preserved Tablet)!"

(Quran, Constellations 85: 21-22)

The Second Stage

With the Quran written by the order of Allah into the 'Preserved Tablet', the next stage of revelation of the Quran occurred when Allah ordered the Quran to be revealed to the lower heavens in a place called 'The House of Honour' (*al-Bayt al-Izza*). This revelation took place in the month of Ramadan during the 'Night of Decree' (*Laylat al-Qadr*).

"The month of Ramadan in which was revealed the Quran, a guidance for mankind and clear proofs for the guidance and the Criterion (between right and wrong)..."

(Quran, The Heifer 2: 185)

"By the manifest Book (this Quran) that makes things clear. We sent it (this Quran) down on a blessed night."

(Quran, Smoke 44: 2-3)

The Third Stage

The final stage of revelation took place when the Quran was gradually revealed to Prophet Muhammad (ﷺ). The Quran was brought down as ordered by Allah through the Angel Gabriel and inspired directly into the heart and mind of Prophet Muhammad (ﷺ).

Allah refers to this stage in many verses of the Quran. In one such verse Allah Says:

"And indeed, the Quran is the revelation of the Lord of the worlds. The Trustworthy Spirit has brought it down upon your heart, (O Muhammad) that you may be of the warners. In a clear Arabic language."

(Quran, The Poets 26: 192-194)

Preservation of the Quran

The Quran is unchanged and remains in its original language, without the revision, addition or omission of a single letter since the time of Prophet Muhammad (ﷺ). The Quran is unique in this way. Allah, The Guardian, has perfectly preserved the Quran and guaranteed it from corruption until the end of time.

The Quran is regarded not just by Muslims but also by historians of religion, as the most authentic religious text among the world's religions. None of the other revealed books have reached us in their original form or language. Some of them, like the scrolls that were revealed through Abraham (ﷺ), have not reached us at all. Over the course of time, parts of other scriptures were rewritten or removed, distorting their message.

Mechanism of Preservation - Memorisation

Throughout the centuries the mechanism of preservation has been two fold: memorisation and writing. Whenever a verse of the Quran was revealed, Prophet Muhammad (ﷺ) would be divinely caused to memorise it. He would then convey the message to his companions, many of whom would also instantly memorise it by heart.

The people of Arabia had been blessed with the capacity to memorise thousands of poetic lines. Common villagers were able to remember by heart their genealogies and those of their families and even those of their horses!

This power to memorise was well utilised for the conservation and protection of the Quran. The result today is that the Quran exists as an unbroken chain of oral transmission back to Prophet Muhammad (ﷺ).

> **"And We have made the Quran easy to understand and remember"**
>
> (Quran, The Moon 54: 22)

> **"Do they not Ponder over the Quran? Had it been from any other than Allah, surely there would have been many contradictions in it."**
>
> (Quran, Women 4: 82)

Opposite page: There are six basic styles of Arabic script, *thulth, muhaqqaq, tawqi, naskh, rayhan* and *riqa*. From these many other forms have developed such as, *nast'aliq, shikaste, divani, ta'liq, ijaze* and *ruq'a, maghribi, sudani* and *andalusi*.

Far right: Decorated marker from a 15th century Quran written in India (Exhibition Islam collection).

The Six Classical Hands
of Arabic Script.

Thulth

اللَّهُمَّ بِنُورِكَ اَهْتَدَيْنَا وَبِفَضْلِكَ

Muhaqqaq

Tawqi

اللَّهُمَّ بِنُورِكَ اَهْتَدَيْنَا وَبِفَضْلِكَ اَسْتَغْنَيْنَا وَفِي كَنَفِكَ اَصْبَحْنَا وَاَمْسَيْنَا
اَنْتَ الاَوَّلُ فَلاَ شَيْءَ قَبْلَكَ وَاَنْتَ الاَخِرُ فَلاَ شَيْءَ بَعْدَكَ نَعُوذُ بِكَ
مِنَ الْفَشَلِ وَالْكَسَلِ وَمِنْ عَذَابِ الْقَبْرِ وَمِنْ فِتْنَةِ الْغِنَى وَالْفَقْرِ

Naskh

اللَّهُمَّ بِنُورِكَ اَهْتَدَيْنَا وَبِفَضْلِكَ اَسْتَغْنَيْنَا وَفِي كَنَفِكَ اَصْبَحْنَا وَاَمْسَيْنَا
اَنْتَ الاَوَّلُ فَلاَ شَيْءَ قَبْلَكَ وَاَنْتَ الاَخِرُ فَلاَ شَيْءَ بَعْدَكَ نَعُوذُ بِكَ
مِنَ الْفَشَلِ وَالْكَسَلِ وَمِنْ عَذَابِ الْقَبْرِ وَمِنْ فِتْنَةِ الْغِنَى وَالْفَقْرِ

Rayhan

اللَّهُمَّ بِنُورِكَ اَهْتَدَيْنَا وَبِفَضْلِكَ اَسْتَغْنَيْنَا وَفِي كَنَفِكَ اَصْبَحْنَا وَاَمْسَيْنَا اَنْتَ الاَوَّلُ فَلاَ شَيْءَ قَبْلَكَ وَاَنْتَ الاَخِرُ
فَلاَ شَيْءَ بَعْدَكَ نَعُوذُ بِكَ مِنَ الْفَشَلِ وَالْكَسَلِ وَمِنْ عَذَابِ الْقَبْرِ وَمِنْ فِتْنَةِ الْغِنَى وَالْفَقْرِ

Riqa.

Mechanism of Preservation - Writing

During the era of the third Caliph of Islam, Uthman ibn Affan (ﷺ), a definitive reference copy of the Quran was compiled from the original writings. Eight copies of the scripture were compiled and then sent to all provincial parts of the Islamic world to ensure that all copies of the Quran were exact. The original reference copy of the Quran, upon which all Quran's are based, was retained in Madinah. It remained in Madinah until it was taken to Istanbul, Turkey, in the early part of the twentieth century, where it can still be viewed at the Topkapi museum. The results of Uthman ibn Affan's (ﷺ) endeavours are clear in at least two ways. Firstly, every Muslim province gained access to the Quran and secondly, this ensured that the skeletal text of the Quran would not be altered in any way.

Over time surface alterations such as verse separators began to materialise in the Quran's in circulation. These bore no effect on the pronunciation of words or the meaning of verses. Caliph Uthman ibn Affan (ﷺ) himself may have been familiar with aspects of this phenomenon; his decision to minimise written vowels and avoid the use of verse separators and dots was most likely meant as a deterrent to those who would memorise the Quran by themselves without proper guidance. With the passing of time, as Islam spread to other parts of the world, the inclusion of vowel marks, a dotting scheme and verse separators has become the norm to aid correct pronunciation of the Quran.

Above: An example of a leather Quran page from a rare 7-8th century Quran written in a hybrid Kufic-Hijazi script. Chapter 109 verse 3 to the end of chapter 111 are shown (Exhibition Islam collection).

Opposite page: The original reference Quran, compiled by the third Caliph of Islam, Uthman ibn Affan (ﷺ), is still in existence today and is held at the Topkapi Museum, Turkey. Chapter 2 (Al-Baqarah) verses 40-48 are shown. The red dotting scheme was most likely added at a later date. Although many different font styles have been used in the Quran over the centuries, to this day the Arabic itself has remained the same since its' revelation over 1,400 years ago.

Above: A fine example of a 15th century Quran handwritten during the Timurid/Saffavid period (Exhibition Islam collection).

Above: A folio written around 800 years ago in Maghribi Quranic script from North Africa.

إنا نحن نزلنا الذكر وإنا له لحفظون

إنا نحن نزلنا الذكر وإنا له لحفظون

إنا نحن نزلنا الذكر وإنا له لحفظون

إِنَّا نَحْنُ نَزَّلْنَا الذِّكْرَ وَإِنَّا لَهُ لَحَفِظُونَ

Above: The development of Quranic reading aids through the ages. Although the font type used today may have developed over time to make the Quran easier to read, the actual Arabic words have remained the same. All four fragments are the same verse, "Surely We have revealed the Reminder and We will most surely be its guardian." (Quran, Stoneland 15:9). The top most fragment from the Quran is from the early Islamic period and lacks skeletal dots and vowel markings. The second, third and fourth lines show the addition of reading aids to help correct pronunciation. The reading aids have no impact on the meaning of the words, which have remained the same for over 14 centuries (adapted from the cover of Professor Muhammad Al-Azami's monumental work; *The History of The Quranic Script from Revelation to Compilation, A comparative study with the Old and New Testament.* UK Islamic Academy, 2003).

Divine Protection

Islam holds that the Quran is divinely protected by the Creator and has remained preserved in its true original form since its revelation over 1,400 years ago. This is evidenced by the existence of original Quranic manuscripts dating back to the very first time it was compiled. When historic Quranic manuscripts dating back to its revelation in the 7th century are compared to the Quran that is available today, they show that the Quran has not changed. Remarkably, there is not even one letter, let alone one word, missing or out of place when compared to the original.

Muslims believe that no one can forge even a small part of the Quran and that no alterations can appear in it. This is because Allah has not allowed the Quran to be tampered with or contaminated in anyway. The Quran is Allah's final book for all of humanity until the Day of Judgment. No new Prophet or Messenger will be sent in the future. If Allah had not protected the Quran, it would never have reached us in its original form.

No Versions of the Quran

Although there are numerous translations in English and in many other languages, these are neither the Quran nor a version of the Quran, they are only 'translations of the meaning'. There are no alternative versions of the Quran. It exists only in the pure Arabic form in which it was revealed.

Free of Corruption and Distortion

For Muslims, it is a miracle that the Noble Quran has remained unchanged and unaltered and it shall remain so. For Allah has taken it upon Himself to protect it. It says in the Quran;

"Then do they not reflect upon the Quran? If it had been from (any) other than Allah, they would have found within it much contradiction."

(Quran, Women 4: 82)

Above: A page from a 7th century Quran attributed to Ali bin Abi Talib (☝), who was the cousin of the Prophet Muhammad (☝) and the fourth of the rightly guided Caliph's of Islam.

Opposite page: A Quranic manuscript dating back to the 10th century. Hand written in elegantly flowing Kufic Arabic script.

"Surely We have revealed the Reminder (the Quran) and We will most surely be its guardian."

(Quran, The Rocky Tract 15: 9)

Opposite page and right: A series of images from a magnificent 800 year old Quran. This is one of the oldest Qurans in Exhibition Islam's renowned Quranic manuscript collection. This rare Quran dates back to the Mamluk period and is beautifully hand written in traditional Mamluk style Arabic script. The manuscript is highly decorated with extensive gold and floral illumination throughout. The opening chapter of the Quran is shown on the opposite page.

What Does The Quran Say?

An Invitation

The Quran does not conform to the normal form, style or structure contained in other books. It deals with man and his ultimate purpose in life. It contains principles, doctrines and guidance in every sphere of human life. It narrates stories of the previous Prophets, lays down social obligations and economic laws, covers a wide range of sciences from egyptology to embryology and contains vivid descriptions of heaven and hell. In short the Quran invites man to accept Allah spiritually as well as intellectually and to worship Allah alone.

"O you who believe! answer (the call of) Allah and His Messenger when he calls you to that which gives you life; and know that Allah intervenes between man and his heart and that to Him you shall be gathered."

(Quran, Spoils of War, 8: 24)

The invitation to reflect on Allah's signs present in creation is well pronounced throughout the Quran. The Quran condemns dogmatic and un-verified convictions.

"And follow not that of which you have not the knowledge; surely the hearing and the sight and the heart, all of these, shall be questioned about that."

(Quran, The Night Journey, 17: 36)

The teachings of the Quran cover life, death and the life after death. It contains Allah's law: the rituals and practices of worship and the means to attain nearness to Allah and righteousness by enjoining good and forbidding evil. The Quran consistently offers firm and clear answers and is not concerned with partial solutions.

"Those who follow the Messenger, the unlettered prophet, whom they find written in what they have of the Torah and the Gospel, who enjoins upon them what is right and forbids them what is wrong and makes lawful for them the good things and prohibits for them the evil and relieves them of their burden and the shackles which were upon them. So they who have believed in him, honoured him, supported him and followed the light which was sent down with him, it is those who will be the successful."

(Quran, The Heights 7: 157)

Main subjects in the Quran

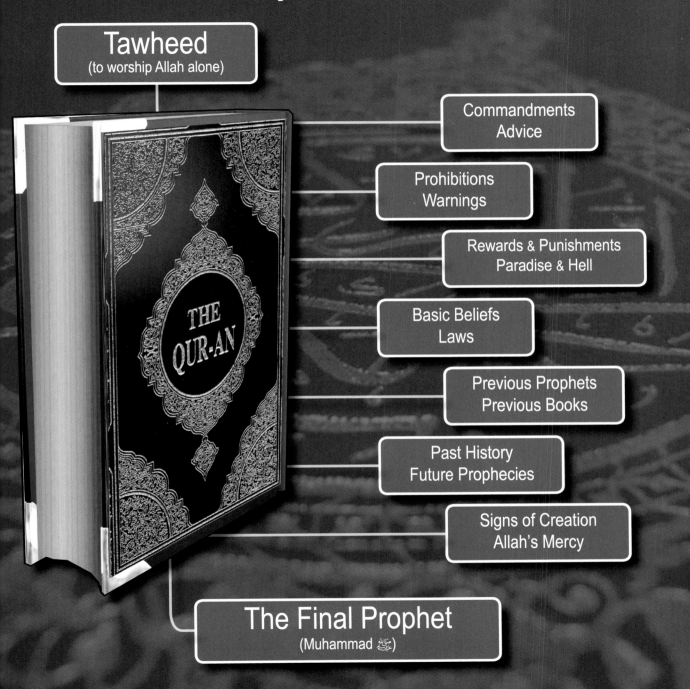

Tawheed (to worship Allah alone)

Commandments
Advice

Prohibitions
Warnings

Rewards & Punishments
Paradise & Hell

Basic Beliefs
Laws

Previous Prophets
Previous Books

Past History
Future Prophecies

Signs of Creation
Allah's Mercy

The Final Prophet (Muhammad ﷺ)

Scientific Phenomena

The idea of reading, reflecting and verifying Allah's revelation is unique to the Quran. Not a single verse of the Quran has been proven to contradict the established facts of science. In the past the Quran has pointed out many scientific and historical facts which were not only unknown, but could not even have been contemplated at the time.

> **"We will show them Our signs in the horizons and within themselves until it becomes clear to them that it is the truth. But is it not sufficient concerning your Lord that He is, over all things, a Witness?"**

(Quran, Ha-Meem 41: 53)

The Quran also describes past events and areas of knowledge which were totally unknown in Arabia at the time. All the Quranic facts have turned out to be absolutely true. Prophet Muhammad (ﷺ) is described in the Quran as follows;

> **"And you were never able to recite any book before this Book (Quran), nor are you able to write, for then those who follow would have doubted."**

(Quran, The Spider 29: 48)

Opposite page: An oil lamp illuminating a page of the Quran. Muslims regard the Quran as literally the "Spoken Word of Allah". As the Quran is meant to be read, understood and implemented, Muslims usually read some of the Quran as part of their daily routine. Moreover, the act of recitation in a melodious voice is itself regarded as an act of worship, so most Muslims will also try to learn and memorise parts or the complete Quran by heart.

Left: Section from a 15th century handwritten Quran scroll from *Exhibition Islam's* Middle Eastern collection (dimensions: 4.4 cm wide and 740 cm long).

The Great Challenge

Historically, the Arabs of the 6th and 7th centuries were masters of language; eloquence and rhetoric were their lifeblood. The liveliness that marked their gatherings, the gaiety of their fairs and the virtues of which they boasted all found their expression through poetry and literature. They were so proud of their literary accomplishments that they contemptuously dubbed all the non-Arab peoples of the world as "'Dumb" (*Ajam* in Arabic). It was in this climate that Prophet Muhammad (ﷺ) presented before them an oration and declared it to be the Word of Allah.

Such a proclamation was no ordinary thing. It came from a person who had never learnt anything from the renowned poets and scholars of the time, had never recited even a single piece of poetry in their congregations and never attended the company of soothsayers. And far from composing any poetry himself, he did not even remember the verses of other poets.

The challenge of the Quran was therefore, the greatest challenge to their literary prowess and to their pagan creed and beliefs. When the Arab orators and poets were faced with the Quran they were silenced. Not a soul stepped forward to accept the challenge laid down by the Quran, which was issued in three stages; i) to produce an entire book like the Quran; ii) to produce ten chapters like the Quran; iii) to produce just a single chapter. None of these challenges were met. It is worth noting that the shortest chapter of the Quran (108) is just three verses long.

Instead of meeting the Quran's challenge by composing a few verses similar in nature to the Quran, Prophet Muhammad (ﷺ) was called insane, a sorcerer, a poet and a soothsayer. To this day no one has met the challenge of the Quran, although there have been many attempts throughout history to do so.

"And if you are in doubt about what We (Allah) have sent down upon Our Servant (Muhammad), then produce a chapter the like thereof and call upon your witnesses other than Allah, if you should be truthful."

(Quran, The Heifer 2: 23)

Background: High speed photography captures the moment a drop of water impacts on a surface. For Muslims, Allah, is the Creator of the Universe and has unlimited knowledge of everything. The Quran says;

"And if all the trees on earth were pens and the ocean (were ink), with seven oceans behind it to add to its (supply), the words of Allah would not be exhausted: for Allah is Exalted in Power, full of Wisdom."

(Quran, Luqman 31: 27)

Quran's Structure & Language

In the month of Ramadan during the last year of his life, Prophet Muhammad (ﷺ) recited the Quran twice behind the Angel Gabriel, in the order that it exists today. The verses of the Quran were not arranged in order of revelation or by subject matter. Many of the later revelations were placed at the beginning whilst the earlier Makkan chapters were placed at the end of the Quran.

Division into Chapters and Verses

Structurally, the Quran is divided into chapters (*Surahs*) and verses (*Ayahs*). The Arabic word, *Ayah* actually means 'miracle' or 'sign' emphasising that the sentences are not just verses of some poem but each phrase is a sign from the Almighty Creator. Each of the Quran's 114 chapters are given a title according to its contents. There are other useful divisions of the Quran, for example the 30 equally sized 'parts' called *Juz*, or 7 equally sized parts called *Manzil*. These divisions are helpful for memorisation and for those who wish to complete recitation of the Quran in a month or in a week.

> **"And (it is) a Quran which We have separated (by intervals) that you might recite it to the people over a prolonged period. And We have sent it down progressively."**
>
> (Quran, The Night Journey: 105-107)

Above: A 9th century Quran manuscript hand written in elegant Kufic style. The end of chapter 9 (Repentance) and the beginning of chapter 10 (Jonah) is shown on this parchment (Maktabat al-Jami' al-Kabir, San'a', Yemen).

Opposite page: Original manuscript leaf from an early 18th century Arabic Quran. Written on fine hand-made paper, in an unusual Maghribi Sudani script with letter-pointing and full vocalization in red and highlighted with saffron (Exhibition Islam collection).

عَلَى أَنفُسِكُم مَّتَاعَ الْحَيَاةِ الدُّنْيَا ثُمَّ إِلَيْنَا مَرْجِعُكُمْ فَنُنَبِّئُكُم بِمَا كُنتُمْ تَعْمَلُونَ

إِنَّمَا مَثَلُ الْحَيَاةِ الدُّنْيَا كَمَاءٍ أَنزَلْنَاهُ مِنَ السَّمَاءِ فَاخْتَلَطَ بِهِ نَبَاتُ الْأَرْضِ مِمَّا يَأْكُلُ النَّاسُ وَالْأَنْعَامُ حَتَّىٰ إِذَا أَخَذَتِ الْأَرْضُ زُخْرُفَهَا وَازَّيَّنَتْ وَظَنَّ أَهْلُهَا أَنَّهُمْ قَادِرُونَ عَلَيْهَا أَتَاهَا أَمْرُنَا لَيْلًا أَوْ نَهَارًا فَجَعَلْنَاهَا حَصِيدًا كَأَن لَّمْ تَغْنَ بِالْأَمْسِ كَذَٰلِكَ نُفَصِّلُ الْآيَاتِ لِقَوْمٍ يَتَفَكَّرُونَ

وَاللَّهُ يَدْعُو إِلَىٰ دَارِ السَّلَامِ وَيَهْدِي مَن يَشَاءُ إِلَىٰ صِرَاطٍ مُّسْتَقِيمٍ

لِّلَّذِينَ أَحْسَنُوا الْحُسْنَىٰ وَزِيَادَةٌ وَلَا يَرْهَقُ وُجُوهَهُمْ قَتَرٌ وَلَا ذِلَّةٌ أُولَٰئِكَ أَصْحَابُ الْجَنَّةِ هُمْ فِيهَا خَالِدُونَ

وَالَّذِينَ كَسَبُوا السَّيِّئَاتِ جَزَاءُ سَيِّئَةٍ بِمِثْلِهَا وَتَرْهَقُهُمْ ذِلَّةٌ مَّا لَهُم مِّنَ اللَّهِ مِنْ عَاصِمٍ كَأَنَّمَا أُغْشِيَتْ وُجُوهُهُمْ قِطَعًا مِّنَ اللَّيْلِ مُظْلِمًا أُولَٰئِكَ أَصْحَابُ النَّارِ هُمْ فِيهَا خَالِدُونَ

181

The Quran's Beautiful Language

Usually a different style of writing is adopted when writing a speech, literary prose or academic article. The amazing fact about the Arabic of the Quran is that it combines all three styles. The Quran contains powerful oration, eloquent words and the weight of an academic piece, resulting in a unique text. It is also accessible to people of all backgrounds and abilities. From rustic villagers, to educated persons, learned scholars and experts in science, its unique style captures them all. Its ability to penetrate the innermost soul and to bring comfort and peace, represents one of the most outstanding properties of the Quran.

There is a tendency in Arabic poetry and prose to exaggerate facts to such an extent that they become obscured. The Quran, however, is unique in that it does not follow the normal pattern of Arabic poetry and prose. The flow of the Quran is not interrupted by the repeated detail contained in many of its verses. In fact part of the beauty of the Quran can be attributed to its precise detail and accuracy.

"And We have revealed to you, (O Muhammad), the Book in truth, confirming that which preceded it of the Scripture and as a criterion over it. So judge between them by what Allah has revealed and do not follow their inclinations away from what has come to you of the truth.

(Quran, The Table Spread 5: 48)

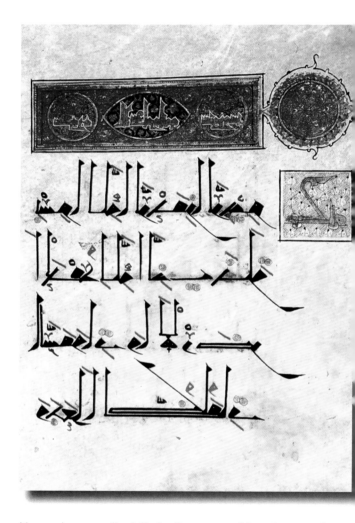

Above: A very stylized Kufic Quran page. Note the use of different colours for the vowel marks and dotting scheme.

A Pinnacle of Literary Excellence

It is regarded as the most eloquent piece of Arabic literature in existence. It has a style like no other work in the Arabic language, a style that cannot be reproduced. The Quran treats with the height of eloquence those topics to which the human mind could not give literary beauty, whatever may be tried to achieve it. For example, the law of inheritance can be a dry and intractable subject that it is impossible to create any rhythm and literary elegance while dealing with it. Yet the Quran deals with this type of subject in such a beautiful and awe-inspiring manner that people can feel deeply moved. No human being has ever composed a book that discusses such diverse topics in a language with so much rhythm, beauty and style.

A Living Language

The Quran is still read and understood in the language in which it was revealed more than 1,400 years ago. Not a single Arabic word, phrase or idiom of this revealed Book has become obsolete or has lost its original meaning. As the word 'Quran' means 'recitation', this alludes to the fact that it is a recitation alive upon the tongues, hearts and limbs of its people.

بِسْمِ اللهِ الرَّحْمٰنِ الرَّحِيْمِ

الٓمّٓ ۚ ذٰلِكَ الْكِتٰبُ لَا رَيْبَ ۛ فِيْهِ ۛ هُدًى لِّلْمُتَّقِيْنَ ۙ الَّذِيْنَ يُؤْمِنُوْنَ بِالْغَيْبِ وَيُقِيْمُوْنَ الصَّلٰوةَ وَمِمَّا رَزَقْنٰهُمْ يُنْفِقُوْنَ ۙ وَالَّذِيْنَ يُؤْمِنُوْنَ بِمَا أُنْزِلَ إِلَيْكَ وَمَا أُنْزِلَ مِنْ قَبْلِكَ وَبِالْآخِرَةِ هُمْ يُوْقِنُوْنَ ۗ أُولٰٓئِكَ عَلٰى هُدًى مِّنْ رَّبِّهِمْ ۖ وَأُولٰٓئِكَ هُمُ الْمُفْلِحُوْنَ

184

In the name of Allah, the Compassionate, the Merciful.

"Alif Lam Meem.

This is the Book; in it is guidance sure, without doubt, to those who fear Allah;

Who believe in the Unseen, are steadfast in prayer and spend out of what We have provided for them;

And who believe in the Revelation sent to you and sent before your time and (in their hearts) have the assurance of the Hereafter.

They are on (true) guidance, from their Lord and it is these who will prosper.

As to those who reject Faith, it is the same to them whether you warn them or do not warn them; they will not believe.

Allah has set a seal on their hearts and on their hearing and on their eyes is a veil; great is the penalty they (incur)."

(Quran 2, The Heifer 2: 1-7)

Opposite page: A complete handwritten Quran from the 19th century showing the first page of Chapter 2, The Heifer (translation given above). Originating from the Ottoman Empire, it is highly decorated throughout using precious gold and a variety of colours. Written on polished paper and bound in a leather hardcover with gold insets (Exhibition Islam collection).

Quran's Rhythmic Style

The Quran is like no other book that any man has written. It is easier to follow and understand it if one accepts it as the word of Allah. Whereas, it is far more difficult to read if one has preconceived ideas about human literary style. Some people however, are instantly moved by the teachings of the Quran.

The Quran follows no set rules of any type of poetry, yet it somehow has an infinitely more rhythmic and appealing elegance than any poem or musical score. It is difficult to describe the sounds and rhythm used in the Quran. However, the effect that the Quran has on people is undeniable. Whoever recites it according to its rules or hears its proper recitation is instantly moved by it.

Inimitability

All of the verses of the Quran are uniformly eloquent, beautiful and impressive. History bears testimony to the fact that it is not humanly possible to write a book of over 6,000 verses with such superbly sublime diction and absolute command of the language.

Say, "If mankind and the jinn gathered in order to produce the like of this Quran, they could not produce the like of it, even if they were assistants to each other."

(Quran, The Night Journey 17: 88)

Above: A 13th century African Maghribi/Andalusian Quran leaf illuminated with gold.

Following pages: Dating back to around 1780 this beautiful Afghan Quran, handwritten in *Naskhi* style Arabic script, has a *Farsi* translation in red ink. The English translation of the Arabic is given on the left.

The Most Memorised Book in the World

Another divine feature of the Quran is its capability of being completely memorised in full, including millions of people who do not understand the Arabic language. In fact the Quran is the most memorised book in the world.

An Ocean of Knowledge

The Quran is like a vast ocean. Children collect pebbles and shells from its shores. The scholars and thinkers, like pearl divers, take from it the most advanced philosophy, wisdom and rules of a perfect way of living.

It is also the most explained book in history with thousands of volumes elucidating on its many wonders. Commentaries such as *Tafseer al-Tabari* (30 volumes), *Tasfeer Al-Qurtubi* (20 volumes) and *Tafseer Ibn Kathir* (4 volumes) are renowned worldwide as classical works of Arabic literature.

In the Name of Allah, Most Compassionate, Most Merciful.

"By those (angels) lined up in rows
And those who drive (the clouds)
And those who recite the message,
Indeed, your God is One, Lord of the heavens and the
earth and that between them and Lord
of the sunrises.
Indeed, We have adorned the nearest heaven with an
adornment of stars
And as protection against every rebellious devil
(So) they may not listen to the exalted assembly [of
angels] and are pelted from every side,
Repelled; and for them is a constant punishment,
Except one who snatches (some words) by theft, but
they are pursued by a burning flame,
piercing (in brightness).
Then inquire of them, (O Muhammad), "Are they a
stronger (or more difficult) creation or those (others)
We have created?" Indeed, We created men
from sticky clay.
But you wonder, while they mock,
And when they are reminded, they remember not.
And when they see a sign, they ridicule
And say, "This is not but obvious magic.
When we have died and become dust and bones, are
we indeed to be resurrected?
And our forefathers (as well)?"
Say, Yes and you will be (rendered) contemptible."
It will be only one shout and at once they
will be observing.
They will say, "O woe to us! This is the
Day of Recompense."
(They will be told), "This is the Day of Judgement
which you used to deny."

(Quran, Drawn up in Ranks 37: 1-21)

Following page: Everything in the Universe glorifies and
submits to the will of the Creator, Allah. Delicate goatsbeard
seedheads provide the background for the translation of the
Quranic chapter 'The Ornaments of Gold'.

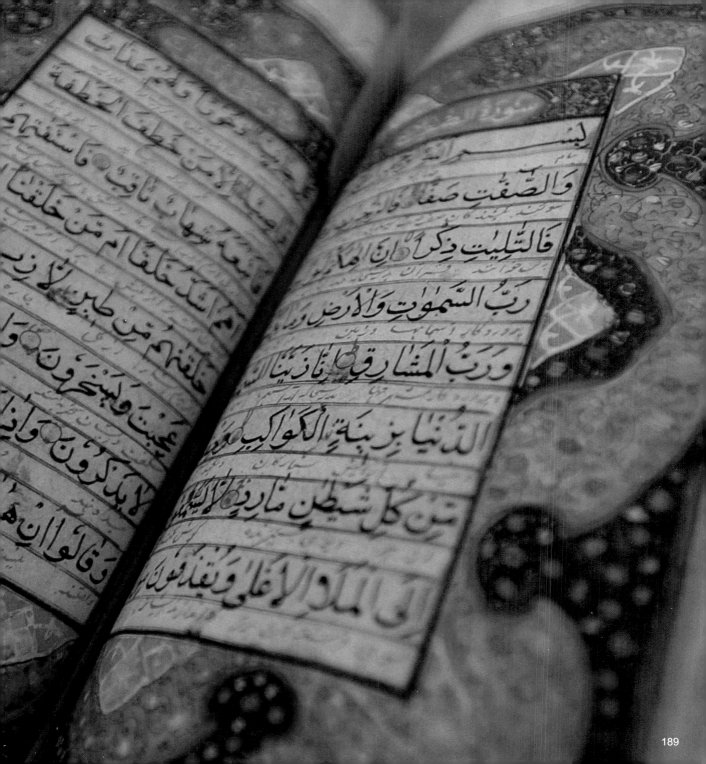

بسم الله

والصّافّات صفّا

فالتّاليت ذكرا إن إلهكم

رب السموت والأرض وما

ورب المشارق إنا زينا

الدّنيا بزينة الكواكب

من كل شيطن مارد لا يسمعون

إلى الملأ الأعلى ويقذفون

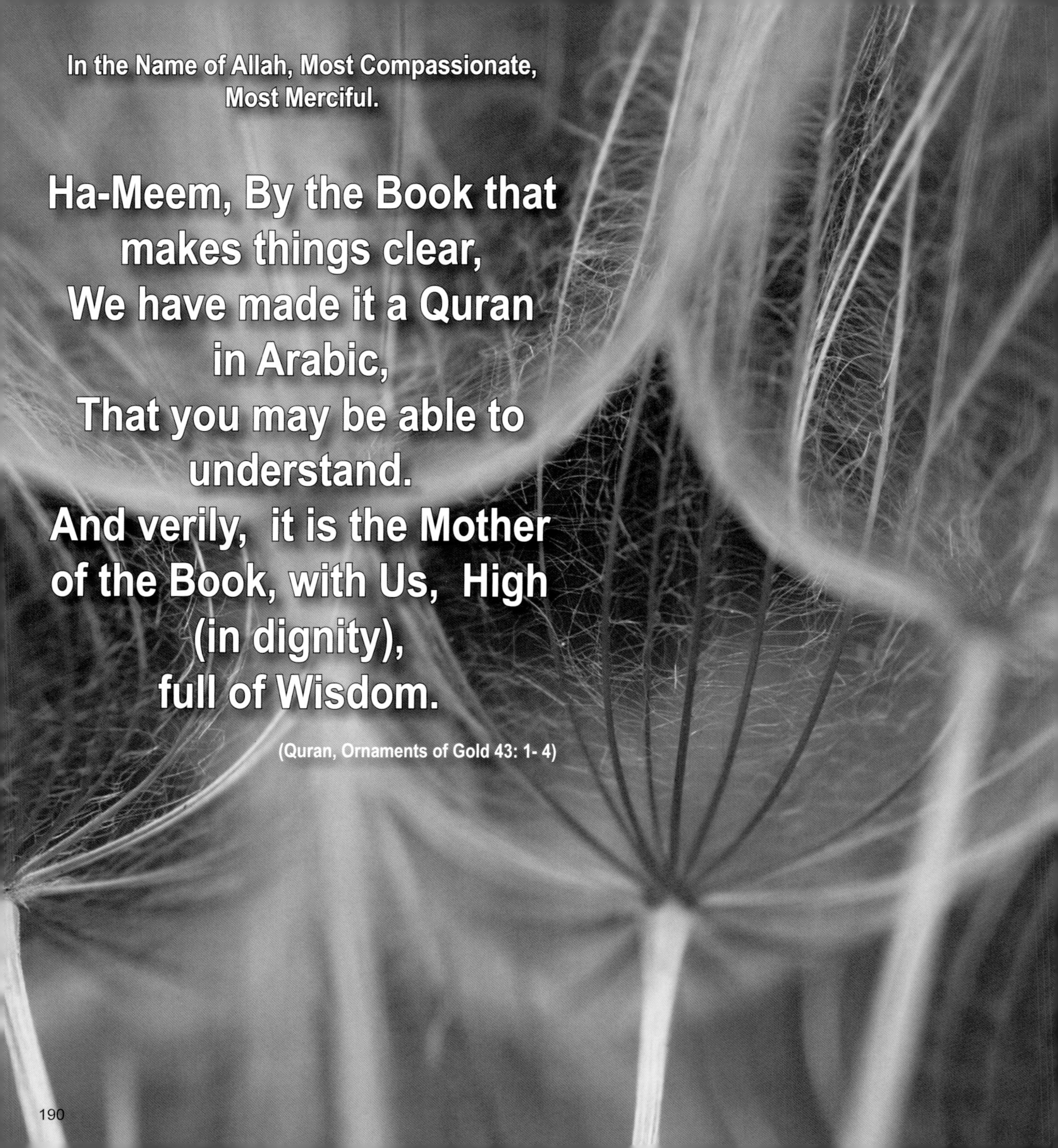

In the Name of Allah, Most Compassionate, Most Merciful.

Ha-Meem, By the Book that
makes things clear,
We have made it a Quran
in Arabic,
That you may be able to
understand.
And verily, it is the Mother
of the Book, with Us, High
(in dignity),
full of Wisdom.

(Quran, Ornaments of Gold 43: 1- 4)

190

Chapter 9

Scientific Signs
in the Quran

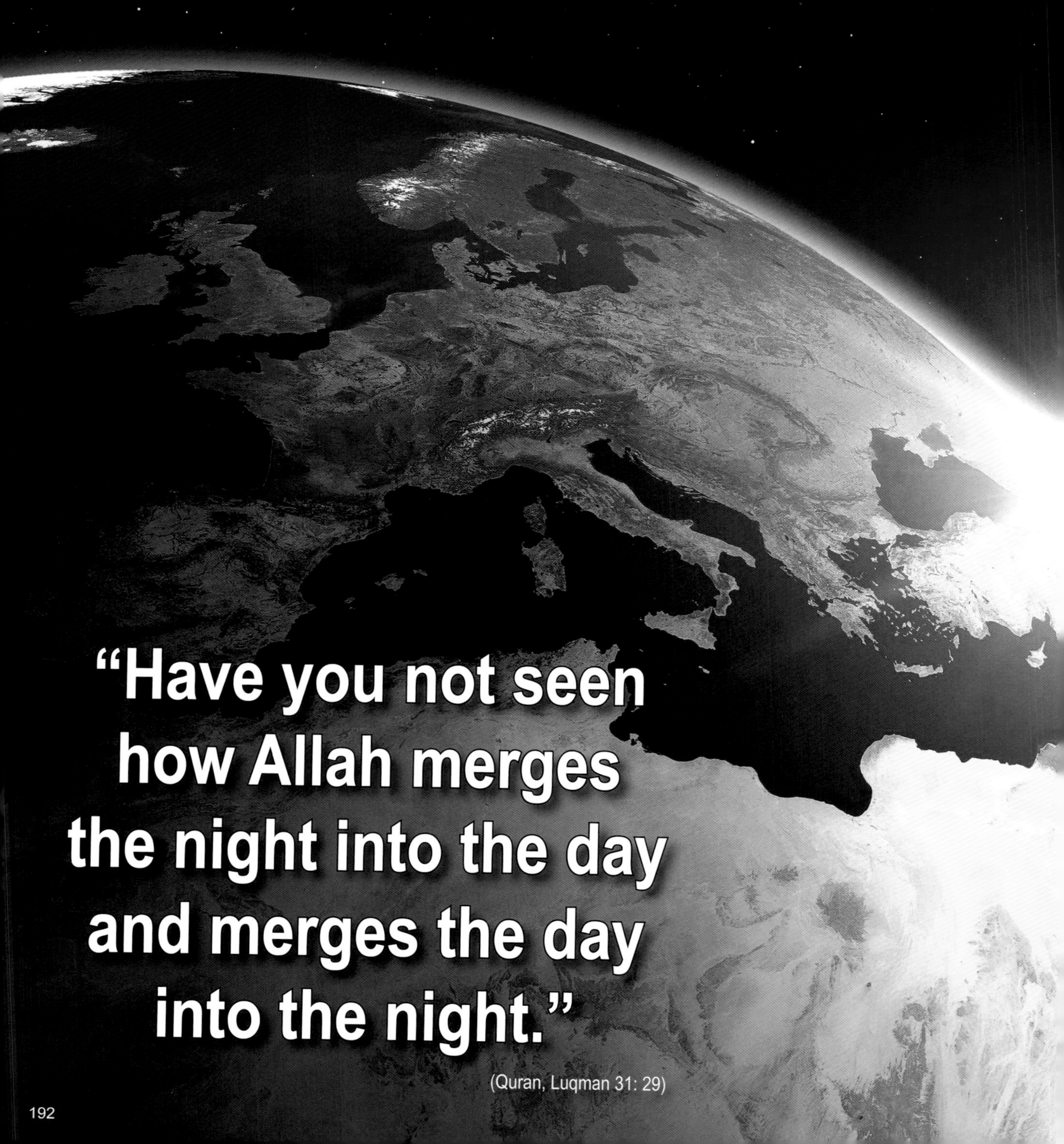

"Have you not seen
how Allah merges
the night into the day
and merges the day
into the night."

(Quran, Luqman 31: 29)

Introduction

Muslims view the Quran as the final revelation from the Creator to mankind. It was revealed during the early part of the 7th century to Prophet Muhammad (), who is regarded as the last Prophet and Messenger sent by Allah. Although not a scientific reference, the Quran contains an abundance of scientific information that was not known to man at the time of revelation, simply because the technology was not available in the 7th· century to verify it. Remarkably, the information contained within the Quran has proven to be accurate.

Quranic verses include information on topics such as astronomy and embryology, conveyed in a simple and comprehensive manner. The information contained in the Quran provides further overwhelming evidence that a human being did not author it. Furthermore, the Quran can be regarded as a 'book of signs.' It provides an insight into the workings of nature. The study of the natural world and the 'signs' in the Quran lead us to conclude that the Universe was created by an All-Knowing and All-Powerful Creator. These 'signs' which guide the reader to the path of discovery and deeper understanding of the sciences has provided enormous inspiration to Muslims for centuries. Muslim scientists have made ground-breaking contributions to the sciences and arts. The extent of this contribution to world civilisation was so great that it inspired the scientific renaissance of 'Dark age' Europe.

Astronomy in the Quran

The Origin of the Universe as One Entity

Today, there are various theories that explain the existence of the beginning of the universe. In the Quran, revealed to the Blessed Prophet Muhammad (ﷺ) over 1,400 years ago, we are given a clue to the possible beginnings. The Quran states that the heavens and the Earth were one connected entity, which were separated from each other.

"Have not those who disbelieved known that the heavens and the Earth were one connected entity, then We separated them?"

(Quran, The Prophets 21: 30)

Beginning of the Universe as a Gaseous Mass

The Quran also refers to the heavens as 'smoke' This suggests that the heavens, which includes the galaxies, stars and planets, were nothing but a cloud of smoke or a highly dense and hot gaseous mass. It is now possible for scientists to observe new stars forming out of remnants of that 'smoke'.

Opposite: One of the many wonders of creation and arguably the most famous dark nebula in the night sky, the Horse Head Nebula. Located in the Orion constellation 1,500 light years from Earth, it is part of a swirling cloud of dark dust and gases, which is approximately 3.5 light years wide and shaped like a horse's head (hence its name). The unusual shape was first discovered in 1888 on a photographic plate taken at the Harvard College Observatory. The red glow originates from hydrogen gas predominantly behind the nebula, ionized by the nearby bright star Sigma Orionis. Bright spots in the Horse Head Nebula's base are young stars just in the process of forming.

IMAGE CREDIT: SCIENCE PHOTO LIBRARY.

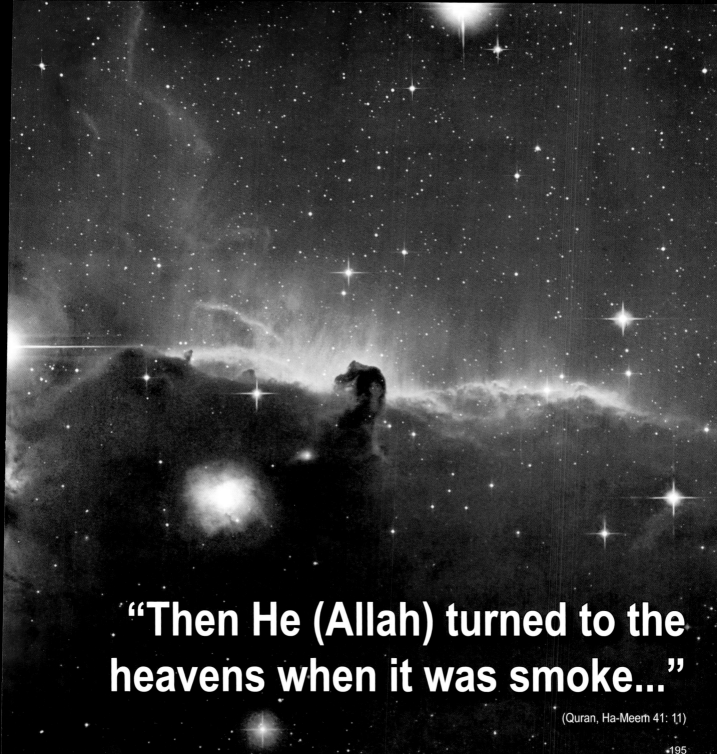

"Then He (Allah) turned to the heavens when it was smoke..."

(Quran, Ha-Meem 41: 11)

"And among His Signs is the creation of the heavens and the earth and the variations in your languages and your colours; verily in that are Signs for those who know."

(Quran, The Romans: 30: 22)

Background: Billions of stars shine out from the Whirlpool Galaxy (M51), each one glorifying the Creator of the Universe in its own unique way. Located at a phenomenal distance of 37 million light-years in the constellation Canes Venatici, the large spiral galaxy is interacting with its small companion (NGC 5195, right). The spiral arms of M51 are studded with pink starbirth regions, which glow as radiation from the newborn stars within them ionises the hydrogen they contain. The regions between the spiral arms look relatively empty, but they are actually criss-crossed by dark dust lanes. A black hole surrounded by a ring of dust exists at the heart of the spiral.

IMAGE CREDIT: HUBBLE TELESCOPE, NASA/ESA/STCI.

The Heavens, the Earth and Matter in Between

The Quran also mentions the existence of an intermediate creation between the Heavens and the Earth.

"Allah is the One Who created the Heavens and the Earth and all that is between them in six days (periods of time)."

(Quran, The Criterion 25: 59)

The existence of an intermediary creation would appear to correspond with the modern discovery of nebulae (clouds of gas and dust). In fact the voids which separate the stars in our Galaxy are not actually empty at all, there is diffuse gaseous matter everywhere.

Appointed term for the heavens

The Quran highlights that the Sun and Moon have a limited existence in the following verse:

"...God subjected the Sun and the Moon: each one runs its course to an appointed term..."

(Quran, The Thunder 13: 2)

Scientists predict that the Sun's hydrogen will start to become exhausted after 5 billion years. When all of the Sun's nuclear energy is exhausted it will collapse into a small dense star of the type known as a `white dwarf'. In the final stage, the Sun will become a `black dwarf' radiating no light or heat. The main point to be noted from the above description is not the appointed time before the Sun and the Moon run its course but of the limited existence of the Sun and the Solar System.

197

The Formation of Multiple Worlds

According to modern science there is a strong possibility that the initial formation of the Universe resulted in the formation of multiple worlds. Over one thousand four hundred years ago, the Quran already gave us this notion as in the following verse;

> **"Praise be to Allah, the Lord of all the Worlds."**
>
> (Quran, The Opening 1: 1)

The Expanding Universe

In the 1920's at the Mount Wilson Observatory, Edwin Hubble (1889 to 1953) used the 100-inch Hooker telescope to show that there were celestial bodies lying beyond our own Galaxy and that these were receding from us. This led to further support for the idea that the Universe was expanding. However, the Quran, revealed centuries earlier, has already mentioned these recent findings by scientists, telling us that the Universe is expanding all the time.

"And the heaven We (Allah) constructed with strength and indeed, We are (its) expander."

(Quran, The Winnowing Winds 51: 47)

Background: View from a particle of light travelling at 186,282 miles per second from the outer rim of our Galaxy. Distances are so phenomenal that even at the speed of light it will still take another fifty thousand years before the light particle reaches planet Earth on the other side of the Galaxy.

Galaxies are huge gravitational bound systems of stars, interstellar gas and dust, plasma and (possibly) unseen dark matter. Typical galaxies contain 10 million to one trillion stars, all orbiting a common centre of gravity. In addition to single stars and a tenuous interstellar medium, most galaxies contain a large number of multiple star systems and star clusters as well as various types of nebulae. Most galaxies are several thousand to several hundred thousand light years in diameter and are usually separated from one another by distances on the order of millions of light years.

Our solar system is located in the Milky Way, a barred spiral galaxy with a diameter estimated at about 100,000 light years containing approximately 200 billion stars. The galaxy is a spiral and our Sun resides in one of the outer spiral arms, known as the Orion Arm or Local Spur.

Allah the Creator, has placed our solar system in a very remarkable orbit between the spiral arms well outside the star-encrusted Galactic centre. The radiation from supernovae in the spiral arms could theoretically sterilise planetary surfaces, ending the existence of all life.

The Sun and the Moon

The Sun is a massive thermonuclear reactor generating a tremendous amount of light and heat with a core temperature of approximately 10 million degrees. The Moon, on the other hand, is a small inert body, which reflects the light of the Sun. The fine distinction between the Sun and the Moon was unknown in the 7th century. It was thought that the Sun was the greater light which lit up the day and that the Moon was the lesser light which lit up the night. This indeed is how the Sun and the Moon were described in books before the Quran.

The simplicity and comprehensive detail of the Sun and the Moon in the Quran is astounding. It describes the Sun as a torch (*Siraj*) and a blazing lamp (*Wahhaj*) ie. a source of generated light, whilst the Moon is described as a light (*Nur*). It has now been discovered that, this is the true nature of the Sun and Moon as first revealed in the Quran.

Right: The average distance from the Moon to the Earth is 384,403 kilometres (238,857 miles). The Moon's diameter is 3,476 kilometres (2,160 miles) which is about 3.7 times smaller than the Earth, making it the Solar System's fifth largest moon, in both diameter and mass, and ranking behind Ganymede, Titan, Callisto and Io. Sunlight reflected from the Moon's surface reaches Earth in 1.3 seconds.

Opposite page: While the Sun is an average sized star with a near-perfect spherical shape, it contains approximately 99% of the total mass of the solar system. About 74% of the Sun's mass is hydrogen, 25% is helium and the rest is made up of trace quantities of heavier elements. The Sun has a spectral class of G2V. 'G2' means that it has a surface temperature of approximately 5,200 °C, giving it a white colour. Atmospheric scattering causes the Sun to appear yellow to us on Earth.

"Blessed is the One Who placed the constellations in heaven and placed therein a lamp (siraj) and a moon giving light (Nur)."

(Quran, The Criterion 25: 61)

"We (Allah) have built above you seven strong (heavens) and placed therein a blazing lamp (Siraj)."

(Quran, The Tidings 78: 12-13)

"The Sun runs its course to a settled place.
This is the decree of the
Almighty, the full of knowledge."

(Quran, Ya-Sin 36: 38)

The Quran also mentions that the Sun is running to a settled place. We know today that the Solar System is actually travelling in space at a speed of 12 miles per second towards a point situated near the current location of the bright star Vega in the constellation of Hercules Lyrae. The verse can also be translated as; "The Sun runs on its fixed course for a term", giving us the sense that the Sun has limited existence.

Today, it is common knowledge that the Moon, like a satellite, orbits around the Earth. It was once believed that the Sun was stationary. However, modern science has discovered that the Sun also has an orbit. It is estimated that the solar system is between 25,000 and 28,000 light years away from the galactic centre. We know today that the Sun revolves around the centre of our Galaxy, taking 225 million years to complete one circular orbit. Remarkably, the Quran mentions both of the orbits of the Sun and the Moon, travelling with their own Motion.

"The Sun must not catch up the Moon, nor does the night outstrip the day. Each one is travelling in an orbit with its own motion."

(Quran, Ya-Sin 36: 40)

The Quran revealed this piece of information over 1,400 years ago. It would be centuries later before modern technology discovered these facts of the Quran. For Muslims, this provides further support for the Quran's divine origin. The most widely held view during Prophet Muhammad's (ﷺ) time was that, the Earth must be flat and located at the centre of the Universe. It was further thought that the Sun travelled around the Earth once every day. So, why weren't these theories mentioned in the Quran if it indeed originated from man. These erroneous theories existed for many centuries but were finally abandoned after the publication of Nicolaus Copernicus' book 'On the Revolutions of the Heavenly Spheres' in 1543. There is also substantial evidence to support the notion that Copernicus relied heavily on the translated works of the 13th century astronomer Nasir al-Din al-Tusi and the 14th century astronomer Ibn Shatir. Before Copernicus, these two Muslim astronomers were the most influential astronomers in the world.

Background: Fiery sunset over distant mountains creates a breathtaking display. In Islamic tradition there are two phrases most loved by the Almighty Creator, which are light on the tongue, yet heavy on the scale of good deeds: 'Glory be to Allah' and 'All Praise is due to Him'

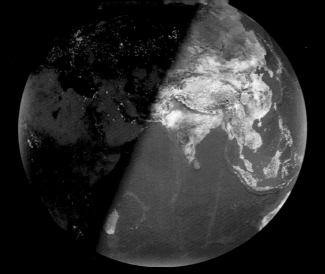

The Rotation of the Day and the Night

In the Quran, there are a number of verses that refer to the sequence of the night and day, yet no mention is made of the movement of the Sun around the Earth. When it is considered that the most widely held view at the time was that the Earth was the centre of the Universe and that the Sun moved around it, a human author of the Quran would not have failed to refer to the Sun's apparent movement around the Earth when discussing the sequence of the night and day.

"Have you not seen how Allah merges the night into the day and merges the day into the night..."

(Quran, Luqman 31: 29)

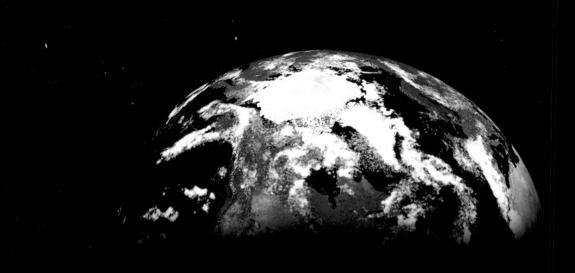

Background: The Earth from the Moon. The Earth's shape is that of an oblate spheroid, with an average diameter of approximately 12,742 km. The rotation of the Earth causes the equator to bulge out slightly so that the equatorial diameter is 43 km larger than the pole to pole diameter. The Moon is Earth's only natural satellite. It has no formal English name other than 'the Moon'.

Opposite page: View of the Earth with half of the hemisphere in darkness.

Biology in the Quran

From lush tropical rainforests to stark desert lands, lofty mountain tops to shimmering seashores, we find an enormous variety of animals and plants. The astounding diversity of life on Earth has enthralled and captivated mankind since the beginning of creation. This wondrous array is reflected in many verses of the Quran and for Muslims it confirms the Magnificence and Greatness of the Creator, Allah.

Plants, in particular, are the colourful garments of the earth and play a key role in protecting life on this planet. Trees, for example, cover a third of the Earth's surface and regulate the climate by absorbing carbon dioxide and releasing oxygen. In addition, plants provide nourishment, medicine, shelter, fuel and clothing to humans and animals alike. The presence of the photosynthetic pigment chlorophyll, gives plants their green appearance. In fact, the process of photosynthesis itself is further proof of a finely tuned biological system that shows all the characteristics of being created by intelligent design rather than having evolved through blind chance.

Opposite page: Images depicting some of the diverse forms of vegetation mentioned in the Quran.

Above right: The date palm, mentioned more than any other fruit-bearing plant in the Quran, is often associated with Islam and Muslims. Throughout the month of Ramadan, dates are a common ingredient in the Muslim diet. Grapes are also mentioned in a number of Quranic verses. Although production and consumption of wine is not allowed in Islam, the cultivation of grapes as a food source is perfectly legitimate.

Above left: Olives have been mentioned seven times in the Quran and their health benefits have been stated by the Prophet Muhammad (ﷺ). The olive, like the date, holds great value in ancient and modern culture. In the Mediterranean culture for instance, it has served as medicine and even money for several thousand years.

Below right: Figs provide an excellent source of nutrition and have been used for many centuries to aid digestive problems. The fig is highly symbolic in Islam as, there is a Quranic chapter named after it. Allah says; **"By the fig and the olive. And (by) Mount Sinai. And (by) this secure city (Makkah), We have certainly created man in the best of stature."** (Quran, The Fig 95: 1-4).

Below Left: The pomegranate is mentioned three times in the Quran and is considered in Islam to be a sample of one of the many wondrous fruits of paradise. The most fascinating aspects of the pomegranate is the structure inside the fruit. The shiny, leathery skin, once removed, reveals a myriad of red jewel-like juicy sacs with a fresh, sweet-sour pleasant taste.

"It is He (Allah) Who sends down rain from the skies: with it We produce vegetation of all kinds: from some We produce green (crops), out of which We produce grain, heaped up (at harvest); out of the date-palm and its sheaths (or spathes) (come) clusters of dates hanging low and near: and (then there are) gardens of grapes and olives and pomegranates, each similar (in kind) yet different (in variety): when they begin to bear fruit, feast your eyes with the fruit and the ripeness thereof. Behold! in these things there are signs for people who believe."

(Quran, Cattle 6: 99)

The Honey Bee

It was once believed that worker bees were male soldiers and answered to a King. In 1637 however, Richard Remnant discovered that worker bees were in fact females (Richard Remnant; *A Discourse of Historie of Bees*, London: Printed by R. Young for T. Slater, 1637).

Over one thousand years before this discovery, during the 7th century when the Quran was revealed to Prophet Muhammad (ﷺ), Allah had already mentioned this fact. In the verse on the next page, the Quran uses a female word, *al-Nahl*, when describing the bee (note: Arabic words can have male or female genders). We know that the Quran is referring to the worker bee because the bee is said to leave it's home to gather food.

The bee is also known to collect nectar from various kinds of flowers and form honey within its body, which it then stores in wax cells. The process of honey production was discovered only a few centuries ago. However, a clue to this mechanism was given in the Quran, which informs us that honey is made within the bee itself. Furthermore, we are now aware that honey has healing properties. This is also mentioned in the opposite verse, further highlighting the miraculous nature of the Quran.

"And your Lord inspired the bee (*al-Nahl*), "Take for yourself among the mountains, houses and among the trees and (in) that which they construct. Then eat from all the fruits and follow the ways of your Lord laid down (for you)." There emerges from their bellies a drink, varying in colours, in which there is healing for people. Indeed in that is a sign for a people who give thought."

(Quran, The Bee 16: 68-69)

Opposite page: Honeycomb consists of rigid hexagonal cells made largely from wax secretions from the worker bees body. They are used for rearing young and for storing pollen and honey. To make one gram of bees wax, a honey bee must consume over sixteen grams of honey and an unknown amount of pollen. Honey is made by worker bees who ingest nectar from flowers, convert it into honey in special 'sacs' in their gut and place it in the cells to mature.

Communication Between Ants

In the past, people would probably have mocked the idea that ants can communicate via sophisticated messages to each other. However, recent research has revealed that ants do in fact communicate. It is remarkable therefore, that in the verses shown opposite, the Quran reveals this very point. It is also known that ant colonies have complex divisions of labour, composed of managers, supervisors, foremen, workers and even soldiers.

Above: Ants communicate directly by touching various segments of their antennae together and indirectly by releasing chemicals (pheromones) onto the surfaces on which they walk. Their sense of smell is highly developed. The cells that detect smell are located in the antennae and the mouth.

Opposite page: Highly magnified image of an ant covered in pollen grains.

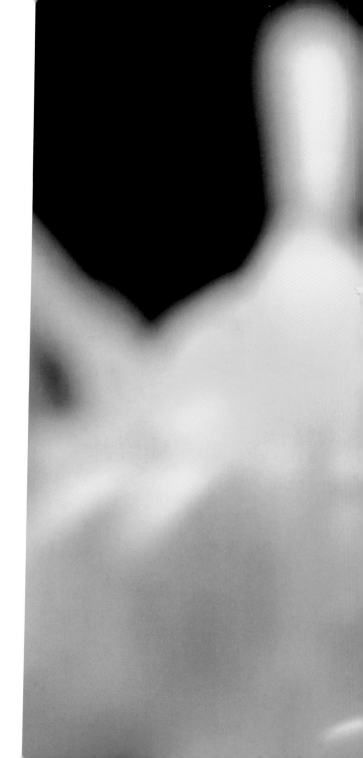

And there were gathered before Solomon his hosts of jinn and men and birds and they were set in battle order (marching forward). Till, when they came to the valley of the ants, one of the ants said: O ants! Enter your dwellings, in case Solomon and his hosts should crush you, while they perceive not."

(Quran, The Ant 27: 17-18)

The Source of Milk

The first Muslim scientist to accurately describe blood circulation was Ibn Nafees in the 13th century. Over three hundred years later William Harvey (1628) brought this understanding to the Western world. These discoveries helped to develop our understanding of digestion. We know today that food is digested in the stomach and intestine before being absorbed by blood vessels passing through the intestine.

However, the Quran using simple language gave us an indication of the mechanism of digestion. Before this scientific discovery was made, the Quran hints that between the excretions and the blood there is something which is used in milk production. This agrees perfectly with the fact that food is broken down in the digestive system and nutrients are released. Any waste material passes through the digestive system and is excreted. The nutrients are absorbed by intestinal blood vessels and transported to the mammary glands for milk production.

> "Verily, in cattle there is a lesson for you. We give you to drink of that which is in their bellies, from between excretions and blood, pure milk; palatable to the drinkers."
>
> (Quran, The Bee 16: 66)

Background picture: A splash crown formed by a drop of milk; high speed photography captures the moment of impact.

Presence of Sensory Nerves in the Skin

Modern scientific research has shown that there are more pain and heat sensitive nerve endings in the superficial layers than in the deeper tissues of the skin (*Textbook of Medical Physiology*, A.C. Guyton, 7th ed, W.B. Saunders Co., 1986, p. 593). It is also known that if the skin is burnt completely then these nerve endings can be destroyed. The Quran mentions that if the skin is burnt through then Allah will change them for "other skins", indicating that the sensitivity of the burnt skin is reduced. For Muslims, fearing Allah's punishment but hoping and praying for his mercy and forgiveness are essential components of belief.

Below: Cross section through the skin. The skin is often known as the largest organ in the human body. This applies to exterior surface, as it covers the body, appearing to have the largest surface area of all the organs. Moreover, it applies to weight, as it weighs more than any single internal organ, accounting for about 15 percent of body weight.

"Surely, those who disbelieved in Our signs, We (Allah) shall burn them in fire. As often as their skins are roasted through, We shall change them for other skins that they may taste the punishment. Truly, Allah is Ever Most Powerful, All-Wise."

(Quran, Women 4: 56)

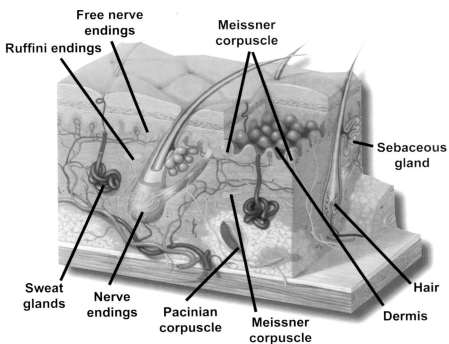

Free nerve endings

Ruffini endings

Meissner corpuscle

Sebaceous gland

Sweat glands

Nerve endings

Pacinian corpuscle

Meissner corpuscle

Hair

Dermis

Wind Pollination

Between 1760 and 1766, Joseph Koelreuter carried out various plant breeding experiments. During this period, he was the first Western scientist to discover the role played by wind in flower pollination. However, this process was already familiar to Muslims over one thousand years before these experiments were carried out, as in the Quran Allah had mentioned the winds as 'fertilising'.

"And We (Allah) have sent the winds fertilising..."

(Quran, The Rocky Tract 15:22)

Background: As well as dispersing pollen grains, wind is also involved in spreading seeds. The Dandelion flower, for example, matures into a globe of fine filaments that are usually distributed by wind, carrying away the seed.

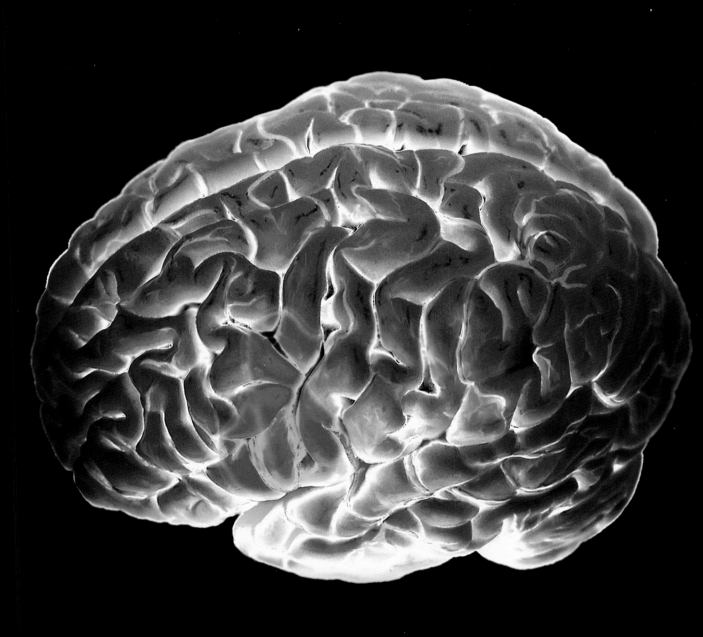

Fingertips

Fingerprints are specific to every individual and were first used in Argentina in the 1890's to solve crime. No two persons in the world have ever been known to have exactly the same fingerprint pattern. In the verse below, the Quran addresses those who say, "when we die and turn to dust, how can Allah resurrect us?" Allah informs us that not only can He bring together our bones, but He can even reconstruct specific features such as the fingertips. This verse is all the more remarkable when one considers the fact that the fingertip is the place which bears a mark that is unique to each individual.

> **"I swear by the Day of Resurrection. And I swear by the self-reproaching soul. Does man think that We shall not assemble his bones? Yes, We (Allah) are able to put together in perfect order the tips of his fingers"**
>
> (Quran, The Rising 75: 1-4)

Opposite page: A composite of a 3-D magnetic resonance imaging (MRI) scan (blue) of the brain, overlaid with positron emission tomography (PET) scan data (red/green) showing brain activity whilst thinking about words. The brain is seen from the side, with the front of the brain at left. The active region is in the left cerebral hemisphere, which is associated with language skills. In this test, words are being thought about before being spoken and the frontal cortex region is most active.

The human brain is a very highly developed organ and one of the many miracles of creation. However, evolutionists utterly fail to provide a detailed description of its origin. The brain is not only important as the site of reason and intelligence, it is the source of cognition, emotion, memory, motor and other forms of learning. It also controls and coordinates most sensory systems, movement, behaviour, heart rate, blood pressure, fluid balance and body temperature.

IMAGE CREDIT: SCIENCE PHOTO LIBRARY.

The Function of the Prefrontal Area of the Brain

> **"Let him beware! If he does not stop, We will take him by the *Naseyah* (front of the head), a lying, sinful *Naseyah* (front of the head)!"**
>
> (Quran, Read 96: 15-16)

The verse above informs us that Allah will take the disobedient person physically by the front of the head or forelock (*Naseyah* in Arabic) and subject him to a humiliating punishment. The front of the head is then described as lying and sinful. It is interesting that the frontal area of the brain, known as the prefrontal cortex, is involved in planning and initiating good and bad behaviour (see image opposite). It also plays a role in relation to moral conduct such as speaking truth or falsehood (*Essentials of Anatomy & Physiology*, R. Seeley, 2nd edition, Mosby-Year Book, Inc., 1996, p.211: *Textbook of Medical Physiology*, A.C. Guyton, 7th edition, W.B. Saunders Company, 1986, p. 656).

Scientists started to discover the functions of the frontal area of the brain in the 1930's but, the Creator had already given an indication of its function in the Quran. For Muslims this is further proof of the fact that no human being could have authored the Quran, as there were no scientific aids at the time of revelation to discover these facts.

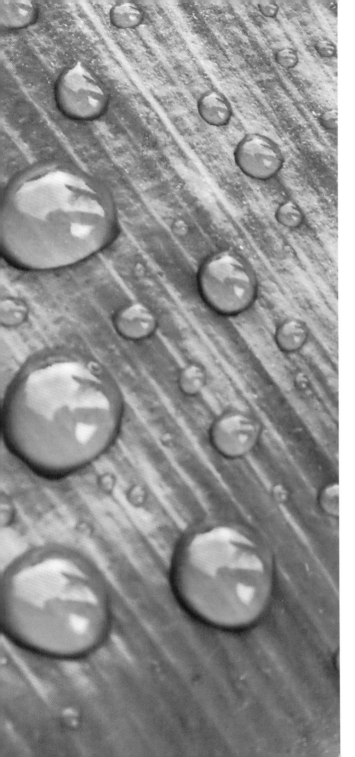

The Importance of Water

It is common knowledge that cells make up the biological structure of all living things. Through modern scientific discovery, we also know that a large percentage of the living cell is composed of water. It is remarkable to read the following verse from the Quran, that gave mankind a clue to the essential role of water.

"...And We (Allah) made from water every living thing. Will they then not believe?"

(Quran, The Prophets 21: 30)

Opposite: Forces of attraction between water molecules help to form drops of water on a leaf. From a biological standpoint, the Creator, Allah, has given water many distinct properties that are critical for the proliferation of life. Water carries out this role by allowing organic compounds to react in ways that ultimately allows replication. It is a good solvent and has a high surface tension and thus allows organic compounds and living things to be transported in it. Fresh water has its greatest density under normal atmospheric pressure at 4°C, becoming less dense as it freezes or heats up. As a stable molecule prevalent in the atmosphere, it plays an important role as a greenhouse gas absorbing infrared radiation without which, Earth's average surface temperature would be −18°C. Water also has an unusually high specific heat which, allows it to play many roles in regulating global and regional climate. Water absorbs strongly in the infrared portion of the light spectrum, a small amount of visible red light is absorbed as well, resulting in a slightly blue colour when seen in mass quantities such as a lake or ocean.

Egyptology in the Quran

Knowledge of Egyptian Hieroglyphics

Hieroglyphics is a system of writing which uses pictures to represent words and ideas. In the period of the 3rd ancient Egyptian dynasty (2650-2575 BCE), many of the principles of hieroglyphic writing were laid down. The writing remained the same for over 2000 years. The rise of Christianity in the 2nd and 3rd centuries led to the decline and eventual demise of hieroglyphics and of the ancient Egyptian religion. An adapted form of the Greek alphabet used by Egyptian Christians also contributed to the widespread decline of the native Egyptian script. The last known use of hieroglyphics can be found on an inscription written in the year 394 (*The Encyclopaedia Britannica*).

No one could read the ancient Egyptian form of writing until after the discovery of the Rosetta Stone in 1799, a text dating from 196 BCE. The Rosetta Stone provided the key to finally unlocking the mystery of Egyptian hieroglyphics. The stone was inscribed in three different scripts: hieroglyphic, demotic and Greek. All three texts are identical in content. However, the most significant advances in translation came from the section written in Greek. It was Jean-Françoise Champollion's interest in oriental languages, especially Coptic, which eventually led him to decipher the writing on the Rosetta stone in 1824. This had the effect of advancing the whole field of ancient Egyptology to a different level. Hence, our current understanding of ancient Egypt and the religious beliefs of the ancient Egyptians is based heavily on the translation work carried out on the Rosetta stone.

The Quran was revealed centuries before the discovery of the Rosetta stone during a time when knowledge of ancient Egyptian hieroglyphics had been totally forgotten. It is striking therefore, to find an amazing degree of historical accuracy when the Quran discusses matters relating to ancient Egypt. Most of the information found in the Quran centres around the story of Prophet Moses (ﷺ) and his meeting with Pharaoh.

Opposite page: With a base area of over 13 acres the 'Great Pyramid' of Giza is the largest in Egypt and one of the largest in the world. It is one of the Seven Wonders of the Ancient World and until the Eiffel Tower was built, it was the tallest structure in the world.

The pyramids were built of brick or stone and functioned as tombs for Pharaohs. The ancient Egyptians capped the peaks of their pyramids with gold and covered the façade with polished white limestone, though many of these stones have fallen or been removed for use in other structures over the millennia.

And Moses said: "O Pharaoh! Verily, I am a messenger from the Lord of the Worlds."

(Quran, The Heights 7:104)

King or Pharaoh?

The stories of the Prophets Joseph (☸) and Moses (☸) are told in the Quran and the Bible. However, there are many differences between the two narratives. One of these is the subtle use in the Quran of the words 'King' and 'Pharaoh' when describing the ruler of Egypt.

Recent research shows that the Kings of Egypt were not always called Pharaoh, which means 'great house' in ancient Egyptian. The title of Pharaoh was only applied to the king himself in the 18th Dynasty (1552 - 1295 BCE) during the new Kingdom (*The Encyclopaedia Britannica*).

Prophet Joseph (☸) is thought to have lived between the middle and second intermediate ancient Egyptian Kingdoms. During this time the Egyptian monarch would have been referred to as a King. The Quran appropriately refers to the ruler of Egypt at the time of the Prophet Joseph (☸) as a 'King'.

"And the king (of Egypt) said: "Verily, I saw (in a dream) seven fat cows, whom seven lean ones were devouring...."

(Quran, Joseph 12: 43)

Prophet Moses (☸) lived during the much later New Kingdom, when the ancient Egyptians had adopted the term Pharaoh when referring to their ruler. It is remarkable therefore, that during the time of Prophet Moses (☸) the Egyptian ruler is referred to as 'Pharaoh' by the Quran.

And Moses said: "O Pharaoh! Verily, I am a messenger from the Lord of the Worlds."

(Quran, The Heights 7:104)

It is also noteworthy that other religious scriptures make no distinction between the title 'King' and 'Pharaoh'. All of the Egyptian Kings are referred to as Pharaoh, regardless of the era. By referring to the sovereign of Egypt who was a contemporary of the Prophet Joseph (☸) as 'King' (in Arabic, *Malik*) and addressing the monarch who ruled during the time of the Prophet Moses (☸) as 'Pharaoh' (Arabic, *Fir'awn*), the Quran retains a remarkable degree of historical accuracy. Bearing in mind that hieroglyphic writing was only deciphered in the 19th century, the above distinction is all the more amazing when one considers that it was made over 1,400 years ago when the knowledge of ancient Egyptian hieroglyphics had been completely lost. This further highlights the amazing historical accuracy of the Quran and utterly refutes the claim that the Quran was copied from any other religious scripture.

Opposite page: The discovery of the Rosetta Stone in 1799 was to provide the key to unlocking the mystery of Egyptian hieroglyphics. The Stone is 114.4 centimetres high at its tallest point, 72.3 centimetres wide and 27.9 centimetres thick. Weighing approximately 760 kg, it was originally thought to be granite or basalt but is currently described as granodiorite. The Stone has been kept at the British Museum in London since 1802.

223

Pharaoh as a 'god'

Champollion's 1824 publication on hieroglyphics 'Precis du systeme hieroglyphique' gave birth to the entire field of modern Egyptology. Since then the world has learnt much regarding ancient Egyptian mythology. None has been more fascinating than the custom of mummification and the great pyramids with their treasures hidden deep within. Details of Egyptian religious beliefs are now fairly well studied. The ancient Egyptians believed that their Pharaoh was a living god, identifying him with their sky god *Horus* and with their sun gods, *Re*, *Amon* and *Aton*. Even after death the Pharaoh was thought to remain divine, becoming transformed into *Osiris*, the father of *Horus*. His sacred powers and position were said to pass to the new Pharaoh, his son. The Pharaoh's divine status was believed to endow him with magical powers. His *uraeus* (the snake on his crown) spat flames at his enemies, he was able to trample thousands of the enemy on the battlefield and he was said to be all-powerful, knowing everything and controlling nature and fertility. He owned a large portion of Egypt and directed its use and he was responsible for his people's economic and spiritual welfare. He also dispensed 'justice' to his subjects. His will was supreme and he governed by royal decree (The Encyclopaedia Britannica).

The story of Prophet Moses (☺) and his meeting with Pharaoh in the Quran, highlights many aspects of ancient Egyptian religion. During the 7th century at a time when knowledge of the ancient religion and history of Egypt had been lost, the Quran had already informed us that Pharaoh considered himself to be a god:

"Then he (Pharaoh) gathered (his people) and cried aloud, Saying, "I am your lord, most high!"

(Quran, Soul Snatchers 79:23-24)

The significance of this fact is that, details of ancient Egyptian mythology were simply not known in 7th century Arabia when the Quran was revealed. For Muslims this type of information further highlights the divine nature of the Quran.

Above: Ancient Egyptians regarded the Pharaoh as divine. The Pharaoh Rameses II is depicted here worshipping his own image. Knowledge of the ancient Egyptian religion only became known during the 19th century when the Rosetta stone was deciphered.

Above: Further examples of hieroglyphic inscriptions.

Right: The mask of the Pharaoh Tutankhamen. The golden mask from the inner tomb was amongst the most splendid of the many treasures discovered in 1923.

225

The Pharaoh at the time of Prophet Moses (ﷺ) regarded himself as a 'god'. He was obsessed with trying to see the 'God of Moses', so he instructed his subjects to build him a high tower. The illustration shows an ancient Egyptian structure dwarfed by the power and glory of the Universe.

The Baking of Bricks in Ancient Egypt

Continuing with the story of Pharaoh in the Quran, we are told in the verse below that Pharaoh arrogantly asks his associate Haman to build a lofty tower, so he can see the "God of Moses". This poses an interesting new question. Were mud bricks ever burnt (or baked) in Egypt at this time? It is a well known fact, borne out by archaeological research that, mud bricks and baked bricks were made in ancient Egypt. According to A.J. Spencer's, *Brick Architecture in Ancient Egypt*, the ancient Egyptians were aware that mud-bricks could be hardened by burning. However, the use of burnt brick did not become common until the Roman period. The earliest examples of Egyptians deliberately preparing burnt brick date from the Middle Kingdom. No other instances of burnt bricks are recorded until the time of the New Kingdom. The New Kingdom period of Egyptian history is associated with Prophet Moses (ﷺ). It is also believed that the art of brick making was imported into Egypt from Mesopotamia to produce some magnificent monuments. A.J Spencer writes "From the foregoing, it must be concluded that burnt brick was known in Egypt at all periods, but used only when its durability would give particular advantage over the mud brick" (A. J. Spencer, *Brick Architecture In Ancient Egypt*, 1979, Aris & Phillips Ltd., UK).

In the verse shown opposite the Quran also clearly mentions that the Egyptians at the time of Prophet Moses (ﷺ) were using baked bricks for building. The interesting point to note here again is that Prophet Muhammad (ﷺ) was not a scholar of Egyptology or any other scientific subject for that matter. Furthermore, he could not have known such accurate and detailed knowledge of ancient Egyptian history that has only come to light in modern times.

Pharaoh's Desire to Ascend to the Sky

As noted earlier recent findings about the mythology of ancient Egypt have shown that Egyptians considered the Pharaohs to be divine beings. It has also been discovered that the Pharaohs believed that they could communicate with the gods if they climbed high towers or palaces (see *Egyptian Magic*: 1985, Aris & Phillips Ltd. (UK) & Bolchazy-Carducci Publishers, Chicago, p. 11).

Centuries before hieroglyphs were deciphered and knowledge of the ancient Egyptian religion came to light. The Quran informed us that Pharaoh, ordered his close associate Haman to build a tower so that he could reach the "God of Moses" and see Him face-to-face. Amazingly the Quran accurately describes another feature of ancient Egyptian religion which would have been unknown at the time of the Quran's revelation.

Pharaoh said: "O chiefs! I know not that you have a god other than me. So kindle for me (a fire), O Haman, to bake (bricks out of) clay and set up for me a lofty tower (or palace) in order that I may look at the God of Moses; and verily, I think that he (Moses) is one of the liars."

(Quran, The Story 28:38)

227

The Mystery of Haman

In the Quranic verse shown previously, it becomes apparent that the person named 'Haman' was someone close to Pharaoh and he was also in charge of building projects. Haman is mentioned six times in the Quran. The question arises, who is Haman? Concerning the question of Haman, the famous French scientist and author, Dr. Maurice Bucaille believed that the only valid investigation was to ask an ancient Egyptian expert for his opinion about the presence in the Quran of this name (Maurice Bucaille, *Moses and Pharaoh: The Hebrews in Egypt*: 1995, NTT Mediascope Inc., Tokyo, pp. 192-193). In his book *Réflexions sur le Coran* (1989, Seghers, Paris), Dr. Maurice Bucaille then narrates an interesting discussion he had with a prominent French Egyptologist:

"I have related the result of such a consultation that dates back to a dozen years ago and led me to question a specialist who, in addition, knew well the classical Arabic language. One of the most prominent French Egyptologists, fulfilling these conditions, was kind enough to answer the question. I showed him the word "Haman" that I had copied exactly like it is written in the Quran and told him that it had been extracted from a sentence of a document dating back to the 7th century, the sentence being related to somebody connected with Egyptian history. He said to me that, in such a case, he would see in this word the transliteration of a hieroglyphic name but, for him, undoubtedly it could not be possible that a written document of the 7th century had contained a hieroglyphic name - unknown until that time - since, in that time, the hieroglyphs had been totally forgotten. In order to confirm his deduction about the name, he advised me to consult the Dictionary of Personal Names of

the New Kingdom by Ranke (Hermann Ranke, Die Ägyptischen Personennamen, Verzeichnis der Namen, Verlag Von J. J. Augustin in Glückstadt, Band I; 1935), where I might find the name written in hieroglyphs, as he had written before me and the transliteration in German.

I discovered all that had been presumed by the expert and, moreover, I was stupefied to read the profession of Haman: "The Chief of the workers in the stone-quarries," exactly what could be deduced from the Quran, though the words of the Pharaoh suggest a master of construction."

Had the Bible or any other literary work, composed during a period when hieroglyphs could still be understood, made reference to 'Haman' and his profession, then the presence of this word in the Quran might not have drawn special attention. The reality is that hieroglyphs had been *totally* forgotten at the time of the Quranic revelation and no one could read them until the 19th century. Thus, the existence of the word 'Haman' in the Quran suggests a special reflection. There is clearly no evidence for the allegations that Prophet Muhammad (ﷺ) copied the Bible. Such false allegations continue to persist and are widely circulated in the media.

Opposite page: Hieroglyph entry for 'Haman' and his profession "Vorsteherder Steinbruch arbeiter" in German, meaning "the chief or overseer of the workers in the stone-quarries" and dates from the New Kingdom Period (W. Wreszinski, *Aegyptische Inschriften* aus dem K.K. Hof Museum in Wien, 1906, J. C. Hinrichs' sche Buchhandlung: Leipzig, I 34, p. 130).

.34. Pfeiler einer Grabthür. № 91. (publ. Reinisch Miramare tab. 39.)

Zeit: NR.

Name und Titel:

Anmerkung: Vorsteher der Steinbrucharbeiter; vgl.

Sethe Urk. I 92, I 113 a. R.

And Pharaoh said: "O Haman! Build me a tower that I may arrive at the ways..."

(Quran, The Forgiver 40: 36)

229

The Drowning of Pharaoh

In the Quranic narration, Prophet Moses (علیه السلام) sets out to leave Egypt with the Children of Israel. However, Pharaoh could not accept their departure without his permission. So the Pharaoh followed them with his army but, they were overwhelmed when they attempted to cross the parted sea. The Quran describes the incident as follows;

"We took the Children of Israel across the sea: Pharaoh and his hosts followed them in insolence and spite. At length, when overwhelmed with the flood, he said: "I believe that there is no god except Him Whom the Children of Israel believe in: I am of those who submit (to Allah in Islam)."

(Quran, Jonah 10: 90)

The verse above reveals how, at the moment of his imminent death Pharaoh finally repents and accepts the Lord of Moses. However, his repentance is in vain, as he is consumed by the sea. Furthermore, the Quranic verse opposite shows how, after he was drowned, Allah caused the lifeless body of Pharaoh to be thrown out onto the shore. The Children of Israel were able to identify him and satisfy themselves that their tormentor was really dead (see the Quranic commentaries by *Ibn Kathîr* and *at-Tabarî*).

The name of the Pharaoh who ruled at the time of Prophet Moses (علیه السلام) is never given in the Quran. Ramesses II and Merneptah are amongst some of the 19th Dynasty Pharaohs that have been suggested over the years. However, the evidence remains inconclusive. It is more than likely that the mummified remains of the Pharaoh lie in the Museum of Egyptian Antiquities in Cairo. Perhaps as the Quran had revealed over 1,400 years ago, as a sign and a warning to successive generations.

"Now (you believe) while you refused to believe before and you were one of the evildoers and corrupters. So this day We (Allah) shall deliver your (dead) body (out from the sea) that you may be a sign to those who come after you! And verily, many among mankind are heedless of Our Signs!"

(Quran, Jonah 10: 91-92)

Opposite page: The mummified remains of the Pharaoh Merneptah displayed in the Museum of Egyptian Antiquities in Cairo. He was discovered in 1898 within the tomb of Amenhotep II (KV35) by Professor Victor Loret. Amenhotep II's mummy was still located in his royal sarcophagus but the tomb also proved to hold a cache of several of the most important New Kingdom Pharaohs such as Thutmose IV, Amenhotep III and Ramesses III.

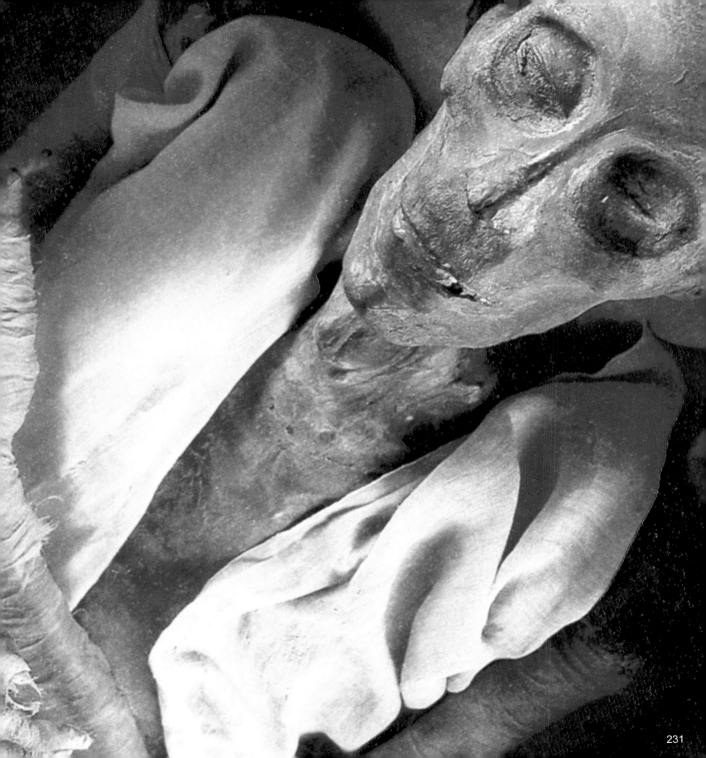

The Quran and Embryology

In the name of Allah, Most Compassionate, Most Merciful.

"We (Allah) then placed him as a drop in a place of settlement firmly fixed.

Then We made the drop into a leech-like structure;

And then We changed the leech-like structure into a chewed-like substance;

Then We made out of that chewed-like substance bones;

Then We clothed the bones with flesh;

Then We developed out of him another creation.

So blessed be Allah the Best to create!

After that, at length you will die.

Again on the Day of Judgement, will you be raised up."

(Quran, The Believers 23: 13-16)

Background: Image of an 8 week old human embryo with the main verses of the Quran that outline human embryonic development.

Introduction

Of all the verses in the Quran that highlight natural phenomena, perhaps the most fascinating are those that deal with the subject of human embryology. Ancient human writings, most notably those of the ancient Greek philosophers, Hippocrates, Aristotle and Galen, contain many inaccurate statements on embryology. Similarly, in the Middle Ages and even in more recent times, reproduction has been surrounded by myths and superstition. This is hardly surprising, as embryo development is a complicated process. Basic sciences such as physiology and embryology were not developed until mankind possessed knowledge of anatomy and invented the microscope . The invention of the microscope in the 17th century by Leeuwenhoek, made it possible to observe sperm for the first time. However, even with this newly invented instrument, inaccurate conclusions were made. Sperm were thought to contain miniature human beings that grew in the womb. Human embryo development was not described accurately until the 20th century. Streeter in 1941 developed the first system of staging embryo development. This has now been replaced by a more accurate system proposed by O'Rahilly (1972).

What will surprise people is that many centuries before the invention of the microscope and other modern instruments, the Quran revealed accurate statements regarding embryology, that modern scientific research has only discovered in the last few decades. Even more remarkably, we find that the Quran contains none of the inaccurate theories held by the ancients, that were popular at the time of revelation. Many different aspects of embryology are discussed in the Quran, using simple yet comprehensive language, that is accessible to everyone regardless of era.

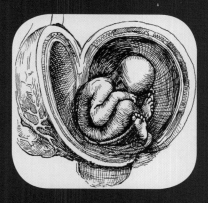

Drawing of foetus in the uterus by Leonardo da Vinci, *circa* 1510.

Photograph and drawing of a microscope made by Leeuwenhoek.

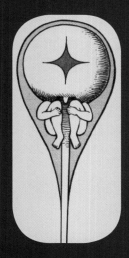

A drawing by Hartsoeker (from "essay de Dioptrique", 1694, Paris) illustrating the preformation doctrine. The sperm containing a miniature human being was thought to enlarge and grow in the womb.

As described in the previous verse (page 232), embryo development in the Quran is divided into three main stages as outlined below. The shaping stage is further divided into four distinct sub-stages.

1. Drop Stage

2. Shaping Stages
i) leech-like structure
ii) chewed-like substance
iii) bone formation
iv) clothing with flesh

3. Growth Stage

1. Drop Stage - *Nutfah*

Human development begins at fertilisation when a male sperm combines with a female egg (ovum) to form a cell called the 'zygote', which has the form of a drop of fluid. The Quran describes in simple language that the basis of creation is a *Nutfah* (drop).

In the verse opposite the Quranic term *Amshaj* means a 'mixture' and the whole verse refers to a mixture of male and female germinal fluid. Hence, the Quran refuted all of the earlier theories about the beginnings of human development because these did not take into account the dual nature of fertilisation.

Opposite page, above right: A scanning electron micrograph of a female ovum ready for fertilisation (x700 magnification).

Above Left: A scanning electron micrograph of a single sperm on the surface of the ovum (x7200 magnification).

Below Left: A scanning electron micrograph of sperm clustered on the surface of a human ovum during fertilisation (x2000 magnification).

"Verily, We created man from a mixture of germinal drop (Nutfah Amshaj)..."

(Quran, Time 76: 2)

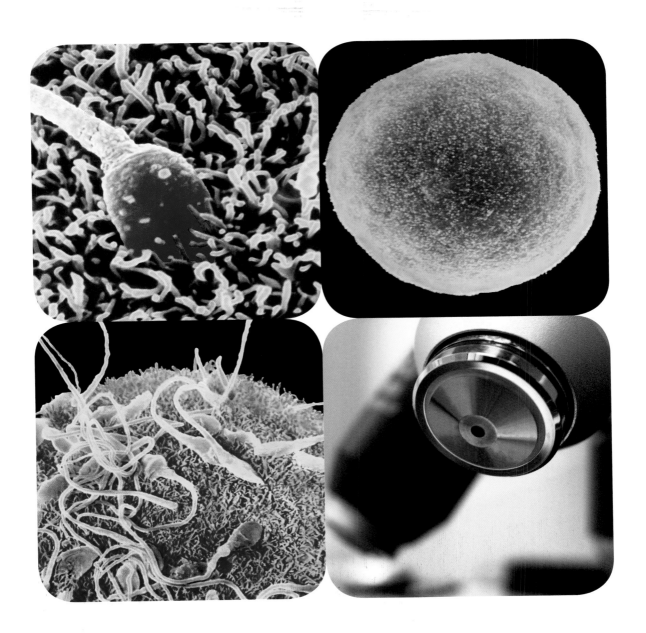

235

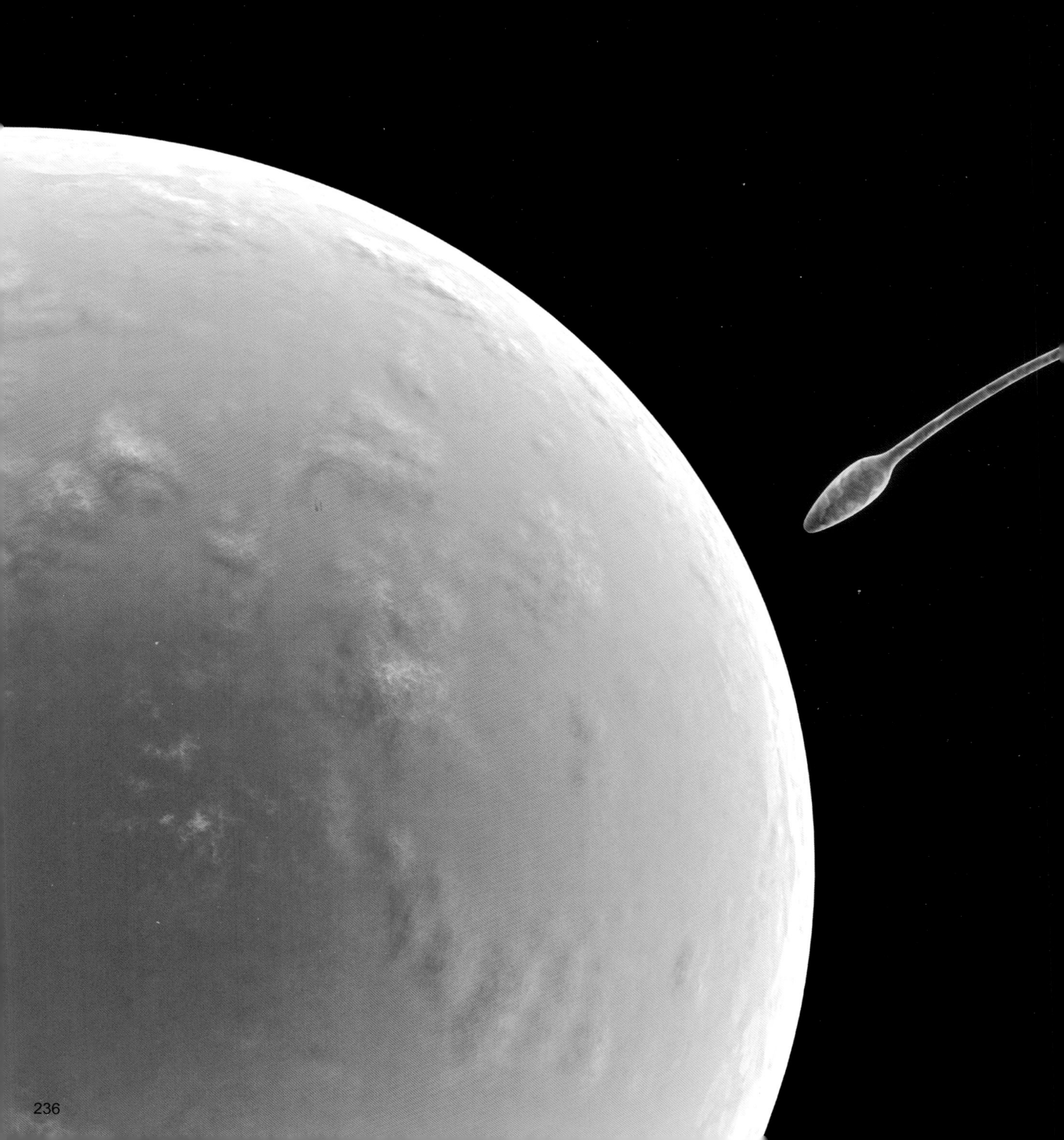

"He created him from (a part of) Nutfah (drop)..."

(Quran, He Frowned 80: 19)

Development from Only Part of the Drop

The Quranic verse shown opposite suggests that only a part of the drop (*Nutfah*) is involved in embryo formation. Remarkably, we know today that the embryo develops from only the inner cell mass, the rest becomes nutritive and protective in function.

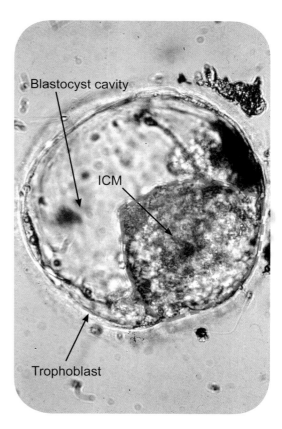

Blastocyst cavity

ICM

Trophoblast

Above: Photomicrograph of a section of a human embryo four and a half days after fertilisation (x600). As described in the Quran, the embryo has the form of a drop of liquid (*Nutfah*) and develops from only the inner cell mass (ICM) part of the *Nutfah*.

Opposite: In a race against time, human sperm swim frantically towards the ovum.

2. Shaping Stage

After the drop stage, the Quran in chapter 23 (The Believers), verse 14, mentions a number of distinct shaping stages. This period begins from the 3rd week until the end of the 8th week of embryo growth and is characterised by rapid cell growth over four distinct sub-stages. It is notable that the terms used to describe the sub-stages are also the main characteristics of the embryo at that precise moment in its development.

i) *Alaqah* (Leech-like structure)

The first sub-stage is termed *Alaqah* and it can either mean a) to attach, cling or hang on to something (opposite image) or b) a leech-like structure. After twenty days, the embryo loses its drop-like shape as it becomes elongated and segmented rather like a leech (Figure 1). Both of these meanings describe the appearance of the embryo and its relationship with the womb with stunning precision. The embryo resembles a leech-like organism surrounded by fluid, that is attached to a host and feeds on its blood. The shaping stages follow in quick sequence with relatively little delay between them. However, the fairly slow change from the drop-like *Nutfah* to the leech-like *Alaqah* is described by the use of the Arabic term *thumma* (thereafter), which indicates a time lag. The subtle indications of time frame throughout the Quranic descriptions of embryology point to an author who has a very detailed and in depth knowledge of the subject at hand.

"Then (thumma) We made the drop into a leech-like structure (Alaqah)"

(Quran, The Believers 23: 14)

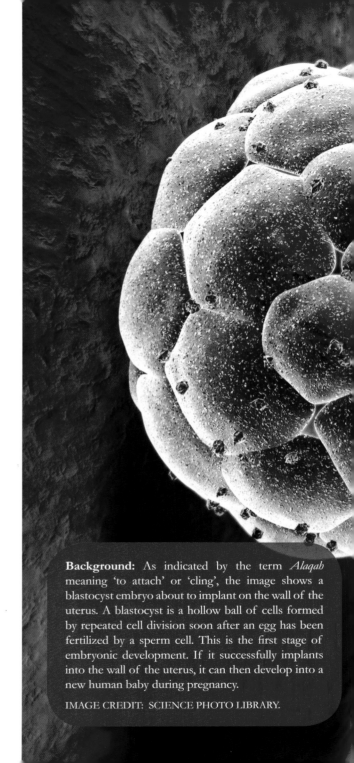

Background: As indicated by the term *Alaqah* meaning 'to attach' or 'cling', the image shows a blastocyst embryo about to implant on the wall of the uterus. A blastocyst is a hollow ball of cells formed by repeated cell division soon after an egg has been fertilized by a sperm cell. This is the first stage of embryonic development. If it successfully implants into the wall of the uterus, it can then develop into a new human baby during pregnancy.

IMAGE CREDIT: SCIENCE PHOTO LIBRARY.

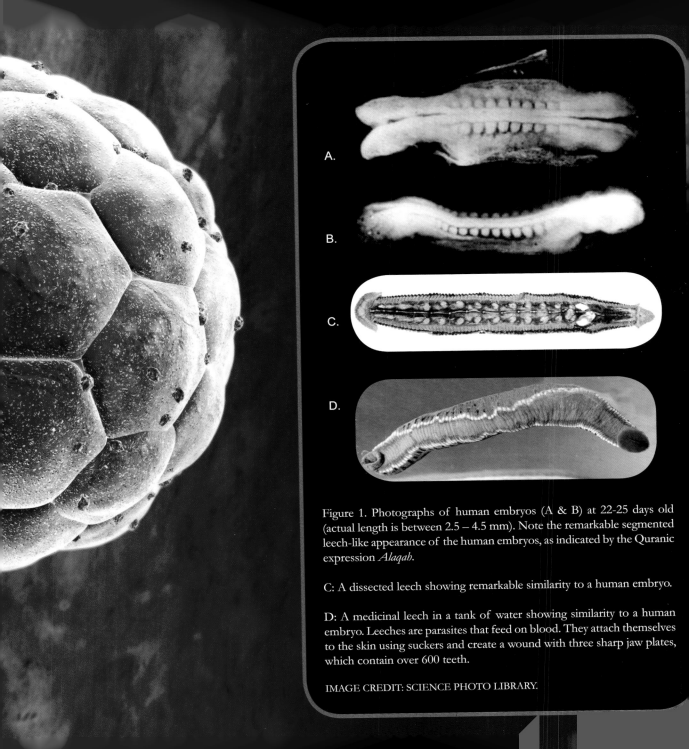

Figure 1. Photographs of human embryos (A & B) at 22-25 days old (actual length is between 2.5 – 4.5 mm). Note the remarkable segmented leech-like appearance of the human embryos, as indicated by the Quranic expression *Alaqah*.

C: A dissected leech showing remarkable similarity to a human embryo.

D: A medicinal leech in a tank of water showing similarity to a human embryo. Leeches are parasites that feed on blood. They attach themselves to the skin using suckers and create a wound with three sharp jaw plates, which contain over 600 teeth.

IMAGE CREDIT: SCIENCE PHOTO LIBRARY.

1) Mudghah (Chewed-like Substance)

Around 26-27 days old, the embryo starts to curve and the leech-like structure described by the word *Alaqah*, rapidly changes into what the Quran describes as a *Mudghah*. The change from *Alaqah* to *Mudghah* is described using the term *fa* (then) which in Arabic indicates a quick sequence of events. The Arabic word *Mudghah* means "chewed-like substance or a chewed lump". The Quranic term is surprisingly accurate as we find that towards the end of the fourth week the human embryo starts to resemble a chewed lump of flesh. The chewed-like appearance results from the irregular surface of the embryo and the development of a set of somites which resemble teeth marks (see image on the opposite page).

Verse fourteen also uses the verb *Khalaqa* (meaning creation, formation & initiation) to indicate an active process of development. In fact throughout the embryo there is active differentiation in almost every system during this time period.

> "...Then (fa) We (Allah) changed (Khalaqa) the leech-like structure into a chewed-like substance (Mudghah)..."

(Quran, The Believers 23: 14)

In a further demonstration of an in depth knowledge of human development, the Quran accurately describes the embryos internal state at the *Mudghah* stage as being part formed and part unformed in chapter 22 (The Pilgrimage).

> "...Then out of a chewed-like substance partly formed and partly unformed..."

(Quran, The Pilgrimage 22: 5)

Again this is a very revealing Quranic verse as it underlines the fact that by 28 days old although the precursors of all embryonic organ systems have formed, they are still undergoing an active process of creation, so are not yet in a fully functional state (ie. *"partly formed and partly unformed"*). When reading the remarkably simple yet comprehensive descriptions of embryonic development presented in the Quran it is important to highlight the fact that there were no microscopes or lenses available in the 7th century when the Quran was revealed. So people could not have known that the embryo resembles a leech and then develops into a chewed-like structure.

Opposite page: A photograph of a 36 day old embryo (actual size is 6.0 mm). Note the embryo's irregular chewed like and C-shaped appearance during the *Mudghah* stage of development. The uneven surface and somites give the embryo the appearance of a chewed substance. The partly developed limb buds and heart bulge can also be seen in this image.

IMAGE CREDIT: SCIENCE PHOTO LIBRARY

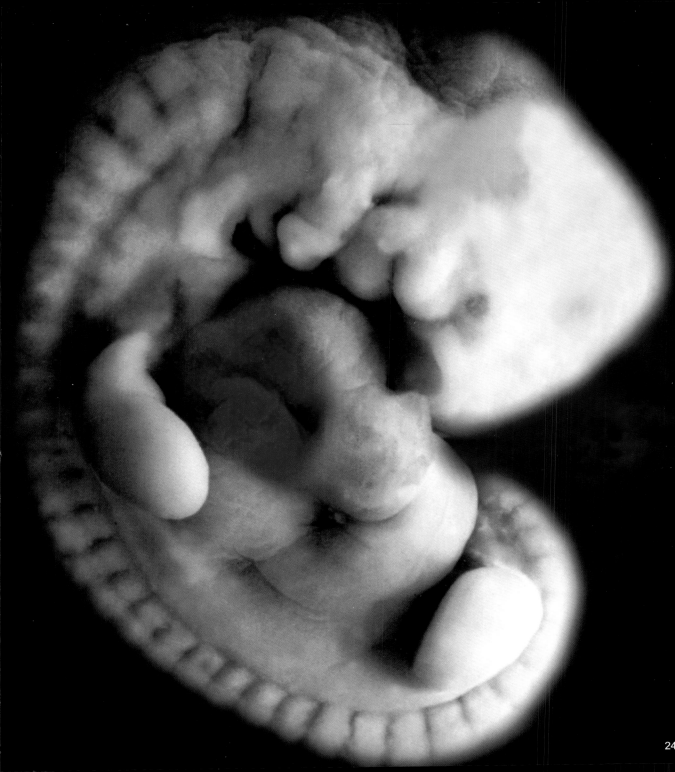

24

iii) *Ižam* (Bone Formation)

Chapter 23 (The Believers, verse 14) continues by mentioning *Ižam* or bone formation, as the third shaping sub-stage. The Quran indicates that out of the chewed-like substance (Figure 2, *Mudghah*) bones are formed. Again the use of the term *fa* indicates a rapid sequence of events. Remarkably this is exactly how the embryo develops in reality. During the 6th week of embryo development skeletal precursors start to rapidly condense and transform into soft skeleton (cartilage). The rapid formation of the skeleton during the 6th and 7th weeks is marked by a very noticeable change in the embryo. The very irregular and curved appearance of the embryo gives way to a more smoother, rounded and straighter shape as the skeleton spreads and develops (Figure 3).

Embryo Straightening

Bearing in mind the complete lack of technology of any type with which to study matters related to embryology, in another verse the Quran uses the term *Sawwak* (meaning to straighten and smooth) when describing the appearance of the embryo after the leech-like and chewed-like stages. The use of this term corresponds with the stage of *Ižam* (bone formation) and accurately describes the embryo as it starts to straighten and the surface becomes more even and smooth.

> "Then he became leech-like and did Allah make him (the Mudghah). And then fashioned him (Sawwak - straightened and smoothed)."
>
> (Quran, Resurrection 75: 38)

> "...Then (fa) We (Allah) made out of that chewed-like substance bones (Ižam)..."
>
> (Quran, The Believers 23: 14)

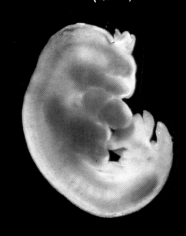

Figure 2 (above). At 5 weeks old the embryo is still in the Mudghah stage. It has an irregular and ragged curved C-shaped appearance.

Figure 3 (opposite page). The human embryo at about 7 weeks, measuring about 3cm. As the skeleton forms and muscles are laid upon the developing bones, the embryo begins to straighten and the surface starts to become more rounded and even. The relatively large and rounded head assumes a more erect position upon the vertebral column. Most of the primitive organ systems & external appendages are formed: the arms & legs have budded; the retina of the eye may be seen. The large dark mass in the body cavity is the enlarged liver, which manufactures red blood cells until the bone marrow (as yet undeveloped) takes over. The brain is undergoing radical divisions.

IMAGE CREDIT: SCIENCE PHOTO LIBRARY.

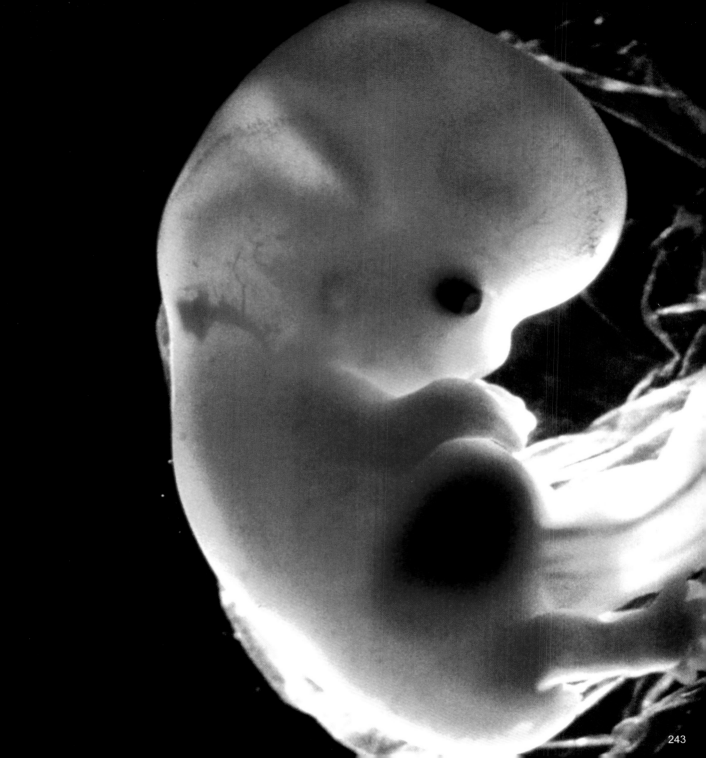

243

iv) *Lahm* (Clothing with Flesh)

The description given in chapter 23 of the Quran continues with the statement that the bones are 'clothed with flesh' as indicated by use of the expression *Lahm*. The *Lahm* stage follows immediately after the *Ižam* (bone formation) stage from the end of the 7th week to the end of the 8th week and represents the last phase of the shaping stage of embryonic development. Remarkably, the Quranic description is simple yet very accurate as, this is exactly how the embryo develops. As the muscles start to form around the bones, this marks the beginning of a new distinct stage as the embryo starts to look human. It is difficult to distinguish between human and animal embryos before the *Lahm* stage.

In the Quranic verse shown on the opposite page, the Arabic word *Addalak* means to straighten, become well proportioned and to modify in form and shape so that a thing becomes definite. As we have seen, the embryo straightens further and various parts such as head and limbs become more proportioned as muscles continue to take form (Figure 4).

The Quran's use of the words, *Alaqah*, *Mudghah*, *Ižam* and *Lahm* combined with the use of the term *fa* in between the four shaping sub-stages, all help to explain that an active process of development is taking place as, the embryo rapidly changes shape from one sub-stage to the next. In addition, the use of verbs *Sawwak* and *Addalak* (see verse opposite) is particularly striking and reveals that the author has detailed knowledge of the whole process. It is further explained in a way that can be easily understood by all people regardless of the era in which they live and the technology available to them.

"...Then (fa) We (Allah) clothed the bones with flesh (Lahm)..."

(Quran, The Believers 23: 14)

Above: The face of the human foetus at about 8 weeks old, at which time the infant roughly resembles the ultimate adult human being. The retina of the eye is visible as a large dark spot, and the features of the nose & mouth are beginning to appear. The hand can also be seen at top right. The cell divisions so rapid in the first 2 months are beginning to slow down: a further doubling in size will take several weeks.

IMAGE CREDIT: SCIENCE PHOTO LIBRARY.

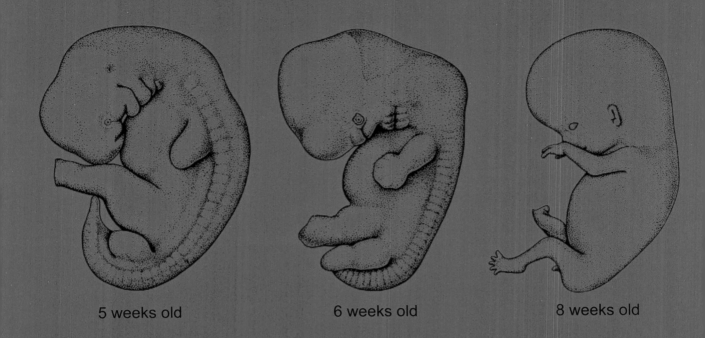

5 weeks old   6 weeks old   8 weeks old

"Who (Allah) created you (the Mudghah), Made you even and straight (Sawwak) and then modified (Addalak) you. In whatever form He wanted He put you together"

(Quran, The Cleaving 82: 7-8)

Figure 4. The above series of diagrams shows how the embryo has to straighten further in order to obtain a human looking shape. The process of straightening and smoothing, described by the words *Sawwak* and *Addalak* continues throughout this period. After 8 weeks, various parts such as the head and limbs have started to become more proportioned as muscles continue to develop.

245

3) Nash`ah - The Growth Stage

Following on from the shaping stage, the Quran mentions the development of 'another creation' described by the verb *Ansha'a* (a derivative of *Nash'ah*). This refers to the foetal period of development. The most obvious difference between the foetal and embryonic periods is that the foetus has acquired definite signs of human appearance.

The growth stage begins in the 9th week of foetal development. It is characterised by a phase of rapid growth and remarkable change. The verb *Ansha'a* has several meanings all of which can be applied to this period.

1. 'To initiate' - This describes the initial functioning of the various organs and systems, such as the kidney.

2. 'To grow and develop' - The embryo undergoes rapid growth and comprehensive development during this period.

3. 'To rise and increase' - This describes the very rapid increase in the foetal size and weight which begins during the 12th week.

The term *thumma* (meaning after some time rather than quickly) between the last shaping sub-stage (*Lahm*) and the growth stage, indicates slow progress following the rapid developments of the previous stages. Thus, 'another creation' is described as a slow process. This presumably covers the whole of the foetal stage.

End Note: Explanation and meaning of the Arabic terms that the Quran uses when describing embryo development can be found in the following dictionaries: *E W Lanes Arabic-English Lexicon; Hans-Weir, Arabic-English dictionary; Mujam Maqayees Al-Lughah; Lisan Al-Arab; Taj Al-Aroos Min Jawahir Al-Qamoos; Al-Moradat Fi Ghareeb Al-Quran.*

"...Then (thumma) We (Allah) developed (Ansha´ nahu) out of him another creation..."

(Quran, The Believers 23: 14)

In conclusion, over 1,400 years ago the Quran expressed in simple layman's terms, statements about embryology which science has only recently discovered in modern times. It becomes quite obvious, after reading the verses in the Quran that science cannot disagree or find any error in them. Also, it should be noted that the Quran contains none of the inaccurate theories and myths of the ancients, concerning human development, which were popular at the time of revelation. On the contrary the Quran signalled the end of all other ideas about embryology.

In view of the limited state of knowledge and lack of technology during Prophet Muhammad's (ﷺ) time, it is inconceivable that the statements in the Quran which are connected with embryology could have been the work of a man. Hence, the Quranic descriptions are clear indications that the Almighty Creator, Allah, revealed this knowledge to the last Prophet, Muhammad (ﷺ).

Opposite: Striking image of a fully grown foetus in the safety of the mother's womb. Despite being surrounded by fluid, cramped and in complete darkness, the human embryo develops vision, body structure and lungs for survival in a completely different environment. Human embryonic growth represents another one of the miracles of creation that defies evolution.

IMAGE CREDIT: SCIENCE PHOTO LIBRARY.

Geology in the Quran

Geology is the science and study of the Earth, its composition, structure, physical properties, history and the processes that shape it. When matters related to the physical Earth are mentioned, the Quran once more uses simple and comprehensive language to enlighten the reader and point the way for further investigation. This unique method is intended to lead a person to discover the mysteries of nature and then acknowledge the Creator.

The Structure of Mountains

The Quran accurately describes the structure of mountains in a very unique way as follows;

"Have We (Allah) not made the earth as a bed and the mountains as pegs?"

(Quran, The Tidings 78: 6-7)

We know today that the roots of a mountain can reach several times their elevation below the surface of the ground (Figures 5 & 6). So the Quranic term 'peg' is a very suitable word to describe mountains on the basis of this information since, most of a properly set peg is hidden under the surface of the ground.

The Role of Mountains

Earth scientists have also discovered that the rock which makes up the roots has a lower density than the rest of the mountain. Therefore, the roots act as foundations providing buoyancy and support for the mountain as well as stabilising the Earth's crust and reducing the shaking of the Earth (*The Geological concept of Mountains in the Quran*, El-Naggar, Z.R., 1991, 1st ed. Herndon: International Institute of Islamic Thought: p.5).

"And He has set firm mountains in the earth so that it would not shake with you"

(Quran, The Bee 16: 15)

Right: A magnificent snow covered peak rises into the clouds, testifying to the power and glory of the Creator, Allah.

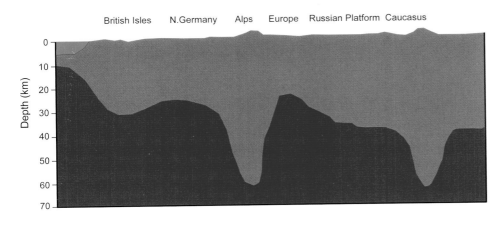

British Isles   N.Germany   Alps   Europe   Russian Platform   Caucasus

Figure 5. Schematic cross section showing the peg-like shape of continental land masses extending deep underground (*Anatomy of the Earth*, Cailleux, A., 1968, London: World University Library: p. 220).

Figure 6. Diagram showing that huge mountain-like continents can have deep roots under the surface of the ground (*Earth*, Press, F. and Siever, R., 1982 3rd ed., San Francisco: W.H Freeman & Company: p.413). The compressional forces in continental collisions may cause the compressed region to thicken, so the upper surface is forced upwards. In order to balance the weight, much of the compressed rock is forced downwards, producing deep 'mountain roots'. Mountains therefore, form downwards as well as upwards. However, in some continental collisions, part of one continent may simply override part of the other.

249

Iron

Iron is the most abundant heavy metal in the universe. It is found in many types of stars, on the Earth and in meteorites in considerable quantities. Iron is also a vital constituent of plant and animal life, being an essential component of the red blood cell molecule, haemoglobin.

The iron found on the Earth and in our Solar System was formed by a process of nuclear fusion in massive stars found in deep space (Figure 7). By comparison, the Sun is a relatively small and cool star with a core temperature of 15 million degrees. Stars with the mass of our Sun can only synthesize helium, carbon and oxygen (Figure 8). They lack the energy needed to produce iron and other heavy metals. Elements heavier than iron are made in supernova explosions from the combination of abundant neutrons with heavy nuclei. Hence, our Sun is unable to produce heavy elements such as iron because it lacks the tremendous amount of energy required to produce a single atom of iron. Hence, all of the iron present in the Solar system was formed in deep space.

Fourteen centuries before modern science discovered the stellar origin of iron, the Quran, using simple terminology specifically referred to iron as having been 'brought forth' by Allah. Iron is also said to have 'mighty power' and to be of great benefit to mankind.

"And We brought forth iron wherein is mighty power, as well as many benefits for mankind, that Allah may test who it is that will help Him (His religion) and His Messengers in the unseen. Verily, Allah is Powerful, Almighty."

(Quran, Iron 57: 25)

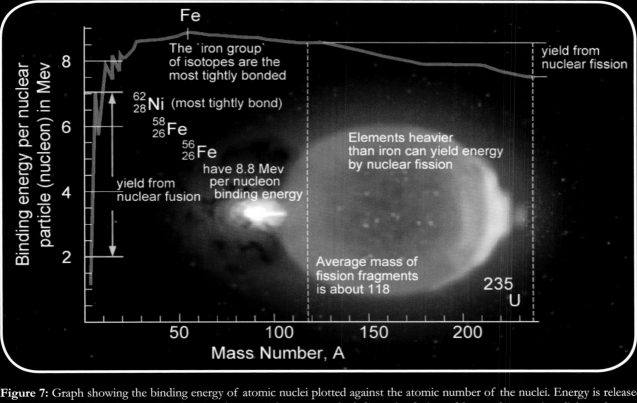

Figure 7: Graph showing the binding energy of atomic nuclei plotted against the atomic number of the nuclei. Energy is released by the fusion of light elements into heavier elements (elements on the left) or the fission of heavy elements into lighter elements (elements on the right). Iron is the highest element on the graph and the most stable. It cannot release energy through either fusion or fission.

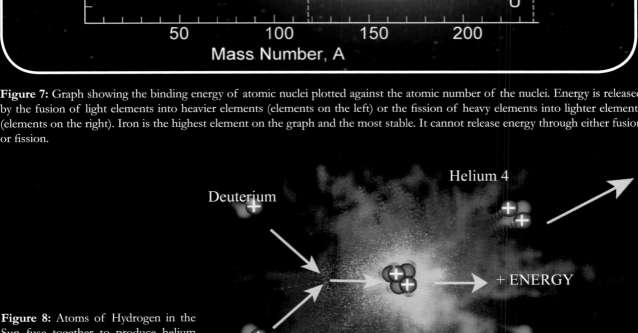

Figure 8: Atoms of Hydrogen in the Sun fuse together to produce helium and release energy. Stars are factories that release huge amounts of energy by taking the simplest element, hydrogen and converting it into heavier ones.

Meteorology in the Quran

Meteorology is the scientific study of the atmosphere that focuses on weather processes and forecasting. The formation of rain clouds is dependent on atmospheric instability and vertical motion. The thunderstorm cloud (cumulonimbus) for example, goes through a series of steps to produce rain. Cumulonimbus clouds (Figure 9) begin to form when wind pushes isolated pieces of cumulus cloud to an area where these clouds converge. Then the small clouds join together forming a larger cloud.

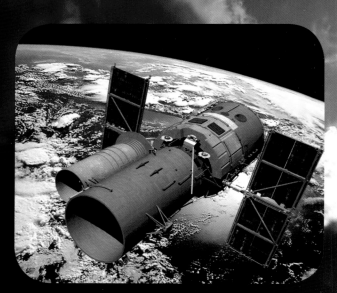

Above: A weather satellite orbits the earth relaying real-time information.

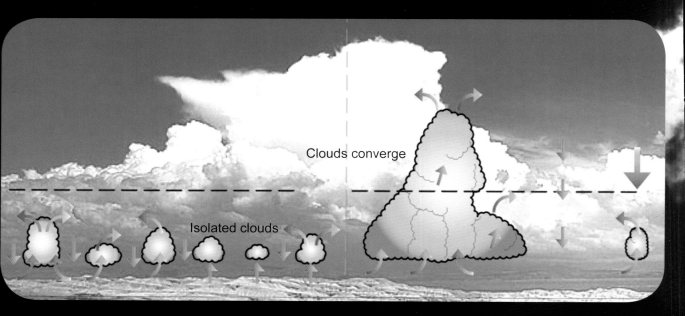

Clouds converge

Isolated clouds

Figure 9. Isolated pieces of cumulus cloud converge to form a larger Cumulonimbus cloud (*The Atmosphere*, Anthes, R.A, Cahir, J.J., Panofsky, H.A., 3rd ed., Columbus: Charles E. Merrill Publishing Company: p.269).

The Quran also mentions unique information about clouds and their formation. This information is surprisingly accurate. The Quran says that clouds are formed into a heap of layers in the following verse;

"See you not that Allah drives the clouds gently, then joins them together, then makes them into a heap of layers and you see the rain comes forth from between them..."

(Quran, The Light 24: 43)

Meteorologists have only recently discovered details of cloud formation, structure and function by using aeroplanes, satellites, computers and weather balloons (Figure 10). Yet, the Quran gave us an insight into this subject many hundreds of years before any of these technologies were invented.

Figure 10. As the small clouds join together, upward movement of air within the larger cloud increases. The up-drafts near the centre of the cloud are stronger than near the edges because they are protected from the cooling effects by the outer portion of the cloud. This upward motion cause the cloud body to grow vertically, so the cloud is stacked up.

The vertical growth causes the cloud body to stretch into cooler regions of the atmosphere, where drops of water and hail form and begin to grow larger. When these drops of water and hail become too heavy for the up-drafts to support them, they begin to fall from the cloud as rain and hail (*The Atmosphere*, Anthes et al., p.269 and *Elements of Meteorology*, Miller, A. and Thompson, J., 2nd ed. Columbus: Charles E. Merrill Publishing Company: pp.141-142).

Hail and Lightning

Hail is a form of precipitation that forms into balls or irregular lumps of ice (Figure 11) and is produced by convective clouds, such as cumulonimbus (thunderstorm cloud). Meteorologists have found that these types of clouds can reach heights of up to 25-30,000 ft (*Elements of Meteorology*, p.141). The Quran refers to these types of clouds as mountains in the sky when describing the formation of hail and lightning.

Figure 11. Hail stones can cause serious damage when they fall to Earth. This large stone has a diameter of 6cm.

" ...And He sends down hail from mountains (clouds) in the sky and He strikes with it whomever He wills and turns it from whomever He wills. The vivid flash of its lightning nearly blinds the sight."

(Quran, The Light 24: 43)

It is also interesting that the Quranic verse mentions lightning with reference to a hailstorm. Radar studies have shown that clouds become electrified as hail falls through a region in the cloud of super-cooled droplets and ice crystals. As liquid droplets collide with particles of hail, they freeze on contact and release latent heat. This keeps the surface of the hail warmer than that of the surrounding ice crystals. When hail comes in contact with an ice crystal, an important phenomenon occurs, whereby electrons flow from the colder object towards the warmer object. Hence, hail stones become negatively charged (Figure 12).

The same effect occurs when super-cooled rain droplets come in contact with a piece of hail and tiny splinters of positively charged ice break off. These lighter, positively charged particles are then carried to the upper part of the cloud by up-drafts. The hail, left with a negative charge, falls towards the bottom of the cloud; the lower part of the cloud becomes negatively charged. These negative charges are then discharged to the ground as lightning (*Meteorology Today*, Ahrens, C.D., 1988., 3rd ed., St Paul West Publishing Company, p.437: *Atmosphere, Weather & Climate*, R.G.Barry, 6th ed, Routledge, 1992, p.80-81).

Hence, the opposite charging of hail and ice crystals plays an important role in producing lightning. For Muslims, the fact that Allah had already provided an insight into the mechanism of lightning production over 1,400 years ago, further highlights the unique and miraculous nature of the Quran.

Figure 12. Radar studies have shown that clouds become electrified as hail falls through a region in the cloud of supercooled droplets and ice crystals. The lower part of the cloud can become more negatively charged compared to the upper part. Negative charges are discharged to the ground as lightning.

Oceanography in the Quran

Over 1,400 years ago the Quran gave us the first clue that sea water might not be as completely mixed as it appears to the naked eye (see the verse below).

The Barrier Between Seas

We know today that where seas, such as the Mediterranean and Atlantic Ocean meet (Figure 13), there is a slanted water barrier between them. We also know that water from each sea passes to the other through this barrier. When sea water from one sea enters the other sea, it loses its distinctive characteristics and becomes mixed with the other water. The barrier serves as a transitional mixing area for the two water masses. However, both seas retain their separate characteristics and do not encroach on one another to become one homogeneous sea. Even open oceans can consist of a number of different layers under the surface (Figure 14).

"He (Allah) has let free the two seas meeting together: Between them is a barrier which they do not transgress."

(Quran, The Mercy Giving 55:19-20)

Figure 13: Diagram showing the movement of Mediterranean sea water. Temperatures are given in degrees Celsius (°C) and salinity is in parts per thousand (‰).

Warm Mediterranean water exits the Gibraltar Straits and spreads throughout the North Atlantic at all depths between 1000 and 2500 metres. As the tongue of Mediterranean sea water enters the Atlantic over the Gibraltar-sill, it moves several hundred kilometres into the Atlantic at a depth of about 1000 metres retaining its own warm, saline and less dense characteristics. (*Marine Geology*, Keunen, H., New York: John Wiley and Sons Inc., 1960, p.43).

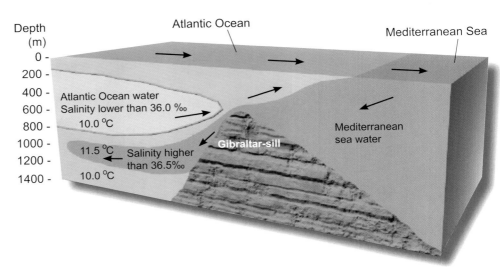

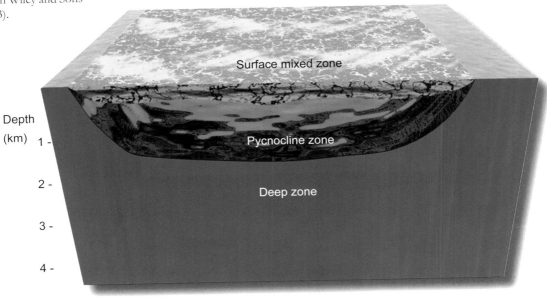

Figure 14: The open ocean consists of three layers: the surface, pycnocline and the deep zones. The surface zone contains the ocean's least dense water. The pycnocline is a very stable zone that lies below the surface zone. Because the pycnocline cannot easily move vertically it acts as a barrier to vertical water movements. The densest waters are near the bottom and are known as the deep zone (*Principles of Oceanography*, M. Grant Gross, 7th edition, Prentice-hall Inc., 1995, p.70).

> "Or (the unbelievers' state) is like the darkness in a vast deep sea, overwhelmed with waves topped by waves, topped by dark clouds (layers of) darkness upon darkness. If a man stretches out his hand, he can hardly see it..."
>
> (Quran, The Light 24: 40)

Darkness in Deep Seas

It was discovered in 1900 that darkness existed in the depths of the deep oceans. Before man was able to dive to these great depths, Allah had already mentioned this information in the Quran, using simple and precise phrases such as "darkness upon darkness". This hints to the fact that the ocean gets progressively darker in layers as a result of, the differential absorption of light (Figure 15). The verse also says "If a man stretches out his hand, he can hardly see it." In deep seas and oceans at around a depth of 200 metres there is almost no light. Below a depth of 1,000 metres there is complete darkness. The verse is all the more remarkable considering that human beings are not able to dive more than forty metres without the aid of submarines or special equipment and cannot survive unaided in the deep and dark part of the oceans.

Internal Ocean Waves

The verse also says "...in a vast deep sea, overwhelmed with waves topped by waves, topped by dark clouds..."

It is clear that the second set of waves are the surface waves that we can see because the verse mentions that above the second waves there are clouds. However, what about the first waves? Scientists have only recently discovered the existence of internal waves which occur on density interfaces between layers of different densities (Figure 16) or "waves topped by waves" as narrated in the Quran. We have only been able to discover these details with the aid of modern technology yet, the Quran has already described this phenomenon many centuries earlier.

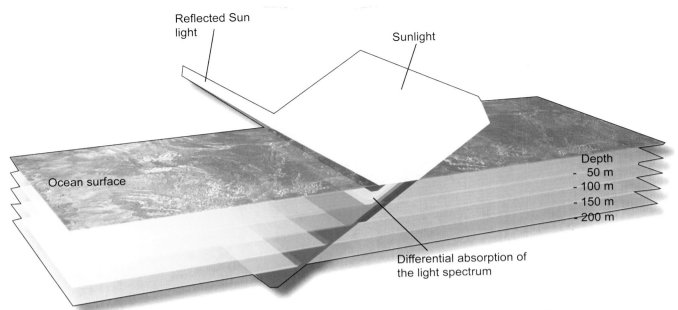

Figure 15: Sun light is made up of several basic colours which can be split up to produce a spectrum. A good example of this is rain dispersing sunlight into its component colours, causing the rainbow effect. As a ray of light reaches the ocean surface some of it is reflected while the rest is absorbed. The absorption of light by the sea is known to take place in stages. The first component of white light to be absorbed is the red wavelength at 10 metres, followed by orange (30 metres), yellow (50 metres), green (100 metres), violet (120 metres) and finally blue at depths greater than 200 metres. The differential absorption of light results in the ocean getting progressively darker in layers of light. Below a depth of 1000 metres there is no light at all (*Oceans*, Elder, D. and Pernetta J., London: Mitchell Beazley Publishers, 1991, p.27).

Figure 16: Internal waves cover the deep waters of seas and oceans because the deep waters have a higher density than the waters above them. Internal waves act like surface waves. They can also break just like surface waves. Internal waves cannot be seen by the human eye, but they can be detected by studying temperature or salinity changes at a given location (*Oceanography, a view of the Earth*, Gross, M., 6th ed. Englewood Cliffs: Prentice-Hall, Inc., 1993, p.205).

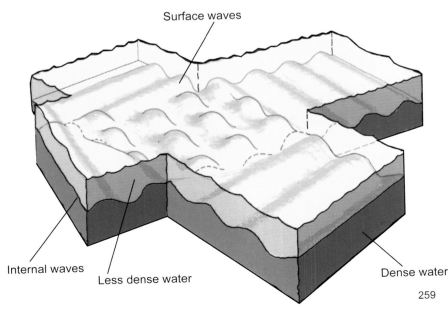

The Barrier Between Fresh and Salt Water

The Quran also provides us with further details of the processes that take place in oceans. It mentions the existence of a barrier which prevents the mixing of fresh water when it meets sea water. We know today that where large rivers flow out into the ocean the mixing of fresh water and sea water can occur very far out at sea (Figure 17). Coastal waters receive river discharges and are thus lower in salinity than the open ocean. They normally exhibit two-way estuarine circulation patterns. Seaward flowing fresh water is less dense and flows above the sea water, which tends to flow along the bottom towards the land. Where river flows are large and tidal mixing is small, the two layers remain quite distinct forming salt-wedge estuaries (e.g. Columbia River, Figure 18). The Quranic description of a barrier would seem to correspond with the existence of an interface between the fresh and salt water in the form of a partition zone that separates the two layers. The partition has a different salinity to the fresh and salt water (*Oceanography, a view of the Earth*, Gross, M., 1993, p.242).

"He (Allah) is the One who has let free the two seas, one sweet and palatable and the other salty and bitter. And He has made between them a barrier and a forbidding partition."

(Quran, The Criterion 25: 53)

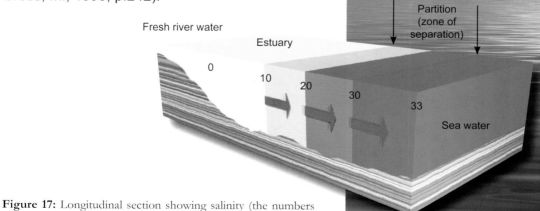

Figure 17: Longitudinal section showing salinity (the numbers represent parts per thousand) in an estuary. Note the partition (zone of separation) between the fresh and the salt water (*Introductory Oceanography*, Thurman, H.V., 5th ed., Columbus: Merrill Publishing Company, 1988, p.301).

The information presented here has been discovered only in recent times using modern instruments to measure factors such as temperature, salinity, density and oxygen solubility. Allah has created these conditions and set the laws governing the distribution of the different types of water and in his wisdom revealed this phenomenon to mankind in the Quran. This therefore shows that the author of the Quran has an intimate knowledge of nature and provides further proof as to the divine origin of the Quran.

Figure 18: Diagram showing different types of estuaries. The numbers represent salinity in parts per thousand. a) Salt wedge estuaries are deep with a large volume flow of fresh water. There is no horizontal gradient in the surface layer, but a strong sloping gradient over the entire depth of the estuary.

b) Well-mixed estuaries are generally shallow, low-volume estuaries that are well mixed vertically and stratified horizontally. The vertically homogeneous sections of water move as a block deeper into the estuary during a flood tide and toward the opening during an ebb tide.

c) Partially-mixed estuaries are relatively shallow, moderately high-volume estuaries in which the salinity increases from the head to the mouth at any depth, but where there is some vertical mixing between the net flow of fresh water out of the estuary at the surface and net flow of sea water into the estuary on the bottom.

d) Highly-stratified (Fjord) estuaries are deep with net flows much like that of the slightly stratified estuary, but where the mixing is from the deeper ocean water up into the surface water, which creates a horizontal surface water salinity gradient that increases toward and equals that of the ocean at the head. The salinity at the bottom of the estuary is oceanic. It is only the salinity at the fresh water interface that changes.

e) Reverse estuary. There is no great salinity gradient in this type of estuary.

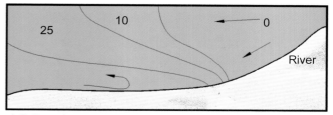

a) Salt wedge estuary

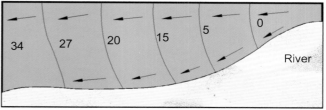

b) Well-mixed estuary

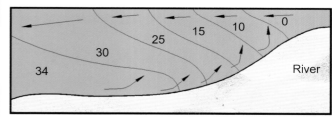

c) Partially mixed estuary

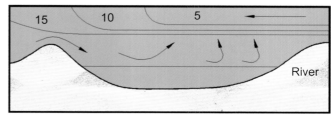

d) Fjord estuary

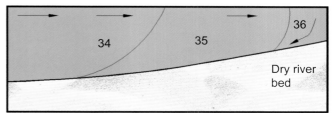

e) Reverse estuary

The Water Cycle

The Quran contains numerous verses that deal with the different roles of water. It is common knowledge nowadays that the Sun's heat causes evaporation of water from the oceans. Water vapour rises on air currents and winds and some of it condenses and falls as rain directly on to the surface of the Earth.

"And We (Allah) have sent down rain from the sky in a measured amount and settled it in the earth. And indeed, We are able to take it away. And We brought forth for you thereby gardens of palm trees and grapevines in which for you are abundant fruits and from which you eat."

(Quran, The Believers 23: 18-19)

Background: A drop of water causes a wave of ripples across the surface.

Following page: A thought provoking verse from the Quran against a dramatic view of outer space.

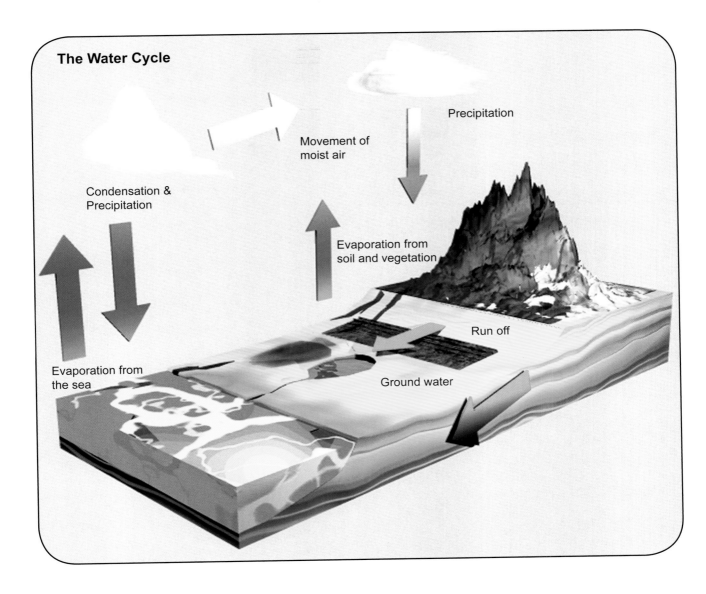

The Water Cycle

Condensation & Precipitation

Movement of moist air

Precipitation

Evaporation from soil and vegetation

Run off

Ground water

Evaporation from the sea

The important point to note from the verse shown on the left is that the Quran does not contain any of the ancient mythical concepts regarding the water cycle. For example, in the 7th century BCE it was thought that rainfall was due to water from the oceans being drawn up by winds and thrust towards the interior of the continents.

The influential ancient Greek philosopher, Plato (427–347 BCE), shared these views and thought that the water returned to the oceans via a great abyss (a mythical bottomless hole), the 'Tartarus'. It was not until 1580 that the first clear view of the water cycle was put forward by Bernard Palissy.

"Indeed, in the creation of the heavens and earth and the alternation of the night and the day and the (great) ships which sail through the sea with that which benefits people and what Allah has sent down from the heavens of rain, giving life thereby to the earth after its lifelessness and dispersing therein every (kind of) moving creature and (His) directing of the winds and the clouds controlled between the heaven and the earth are signs for a people who use reason."

(Quran, The Heifer 2: 164)

Chapter 10
Living Islam

The Journey of Life

For Muslims, life is a brilliant demonstration of Allah's wisdom and knowledge, and a vivid reflection of His Art and Power. He is the Giver and Creator of life. Nothing comes into existence by chance and nobody creates himself or anybody else. Life is very precious and no sensible or reasonable person would like to lose it by choice. Even some of those who feel so desperate and take their lives by committing suicide try in the last minute to regain their existence in order to capture a second chance to live. Life is given to man by Allah and He is the only Rightful One to take it back; no one else has the right to destroy a life. This is why Islam forbids all kinds of suicide and self-destruction and recommends patience and good faith when a dear soul passes away. When a murderer is executed in punishment, his life is taken away by the right of Allah and in accordance with His Law.

When Allah gives life to man, it is not in vain that He endows him with unique qualities and great abilities. Nor is it in vain that He charges him with certain obligations. Allah helps man to fulfil the purpose of life and to realise that the goal of existence is to worship Allah alone. He means to help him to learn the creative art of living and enjoy the good taste of life according to Divine guidance. Life is a trust from Allah and man is a trustee who should handle his trust with honesty and skill and with consciousness of responsibility to Him.

Life may be likened to a journey starting from a certain point and ending at a certain destination. It is a transitory stage, an introduction to the eternal life in the hereafter. In this journey, people should consider themselves as travellers and should be concerned only with what is of use to them in the future life. In other words, we should do all the good we can and make ourselves fully prepared to move any minute to eternity.

The best use of life in Islam therefore, is to live it according to the teachings of Allah and to make it a safe passage to the future life of eternity. Life is important as a means to an ultimate destination. Islam has laid down a complete system of regulations and principles to show men and women how to conduct their lives. All people come from Allah and there is no doubt that they shall return to Him. In one of his comprehensive statements Prophet Muhammad (ﷺ) wisely advised man to consider himself a stranger in this life or a traveller passing by the world.

Allah's Messenger took hold of my shoulder and said, "Be in this world as if you were a stranger or a traveller." The sub-narrator added: Ibn 'Umar used to say, "If you survive until the evening, do not expect to be alive in the morning and if you survive until the morning, do not expect to be alive in the evening and take from your health for your sickness and (take) from your life for your death."

(Saying of the Prophet Muhammad (ﷺ), recorded in Bukhari)

The University of Al-Qarawiyin in Fez was founded in 859. Associated with the city's giant mosque, it is recognized as the oldest university in the world. It is over seventy years older than Al-Azhar University of Cairo. Its construction was funded by a wealthy lady called Fatima al-Fihri. It was here that Pope Sylvester II around the year 999 learnt about Arabic numerals and then introduced them to Europe.

Islam Provides Many Benefits for the Individual and Society

Prophet Muhammad (ﷺ) informed us that the lowest in rank among the dwellers of Paradise will have ten times the like of this world (Saheeh Muslim); and that a space in Paradise equivalent to the size of a foot would be better than the world and whatever is in it (Saheeh Al-Bukhari). Paradise is also said to contain things which no eye has seen, no ear has heard and no human mind has thought of (Saheeh Muslim). The contrasting treatment of the believers compared to the rejectors of faith is also described in many places in the Quran.

"And give good news (O Muhammad) to those who believe and do good deeds, that they will have gardens (Paradise) in which rivers flow..."

(Quran, The Heifer 2:25)

"Indeed those who have disbelieved and died in disbelief, the earth full of gold would not be accepted from any of them if one offered it as a ransom. They will have a painful punishment and they will have no helpers."

(Quran, The Family of Imran 3:91)

Islam asserts that this life is our only chance to win Paradise and to escape from Hellfire. If someone dies in disbelief, they will not have another chance to come back to this world to believe. Allah warns us of the consequences for the unbelievers on the Day of Judgment:

Opposite: Glimpse of paradise on Earth. The Quran is full of vivid descriptions of Heaven and Hell. Heaven is often described as a high garden with rivers flowing underneath. By contrast Hellfire is depicted as a place of torment whose fuel is men and stones.

"If you could but see when they are set before the Fire (Hell) and say, "Would that we might return (to the world)! Then we would not reject the verses of our Lord, but we would be of the believers!"

(Quran, Cattle 6:27)

"But those who believe and do good deeds, We will admit them to gardens (Paradise) in which rivers flow, lasting in them forever...."

(Quran, Women 4:57)

Becoming a Muslim

One converts to Islam and becomes a Muslim simply by saying with understanding and conviction the declaration of faith, *Laa illaaha illal-lah Muhammad-ur Rasoolullah*. This saying means 'There is no god but Allah and Muhammad is the Messenger of Allah'.

When accepting Islam as the truth the person saying the declaration of faith needs to bear in mind a number of important points. Firstly, the person has to deny that there is anything else worthy of worship except Allah alone. This includes denying and rejecting those people who overstep the limits set by the Creator or those people who wish to take an attribute of Allah upon themselves, such as the 'Forgiver' or 'Lawgiver'. The declaration also needs to be said with knowledge and certainty. The person also needs to submit to Allah with love and sincerity.

Forgiveness For All Previous Sins

When someone converts to Islam, Allah forgives all of his/her previous sins and evil deeds. A man called Amr came to Prophet Muhammad (ﷺ) and said, "Give me your right hand so that I may give you my pledge of loyalty." Prophet Muhammad (ﷺ) stretched out his right hand. Amr withdrew his hand. The Prophet (ﷺ) said: *"What has happened to you, O Amr?"* He replied, "I intend to lay down a condition." Prophet Muhammad (ﷺ) asked: *"What condition do you intend to put forward?"* Amr said, "That Allah forgive my sins." Prophet Muhammad (ﷺ) said: *"Didn't you know that converting to Islam erases all previous sins?"* (Recorded in Saheeh Muslim).

"And to Allah belongs all that is in the heavens and all that is in the earth. He forgives whom He wills and punishes whom He wills. And Allah is Oft-forgiving, Most Merciful."

Systems of Islam

The Shariah

The chief characteristic of Islam is that it makes no distinction between the spiritual and the secular in life. Its aim is to shape both individual lives as well as society as a whole in ways that will ensure that Allah's law may really be established on Earth and that peace, contentment and well-being may fill the world. The Islamic way of life is thus based on a unique concept of man's place in the universe. In Islam, man's entire individual and social life is an exercise in developing and strengthening his relationship with Allah by submitting to His will in all aspects of life.

The Islamic code of conduct is known as the *Shariah*. It is compulsory on all Muslims to live, rule and judge by the *Shariah* alone. Its source is the Quran and the teachings of the Prophet Muhammad (ﷺ).

Contrary to popular belief, *Shariah* law is not about administering very harsh punishments. The main objectives of the *Shariah* are to ensure that human life is based on good actions (*Maroof*) and to cleanse these actions of all evil (*Munkar*). The Arabic term for 'good' denotes all the qualities that have always been accepted as 'good' as decreed by Allah and submitted to by His creations. Conversely, the word for 'evil' denotes all those qualities that have always been condemned by Allah.

For Muslims the *Shariah* gives precise definitions of good and evil. The standard of morals which individuals and society should aspire to, are clearly indicated in *Shariah* law. It does not, however, limit itself to an inventory of good and evil deeds; it lays down an entire scheme of life to ensure that good flourishes and evil does not destroy or harm human life.

To achieve this, the *Shariah* has embraced in its scheme everything that encourages the growth of good and has recommended ways to remove obstacles that might prevent this growth. This process gives rise to a subsidiary series of ways of initiating and nurturing good, together with another set of recommendations consisting of prohibitions to evil.

The *Shariah* thus prescribes directives for the regulation of our individual and our collective lives. These directives affect such varied subjects as religious rituals, personal character, morals, habits, family relationships, social and economic affairs, administration, the rights and duties of citizens, the judicial system, the laws of war and peace and international relations.

Opposite page: Diagram showing rights of ownership in Islam. The underlying principle is that everything belongs to the Creator, Allah. Individuals are only given wealth as a trust. The main business of the Islamic leadership is to distribute wealth to those in need and encourage good within the global Muslim community. Key Terms: *Bait al Mal* - the public treasury; *Caliph* - The Muslim ruler; *Ummah* - Global Muslim community.

Islamic Rights of Ownership

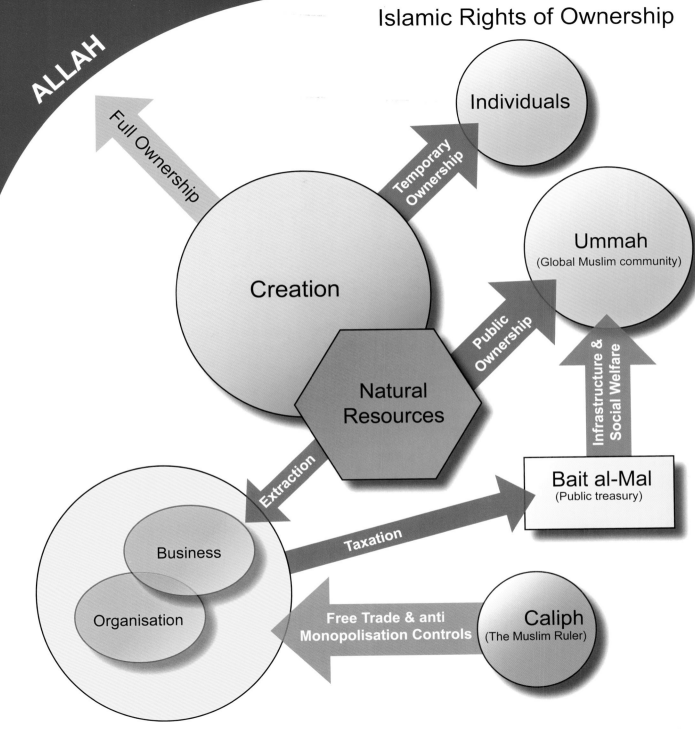

273

These laws tell us what is good and bad; what is beneficial and useful and what is injurious and harmful; what are the virtues which we have to cultivate and encourage and what are the vices which we have to suppress and guard against; what is the sphere of our voluntary, personal and social action and what are its limits; and, finally, what methods we can adopt to establish a dynamic order of society and what methods we should avoid. The *Shariah* is thus a complete way of life and an all-embracing social order.

Another remarkable feature of the *Shariah* is that it is an organic system of life. The entire way of life propounded by Islam is animated by the same spirit and hence any arbitrary division of the scheme is bound to affect the spirit as well as the structure of the Islamic order. In this respect, it might be compared to the human body. A leg separated from the body cannot be called one-eighth or one-sixth man, because after its separation from the body the leg cannot perform its function. Nor can it be placed in the body of some other animal with the aim of making it human to the extent of that limb. Likewise, we cannot form a correct judgment about the utility, efficiency and beauty of the hand, the eye or the nose of a human being outside the context of their place and function within the living body.

Islam is a complete way of life which cannot be split up into separate parts. So it is not appropriate to consider the different parts of the *Shariah* in isolation. The *Shariah* can only function effectively if the whole of one's life is lived in accordance with it. Consequently, Muslims are required to abide by Shariah law and settle any disputes only in accordance with the Islamic legal system as outlined by *Shariah* law.

In Islamic Law, the State is required to cater for the rights and needs of citizens. For example, it should encourage economic activity, provide jobs and education, adequate social welfare mechanisms through *Zakah* (compulsory charity) and similar institutions and to ban whatever is conducive to crime.

The State only has the right to prescribe and mete out punishment if it has good governance and adequate social and welfare provisions in place for society. For example, it would not be just to amputate the hand of a convicted thief found guilty by an Islamic State, unless the State has provided the thief with no excuse to steal such as employment or adequate social welfare for the poor and needy. It must also take into account the age of the thief, the amount stolen and the reason for stealing. Thus a thief is only punished when there is no reasonable excuse for stealing.

A well known tradition records that the Caliph Umar ibn al Khattab (رضي الله عنه) had a thief once brought before him, whereupon he was asked the reason for his theft. The man replied that he was a slave and his master had not provided enough for him. Umar immediately summoned the thief's master and warned him "The next time your slave steals out of hardship, it will be your hand we will cut."

Opposite page: Diagram showing Islamic model of taxation, compulsory charity and wealth distribution to the poor and needy. Key terms: *Bait al Mal* - the public treasury; *Fitrana* - compulsory charity to be paid to the poor and needy prior to the *Eid* celebration after Ramadan; *Ghanima* - Wealth acquired as a result of war; Jizyah - A small charge paid by non-Muslims living under the protection of the Islamic state; *Kharaj* - Tax on agricultural land; *Sadaqat* - Voluntary charity; *Ummah* - Global Muslim community; *Zakah* - compulsory charity amounting to 2.5% of annual savings paid by eligible Muslims.

Islamic System of Taxation, Compulsory Charity and Wealth Distribution

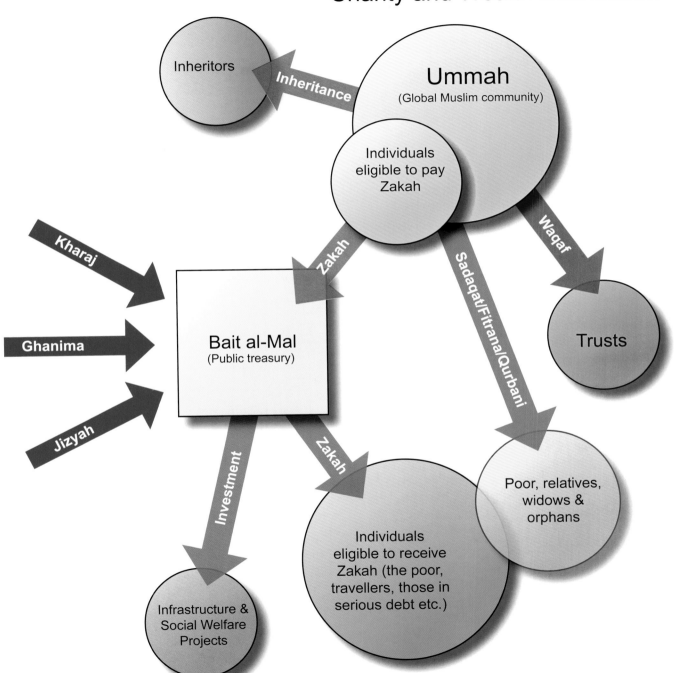

275

The Ruling System of Islam

The Islamic ruling system is based upon a unique system of unity ordained by Allah. It is not a federal, democratic, republican, monarchical or dictatorial system nor is it similar to any man-made ideology. The Islamic State considers people under its authority as citizens, whether they are Muslims or non-Muslims. They have their rights guaranteed by Islam. There is no concept of 'ethnic minority' and people are not discriminated against at all due to their colour, race or religion. There must not be any discrimination against or mistreatment of non-Muslims. Places of worship (such as Churches and Synagogues) must not be attacked or destroyed by other people. This is why we see areas in the Muslim world with churches and synagogues that have lasted for centuries under Islamic rule, such as those seen in Egypt and Jerusalem. It is also a duty of the Islamic State to protect non-Muslim citizens against aggressors if they attack the land. Islam outlaws nationalism and tribalism; there is no such concept as the nation state or borders within the Islamic State. The underlying principle in Islam is that all people regardless of race or colour are united under the banner of one leader: the Caliph.

Leadership and ruling in an Islamic State is centralised, whereas administration is decentralised. The State is made up of a number of provinces headed by governors. The main officials of the State are appointed by the head of state, the Caliph. Every decision must emanate from the head of State. This negates any corruption and confusion within the ruling system. The method of appointing a Caliph is through the process of pledging allegiance (in Arabic - *bayah*), which acts as a binding contract between the people and ruler. The people must obey the ruler as long as he implements Islam.

Opposite page: An overview of the Islamic ruling system showing the relationship between Allah, the Ummah (global Muslim community), the Calpih (Muslim head of state) and the various instruments of government. The global Muslim community elects representatives from among itself to stand on the Majlis al-Ummah (Council of the Ummah), which scrutinises the Caliph in his implementation of Islam and advises him on the affairs of the Ummah.

The Ruling System of the Islamic State is based upon the following:

1. Sovereignty is for Allah alone.
2. The *Sunnah* or example of Prophet Muhammad (ﷺ) is to be followed in everything.
3. Appointing a Caliph is an obligation upon all Muslims.
4. The Caliph alone has the exclusive power to adopt the divine laws - he alone enacts the constitution and various laws.

In Islam, Muslims are required to carry out the orders of the Caliph without reservation or dispute. This is subject to the orders falling within the bounds of Islam, as verified by the *Majlis al-Ummah*, which is the Ummah's representative. A noteworthy point is that in Islam it is forbidden for the global Muslim community to i) be without a Caliph and ii) to have more than one head of state (*Kitab al-Ahkam al-Sultania - The Book of the Rules of Governance*, Abu al-Hasan Ali Ibn Muhammad Ibn Habib al-Mawardi, died 1058).

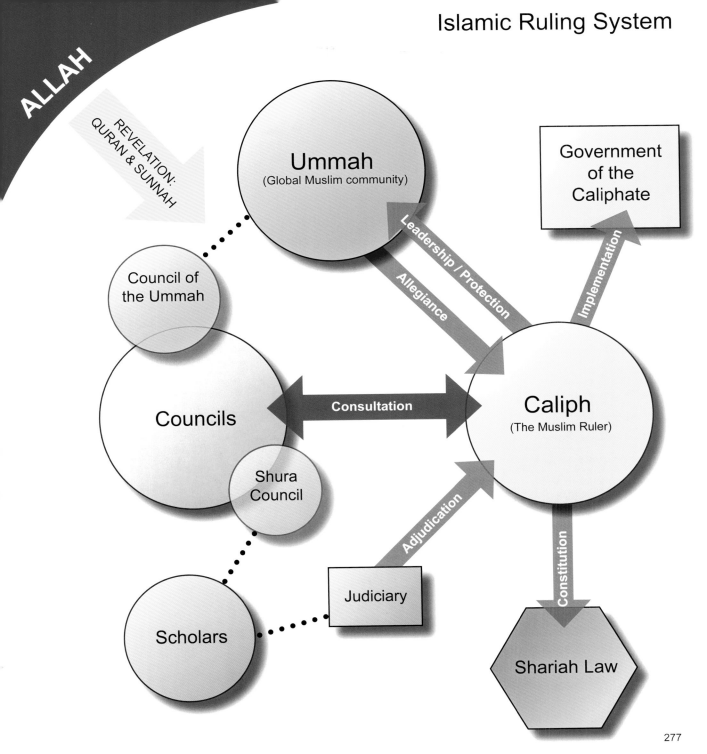

Islamic Ruling System

ALLAH

REVELATION: QURAN & SUNNAH

Ummah
(Global Muslim community)

Council of the Ummah

Councils

Shura Council

Scholars

Caliph
(The Muslim Ruler)

Government of the Caliphate

Judiciary

Shariah Law

Leadership / Protection

Allegiance

Implementation

Consultation

Adjudication

Constitution

Human Rights in Islam

Centuries before the concept of human rights was even discussed, Islamic Laws regulated the mutual rights and duties of members of society in order to ensure social stability. Islam requires a Muslim to take care of fellow Muslims wherever they are, by extending help to them and trying to improve their conditions. The bond between two Muslims is like parts of a house, one part strengthens and holds the other. This is stressed by the following tradition of the Prophet Muhammad (ﷺ):

"Muslims, in their mutual love, kindness and compassion, are like the human body: If one of its parts is in agony, the entire body feels the pain both in sleeplessness and fever." (Recorded in Bukhari & Muslim).

Rights of Guests

Guests have a right to entertainment. This is based upon Prophet Muhammad's (ﷺ) saying;

"One who believes in Allah and the Day of Judgment should honour his guest according to his right. He was asked: O Messenger of Allah! What is his right? He said: A day and night (of good feasting) and hospitality for three days. Thereafter it is an act of charity." (Recorded in Bukhari & Muslim).

Rights of Neighbours

Islam enjoins kindness to neighbours and refrain from causing them any physical and psychological inconvenience, such as by raising one's voice or causing or permitting offensive smells or alarm. Prophet Muhammad (ﷺ) said: *"One who believes in Allah and the Last Day should honour his neighbour."* (Recorded in Bukhari & Muslim).

Rights of Friends and Companions

Islam has also prescribed certain rights that should be fulfilled for a friend, such as kind treatment and sincere advice. Prophet Muhammad (ﷺ) said:

"The best friend in the sight of Allah is he who is the well-wisher of his companions and the best neighbour is he who behaves best towards his neighbours." (Recorded in Tirmidhi).

Rights of Relatives

Muslims are urged to help their relatives by complying with their needs, enquiring about their condition, treating them with kindness and sympathy and sharing their joys and sorrows. The Quran says:

"And fear Allah through Whom you demand (your mutual rights) and do not cut the relations of the wombs (kinship)."

(Quran, Women 4:1)

In line with Prophets Muhammad's (ﷺ) merciful and tolerant behaviour, Muslims are encouraged to treat close relatives kindly, even if they do not return the kindness, forgive them even though they may do wrong and to try seeking their friendship, even though they may be unfriendly.

Opposite page: Diagram showing the relationship between the individual and others in society. The individual has obligations towards others in Islam. Similarly, other people can expect to have certain rights over the individual. Ultimately the individual is held to account by the Almighty Creator, Allah.

Key Terms: *Caliph* - The Muslim ruler appointed by the Ummah: *Sunnah* - The example or way of the Prophet Muhammad (ﷺ): *Ummah* - Global Muslim community.

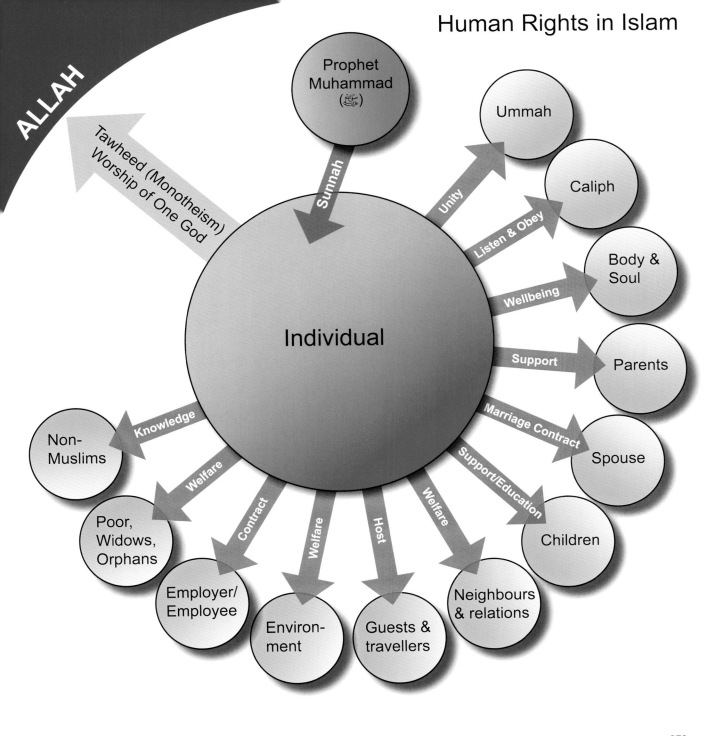

Human Rights in Islam

ALLAH

Prophet Muhammad (ﷺ)

Tawheed (Monotheism) Worship of One God

Sunnah

Individual

Unity — Ummah

Listen & Obey — Caliph

Wellbeing — Body & Soul

Support — Parents

Marriage Contract — Spouse

Support/Education — Children

Welfare — Neighbours & relations

Host — Guests & travellers

Welfare — Environment

Contract — Employer/ Employee

Welfare — Poor, Widows, Orphans

Knowledge — Non-Muslims

Rights of Children

Despite the customary pre-Islamic acceptance of female infanticide among Arab tribes, the Quran forbade this custom and considered it an abominable crime. Although every child's life is sacred in Islam, Allah especially orders the kind and just treatment of daughters.

Prophet Muhammad (ﷺ) said the following about the treatment of daughters:

"Whoever has a daughter and does not bury her alive, insult her and does not favour his son over her, Allah will enter him into paradise."

(Ibn Hanbal).

Prophet Muhammad (ﷺ) was very close to his children and like any father he would take great care in their welfare. He was also a very merciful and compassionate man, forgiving the killer of one of his daughters. Indeed, he remained very close to his children even when they grew into adulthood. He was always concerned about their welfare.

Another important Islamic teaching is that righteous children who outlive their parents can contribute to their parents record of good deeds after the death of their parents.

"When a human being dies, his (good) deeds come to an end, except for three things: ongoing charity, beneficent knowledge, or a righteous child supplicating for him."

(Saying of the Prophet Muhammad (ﷺ), recorded in Muslim).

Children have the right to be looked after by their parents. They must provide for all their basic needs such as food, clothes and shelter. Parents must also give their children proper education and good manners such as teaching modesty, respect for elders, truthfulness, honesty and obedience to parents.

"Everyone of you is a shepherd (of his immediate charge) and is responsible for (the action of) those persons who are committed to his charge."

(Saying of the Prophet Muhammad (ﷺ), recorded in Bukhari & Muslim)

Children also have the right to be treated fairly and equally. Depriving or banning the right of inheritance or other financial gifts during the lifetime of the parents or the preference of a parent for one child over the other is considered as an act of injustice in Islam. Injustice can lead to an atmosphere of hatred, anger and dismay amongst the children in a household. In fact, such an act of injustice is likely to lead to animosity amongst the children and consequently, this can affect the entire family environment.

If parents fulfil their duties towards all their children by meeting their basic needs, this can lead to more caring children and a healthy family atmosphere as well as a better social environment. Neglectful parents risk losing their ties with their own children or in worse cases being subjected to ill-treatment by their children later on in life.

Women's status in Islam

In Islam there is absolutely no difference between men and women as far as their relationship with Allah is concerned, as both are promised the same reward for good conduct and the same punishment for evil conduct. Islam regards men and women as being of the same essence created from a single soul. Their obligations and rights are also similar, with some distinct differences. The Quran says:

"...And they (women) have rights similar to those (of men) over them in kindness..."

(Quran, The Heifer 2: 228)

As in the verse on the opposite page, the Quran, in addressing the believers, often uses the expression, 'believing men and women' to emphasise the equality of men and women in regard to their respective duties, rights, virtues and merits. It also says:

"Enter into Paradise, you and your wives, with delight."

(Quran, Ornaments of Gold 43: 70)

Protecting women's rights is an important theme in the Quran and in the verse shown opposite it admonishes those men who oppress or ill-treat women.

When it is considered that before the advent of Islam, the pagan Arabs used to bury their female children alive, make women dance naked in the vicinity of the *Kaaba* during their annual fairs and treat women as objects of sexual pleasure, possessing no rights or position whatsoever, these teachings of the Quran were nothing short of revolutionary.

"O you who believe! You are forbidden to inherit women against their will. Nor should you treat them with harshness, that you may take away part of the dowry you have given them - except when they have become guilty of open lewdness. On the contrary live with them on a footing of kindness and equity. If you take a dislike to them, it may be that you dislike something and Allah will bring about through it, a great deal of good."

(Quran, Women 4: 19)

Opposite page: The Taj Mahal in Agra, India, is considered one of the most beautiful buildings in the world and the finest example of the late style of Islamic architecture. The Mughal emperor Shah Jahan ordered it to be built after the death (1629) of his wife, Mumtaz Mahal. The building was designed by the local Muslim architect Ustad Ahmad Lahori. Set in its carefully laid out grounds, it was intended to be a reflection of the gardens of Paradise. The entire complex, with gardens, gateway structures and mosque, was completed in 1643.

Following pages: Dramatic reflection of the Wilayah Persekutuan Mosque in Kuala Lumpur, Malaysia. This imposing structure is one of the grandest mosques in the world and can be seen for miles around. The mosque's entrance is a soaring twenty eight metres, a masterpiece of white marble inlaid with dark green granite calligraphy from the Quran. Inside the mosque, the dazzling prayer niche (*mihrab*) wall is a carved marble floral arabesque, inlaid with semi-precious stones.

"Indeed, the Muslim men and Muslim women, the believing men and believing women, the obedient men and obedient women, the truthful men and truthful women, the patient men and patient women, the humble men and humble women, the charitable men and charitable women, the fasting men and fasting women, the men who guard their chastity and the women who do so and the men who remember Allah often and the women who do so for them Allah has prepared forgiveness and a great reward."

(Quran, The Clans 33: 35)

Islam has accorded women rights over 1400 years ago, which we now take for granted. Islam offered women dignity, justice and protection which had long remained out of their reach. If we look at any other civilisation in history, we will not find women playing a major role in its establishment. Islam is the only civilisation where a leading input in terms of the transmission, establishment and support was based upon the efforts of women. This is historical fact which is not open to interpretation. Far from struggling in aggressive campaigns for mere acknowledgement of her existence, the woman in Islam is effortlessly awarded liberties and privileges from her Lord. The carpet of ease and dignity is rolled out under the woman's feet in Islam and she is entrusted with important tasks that beautifully adorn her nature.

The Prophet Muhammad (ﷺ) wanted to put a stop to all cruelties to women, so he preached kindness towards them. He told Muslims:

> "*The best of you are they who behave best to their wives.*"

(Mishkat al-Masabih, Transmitted by Tirmidhi).

The Prophet Muhammad (ﷺ) was most emphatic in enjoining upon Muslims to be kind to their women when he delivered his famous last sermon on the Mount of Mercy at Arafat in the presence of one hundred and twenty-four thousand of his companions who had gathered there for the 'Farewell Pilgrimage' (*Hajj al-Wada*).

> "A *Muslim must not hate his wife and if he be displeased with one bad quality in her, let him be pleased with one that is good.*"

In his sermon he ordered those present and through them all those Muslims who were to come later, to be respectful and kind towards women. He said:

"Fear Allah regarding women. Verily you have married them with the trust of Allah and made their bodies lawful with the word of Allah. You have got (rights) over them and they have got (rights) over you in respect of their food and clothing according to your means."

Financial Status

In Islam a woman is a completely independent personality. She can make any contract or bequest in her own name. She is entitled to inherit in her position as mother, as wife, as sister and as daughter. She has perfect liberty to choose her husband. The pagan society of pre-Islamic Arabia had an irrational prejudice against their female children, many of whom were often buried alive. The Messenger of Allah was totally opposed to this obscene practice. He taught them that supporting their female children would act as a screen for them against the fire of Hell.

Islam teaches that human beings were created to worship and submit to Allah the Creator. There are separate defined roles for men and for women and it is the Creator who defines these roles. Views concerning women are based on divine guidance in the Quran and by the teachings of Prophet Muhammad (ﷺ). The economic rights of women were denied before Islam and continued to be denied in secular cultures after it, only being awarded to women relatively recently. However, over 14 centuries ago, Islam gave women the right to personal ownership of property and wealth. The woman's right to her money, real estate or other property was acknowledged and this right does not change after marriage.

As discussed previously, Islamic civilisation, unlike any other, from its very beginning has been supported and founded by women. For example, the first person to believe in the Blessed Prophet Muhammad (ﷺ) was his wife Lady Khadijah (رضي الله عنها). She was a business woman with her own property and wealth and it was through her money and support that, the Prophet Muhammad (ﷺ) was able to spread the message of Islam in his first year of prophethood.

The Right of Inheritance

Islam gives women the right of inheritance whereas in some cultures, women were themselves considered objects to be inherited! The woman is allotted inheritance and this is hers to retain and manage - no one including her father or her husband, can lay any claim to it. Generally, her share is one half the man's share. This variation in inheritance is consistent with the variations in the financial responsibilities for men and women. Men are justly allotted a larger share because the woman, by divine right, is completely free from all financial responsibility and all her monetary requirements are met by her father, brother or husband as the case may be.

Political Involvement

An objective study of early Islamic history reveals the important political role of women in Islam. Women have always had the right to participate in public affairs. Throughout Islamic history, we find examples of women participating in serious debates. For example, during the Caliphate of Umar Ibn al Khattab (رضي الله عنه), a woman publicly debated with him and proved to be correct in an argument to which the leader, with humility, declared before an audience: "The woman is right and Umar is wrong."

One of Prophet Muhammad's (ﷺ) wives, Lady Ayesha (رضي الله عنها) is regarded as one of the greatest scholars of Islam. She has narrated numerous Prophetic statements and is amongst the few who have given many religious pronouncements and verdicts and has also explained many verses of the Quran.

Another influential woman from the early period of Islamic history was Lady Hafsah (رضي الله عنها). She was an intellectual who collected copies of the Quran as it was dictated by Prophet Muhammad (ﷺ) and written down by his scribes. This was the text which was handed down to Caliph Uthman ibn Affan (رضي الله عنه) and established as the standard text that was circulated throughout the Islamic world.

Opposite page: An arched doorway along the western façade of the Great Mosque of Cordoba in Spain. The construction of the mosque lasted for over two centuries, starting in 784 under the supervision of the first Muslim Caliph Abd ar-Rahman. The building is another magnificent example of Islamic architecture most notable for its giant arches, with over 1,000 columns of jasper, onyx, marble and granite. The mosque reached its current dimensions in 987 with the completion of the outer naves and orange tree courtyard.

Marriage

Prophet Muhammad (ﷺ) encouraged the institution of marriage and good relationships between spouses. The issue of marriage in Islam is often misunderstood by many people. The idea of forced marriage is completely alien and hostile to the teaching of the Prophet Muhammad (ﷺ). Women have the right to choose their marriage partner and the marriage must have her free consent. Upon entering marriage women are also entitled to retain their maiden name; this is symbolic of her unique identity. Together with all the required provisions for her welfare and protection at the time of marriage, Islam additionally gives the woman the right to a dowry (*Mahr*). This is a gift from the husband symbolising his love and affection. The ownership of her wealth does not transfer to the her in-laws, father or husband upon marriage but is entirely at the disposal of the woman.

The Prophet Muhammad (ﷺ) exhorted men to marry women of piety and women to be faithful to their husbands and kind to their children. He (ﷺ) said: "*Among my followers the best of men are those who are best to their wives and the best of women are those who are best to their husbands. To such women is set down a reward equivalent to the reward of a thousand martyrs. Among my followers, again, the best of women are those who assist their husbands in their work and love them dearly for everything, save what is a transgression of Allah's laws.*"

The natural difference between the sexes is acknowledged in Islam and the physically stronger male is given a greater degree of responsibility concerning economic maintenance and protection and overall leadership of the family. This responsibility does not imply superiority over the woman.

Widows

A real test for a woman is when her husband passes away and as a widow, the responsibility of maintaining the children falls upon her. In the Eastern World, where a woman does not always go out to earn her living, the problems of being a widow are very difficult. The Prophet Muhammad (ﷺ) upheld the cause of widows. In fact most of his wives were widows. In an age when widows were rarely permitted to re-marry, the Prophet encouraged his followers to marry them. He was always ready to help widows and exhorted his followers to do the same.

Divorce

Not only is the woman's right to decide her marriage partner recognised, but also the right to terminate an unsuccessful marriage. However, Islam enjoins that both parties observe a waiting period (roughly three months) before a divorce is finalised. This helps to prevent irrational decisions taking place in the midst of a trauma that may be developing and for the sake of the family's stability, especially where children are involved. Both husband and wife can then assess the situation rationally before making any decision. When divorce is unavoidable, Allah instructs the husband to depart from his wife peacefully with no malice.

Opposite page: Courtyard houses are common in the Islamic world and reflect the nomadic influences of the region. Courtyard homes are perhaps more prevalent in temperate climates, as an open central court can be an important aid for cooling the houses in warm weather especially, if it incorporates a water fountain within the courtyard. In some Islamic cultures, private courtyards also provide outdoor space for women to relax unobserved.

"And of His signs is that He created for you from yourselves mates that you may find tranquillity in them; and He placed between you affection and mercy. Indeed in that are signs for a people who give thought."

(Quran, The Romans 30: 21).

Family Life

This is the most important social institution responsible for the upbringing of the next generation of society. The family has the greatest influence on the morality of any generation. Islamic law is therefore very strict with regard to the protection of the objectives of the family. Adultery, being one of the main reasons for family break up and an immorality in itself, is an offence under Islamic law.

The severe punishment for adultery, however, serves more as a deterrent in view of the strict conditions required before it can be enforced. No less than four reliable and dependable witnesses who each saw the physical act taking place are required for a judge to rule such a punishment. Since adultery in the presence of less than four witnesses is still not punishable by Shariah law, it seems that the accusation that Shariah is too severe and barbaric with respect to adultery is simply void.

As a Mother

Islam reminds us to be kind to our parents and in particular to the mother, as she bears the child from one hardship to another, through the difficulties of pregnancy and childhood. When a woman becomes a mother in Islam, her seat of honour and dignity becomes extra special. As shown on the opposite page many sayings of the Prophet Muhammad (ﷺ) emphasise the respect that should be given to the mother.

However, many women today, feel that motherhood is not considered to be a career that brings in financial gains and fulfilment. Yet Allah has filled the life of a mother with opportunities, wonderful challenges, immense reward and constant fulfilment. These are certainly important responsibilities which confirm that her role is varied, rewarding and indispensable.

The difference is that a mother does her duty in an environment of care, love and respect. A mother is also in a unique position to play a substantial part in the way a whole generation is educated, guided and trained. Motherhood itself is a noble profession. It requires skill and professionalism, commitment and care, devotion and dedication. This is why in Islam it is more important to shape the future generation first before pursuing a career outside. However, some women work full time out of financial necessity and still remain responsible for the house work and child-care too.

Opposite page: Newborn babies are able to feel all the different sensations, but respond most enthusiastically to soft stroking, cuddling and caressing. Gentle rocking back and forth often calms a crying infant, as do massages and warm baths.

In Islam, children are a source of delight and an adornment for the world granted by Allah to their parents. They give vigour to the heart, joy to the soul and pleasure to the eyes. All hope for the future lies with our children. Islam has elevated the status of children and has laid down manners for their treatment relating to all their affairs at each stage of their lives.

Following page: A colourful water lily with a beautiful Quranic verse explaining the rights of parents over their children.

"PARADISE LIES AT THE FEET OF YOUR MOTHERS"

(Saying of the Prophet Muhammad ﷺ,
Recorded in ibn Majah and Ahmad).

"And your Lord has decreed that you worship none but Him and that you be dutiful to your parents. If one of them or both of them attain old age in your life, say not to them a word of disrespect, nor shout at them but address them in terms of honour. And lower unto them the wing of submission and humility through mercy and say: "My Lord! Bestow on them your Mercy as they did bring me up when I was young."

(Quran, The Night Journey, 17: 23-24)

Chapter 11

Islam's Contribution to Civilisation

History of Islamic Science

Imagine a world where the modern day system of numbers had never been invented and where there was no knowledge of vaccination or cataract removal or processes such as distillation. Imagine a world where computers, schools, universities, pharmacies and hospitals did not exist. Imagine a world without inventions such as surgical instruments, pointed-arches, hydraulics, water-raising machines, crank-shafts, pin-hole cameras, soap, the toothbrush, fountain pens, carpets, cheques and novels. These are just a few examples of the many hundreds of revolutionary inventions that were introduced by Islamic civilisation. Some of these discoveries were of such magnitude that they laid the foundations for many of the subsequent revolutionary discoveries over the last 1,000 years.

Unfortunately, little is told in the West about the glorious history of Islamic civilisation. From the 7th century, Islam brought people from different nations and cultures together into a society in which the life honour and property of every citizen, Muslim and non-Muslim, was secure. Furthermore, Islam broke the shackles of ignorance that had engulfed humanity and provided for them a system in which they excelled, among other things, in the development of science. One has to only look at the origins of many commonly used words such as alcohol, algebra, algorithm, cipher, earth, monsoon and so on, to realise that these words are derived from Arabic. Scientists from all different backgrounds, Muslims as well as non-Muslims, excelled in numerous fields such as architecture, astronomy, geography, medicine and mathematics. These inventors changed the

world with their numerous innovations that are taken for granted in daily life.

It was between the 8th and 13th centuries that the most ground-breaking scientific inventions were made. The Muslim world was filled with libraries, hospitals and universities. Great centres of learning and excellence were established in the cities of Baghdad, Istanbul, Samarkand, Bukhara and Cordoba. It was a time when the likes of Al-Biruni, Al-Khwarizmi, Ibn Sina, Al-Razi and hundreds more scientists shaped the modern sciences in such a way that in the mind of the historian Briffault, "*science owes a great deal more to the Arab culture, it owes its existence.*" He further comments that "*had it not been for such Muslim upsurge, modern European civilisation would never have arisen at all.* (R Briffault: *The Making of Humanity*, George Unwin and Allen, London, 1928, p.191).

Martin Levey points out the crucial timing of the Muslim scientific upsurge, during the times of darkness elsewhere and how it inspired much of Europe. "*In a time when the movement of ideas was at a relative standstill,*" he says, "*the Muslims came along with a new outlook, with a sense of enquiry into the old and finally to a point where Western Europe could take over this thoroughly examined knowledge and endow its ripeness with a completely fresh approach of its own*" (M.Levey: *Early Arabic Pharmacology*, Leiden, E.J. Brill, 1973, p.71).

Opposite page: From the 8th century onwards, Muslim engineers devised many ingenious methods for transporting, storing and lifting water. In a fusion of old and new, a large water wheel or *norias* is depicted against a circuit board.

Astronomy

In astronomy, the Arabic names of stars and constellations and the Arabic origins of the words 'azimuth' (*as-sumut*), 'nadir' (*nazir*) and 'zenith' (*samt*) all point to the great contribution of the Muslims towards this field.

Over 1000 years ago, scientists in the Islamic world started to develop sophisticated instruments such as the astrolabe, which has been described as the single most important calculating device before the invention of the digital computer. Along with the quadrant and good navigational maps, these instruments paved the way for many Muslim and European voyages of discovery.

Above: Planetary diagrams in an anonymous and untitled Persian treatise on astronomy. The copy was completed on 7 November 1552 by Sadr al-Din al-Mutatabbib (*the medical practitioner*).

Above: Al-Burini's treatise on the astrolabe (14th century).

Below: The manuscript shows a 13th century sketch of the 'Tusi-couple' by Nasir al-Din Tusi. The "Tusi-couple" is one of several late Islamic astronomical devices bearing a striking similarity to models found in *De revolutionibus orbium coelestium* (*On the Revolutions of the Heavenly Spheres*) by the 15th century astronomer Nicolaus Copernicus. Historians suspect that Copernicus or another European author had access to an Islamic astronomical text, however the exact chain of transmission remains obscure.

Botany

In the field of botany, the work of Abu Hanifa al-Dinawari (died 895) from Andalusia in Muslim Spain, was made known by the German scholar Silberberg. He wrote a thesis in Breslau in 1908, which contained Abu Hanifa al-Dinawari's descriptions of about 400 plants. However, what is described by Silberberg is just a small part of al-Dinawari's work, as only 2 out of 6 volumes have survived.

Above and top right: In his treatise on the Earth, Dinawari describes a variety of soils, explaining which is good for planting, its properties and qualities. Dinawari also describes the phases of plant growth, including the production of flowers and fruit. He then covers various crops including cereals, vines and date palms. Relying on his predecessors, he also explains trees, mountains, plains, deserts, aromatic plants, woods, plants used in dye production, honey and bees.

Right: A 14th century Arabic translation of the work of Dioscorides on *materia medica*.

Chemistry

In chemistry, the most fundamental development was the initiation of its practical side. Experimentation differentiated Islamic from ancient Greek science, which was mostly based upon speculation. This development laid down the very foundation of modern chemistry.

Jabir Ibn Hayyam (722 to 815) was one of the earliest Arab chemists. On the crucial role of experimentation Jabir says;

"The first essential in chemistry is that you should perform practical work and conduct experiments..." (E.J Holmyard, *Makers of Chemistry*, Oxford at the Claredon Press, 1931, p. 60).

Some of Jabir's work includes *Khawass al-Jabir* (*Great book of Chemical Properties*) and *al-Mizaj* (*Chemical Combination*). He also built a precise weighing scale and ten centuries before John Dalton, he defined chemical combinations as the union of elements together. Jabir also invented fireproof paper and perfected various chemical processes such as crystallisation, distillation, purification, filtration, sublimation and reduction.

Above right: The *al-inbiq* apparatus was used by Muslim chemists for distillation purposes. The name al-inbiq has been taken into the English language as 'alembic'.

Middle: Ink drawings of a triple alembic with 3 distilling heads. This is taken from a 12th century chemical commentary on a poem composed in Spain by Ibn Arfa` Ra`s.

Bottom: A leaf from a composite volume of alchemical treatises. The upper half of the page has the end of a treatise *Kitab al-Rahib* by Jabir ibn Hayyan, while the lower half is the beginning of an extended extract from Aristotle's Meteorologia in an Arabic translation.

Engineering

There were many creative achievements in the fields of engineering and mechanical technology during the 'Golden Age of Islamic Science'. Amongst the achievements of Islamic engineers are the design and construction of various types of clocks and instruments, segmental gears, sinking floats serving as actuators, hydraulic devices and machines for crushing sugar cane, extracting vegetable oils and lifting water. Some of these machines have survived to this day.

In the field of hydraulic engineering and water management, Muslim mastery of this technology was far more advanced than acknowledged by many historians. Muslim engineers built hundreds of huge dams, bridges, water reservoirs and canals in a variety of structures and forms using techniques which reached great heights of ingenuity.

In the development of mechanical engineering, it is impossible to over emphasise the name of Al-Jazari. In 1206, he completed his famous book in which he describes fifty mechanical devices in six different categories, including water clocks, machines for raising water and a hand washing device .

Above right: A diagram of Al-Jazari's 13th century water raising device.

Middle: An illustration of clock construction.

Bottom: The Pul-i-Bulaiti dam on the Ab-i-Gargar canal, Iran. The dam provides one of the earliest examples of hydropower in the Muslim world. Tunnels cut through the rock on either side of the channel housed mills that provided the power for operating industrial milling processes.

Following pages: A fine example of a 17th century brass astrolabe (Exhibition Islam collection).

Geography

Muslims travelled widely during the Middle Ages. They travelled on pilgrimage to Makkah and on vast caravans for trade across Africa, the Middle East, America and Asia. Therefore, geography and map making (cartography) were important subjects. Al-Idrisi (1099-1166) is best known in the West as a geographer, who made a silver globe weighing 400kg for the Christian King Roger II of Sicily. Some scholars regard him as the greatest geographer and cartographer of the Middle Ages, who put together a geographical encyclopaedia containing many maps.

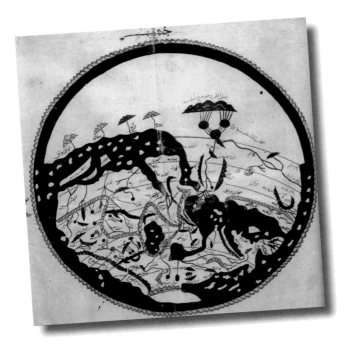

Above: Piri Reis (full name Hadji Muhiddin Piri Ibn Hadji Mehmed) was a famous admiral of the Turkish fleet in the sixteenth century. The surviving fragment of his first world map (1513) shows the western coast of Africa, the eastern coast of South America and the northern coast of Antarctica. The most striking characteristic of the map, however, is the level of accuracy in positioning the continents (particularly the relation between Africa and South America) which was unparalleled for its time. Even maps drawn decades later did not have such accurate positioning and proportions; a quality which can be observed in other maps of Piri Reis in his *Kitab-ı Bahriye* (*Book of Navigation*). The map of Piri Reis perfectly fits an azimuthal equidistant projection of the world centred in Cairo and some believe it's also the oldest surviving map of Antarctica, despite being drawn more than 3 centuries before the official discovery of that continent.

Left: A 12th century world map by Al-Idrisi was drawn with north at the bottom.

Mathematics

Although most Islamic texts on mathematics were written in Arabic, they were not all written by Arabs, as Arabic was used as the written language of non-Arab scholars throughout the Islamic world at the time. Some of the most important Islamic mathematicians were Persian.

Muhammad ibn Musa al-Kwarizmi, a 9th century Persian mathematician and astronomer to the Caliph of Baghdad, wrote several important books on the Hindu-Arabic numerals and on methods for solving equations. His book on 'Calculation with Hindu Numerals', written about 825, along with the work of the Arab mathematician al-Kindi, were instrumental in spreading Indian mathematics and Indian numerals to the West. The word algorithm is derived from the Latinization of his name, *Algoritmi* and the word algebra from the title of one of his works, *Al-Kitab al-mukhtasar fi hisab al-gabr wa'l-muqabala* (*The Compendious Book on Calculation by Completion and Balancing*). Al-Khwarizmi is often called the "father of algebra", for his preservation of ancient algebraic methods and for his original contributions to the field.

Another famous mathematician, al-Batani (850 - 929), travelled widely in the Middle East and India. He was the first person to introduce the Indian numbering system and the concept of the zero to the Middle East. Later this numbering system would replace Roman numerals in Europe. The use of the zero enabled Muslims to denote units of tens, hundreds and so on. When this numerical system was introduced to Medieval Europe it transformed the whole science of mathematics. Even in the West today the numbering system is still known as Arabic numerals.

Above: Pythagorean Theorem in the Arabic translation of Euclid's elements, revised by al-Tusi.

Below: *The Compendious Book on Calculation by Completion and Balancing,* written in the 9th century by Al-Kawarizmi "the father of algebra". The book was first translated into Latin in the 12th century.

Medicine

In the field of medicine two of the most famous physicians that lived in the Islamic world were al-Razi (865-925) and Ibn Sina (980-1037). Considered the world's best clinician of the Middle Ages, al-Razi, during the 10th century, made great advances in the treatment of kidney stones and bladder problems. He also presented the first ever clinical report on smallpox which, included a method for vaccination. Ibn Sina's famous medical book *The Canon of Medicine* (*al-Qanun fi al-Tibb*) was a monumental work. It contained a million words spread over 14 volumes. It is regarded as the single most famous book in the history of medicine; and it remained a standard medical reference text in Europe for over 700 years.

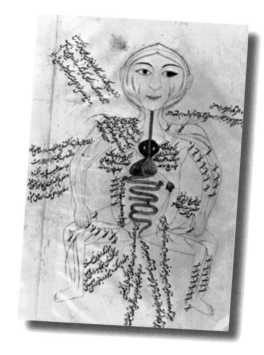

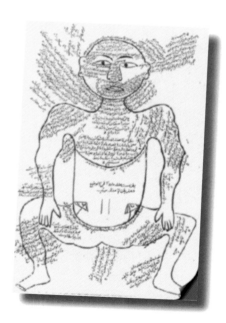

Above: Diagram with extensive text denoting the layout of the muscles, from *The Anatomy of the Human Body* (*Tashrih-i badan-i insan*) written in Persian at the end of the 14th century by Mansur ibn Ilyas.

Above: Anatomical drawing. Arabic medicine was advanced in Europe throughout the Middle Ages. From the very first medical school of Salerno down to Vesalius, Western doctors were taught by the Muslims.

Below: Pages from Ibn Sina's famous medical book, *The Canon of Medicine* (*al-Qanun fi al-tibb*).

Ophthalmology

In the field of Ophthalmology, Muslim scientists produced many original works on the anatomy of the eye. They introduced terms such as Conjunctiva, Cornea and Retina. However, the greatest single contribution by Muslim Ophthalmologists, was in the field of cataracts. As early as the 10th Century cataract operations were being performed in places such as Baghdad.

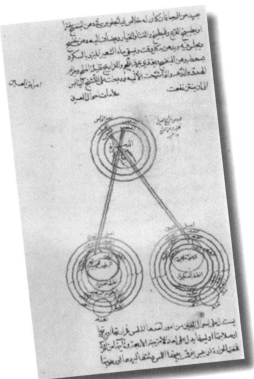

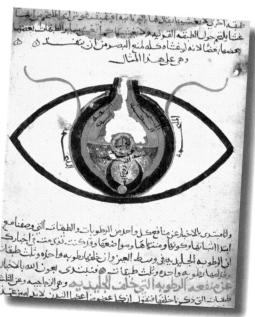

Above: Pages from a book called *The Result of Thinking about the Cure of Eye Diseases* (*Natijat al-Fikar fi `Ilaj Amrad al-Basar*) written in Cairo by Fath al-Din al-Qaysi during the 13th century.

Above right: Eye diagram showing eye function, from an abridgement of the 10th century *Qanun* (*Canon*) of Ibn Sina by Ibn al-Nafis

Right: Arabic manuscript on the *Anatomy of the Eye* written around the year 1200 by al-Mutadibih.

Pharmacy

In pharmacy and pharmacology, Muslim scientists made great contributions. By the 9th century, pharmacy was a recognised profession in the Islamic world. Every major city had numerous pharmacies not only in the market place but also in hospitals and clinics. In the 11th century, al-Biruni wrote one of the most influential books in this field called, *The Book of Pharmacology*. He outlined the properties of drugs and defined the functions and role of a pharmacist. In line with regulations nowadays, by the 12th century, many Islamic cities started to implement and enforce health and safety procedures in pharmacies.

Above: Decorated opening of *The Storehouse of Medicaments Concerning the Explanation of Materia Medica (Makhzan al-Adwiyah Dar-i Bayan-i Adwiyah)* by the 18th Century physician Muhammad Husayn ibn Muhammad Hadi al-`Aqili al-`Alavi, a practitioner in India.

Surgery

Many physicians such as, al-Zahrawi (930 to 1013) and Ibn Sina also practised surgery. These two physicians along with al-Razi greatly inspired Europe. Most of their works were translated into Latin and served as standard medical and surgical references in Europe for hundreds of years.

As far back as the 10th century, when surgery in Europe was dishonourably considered the practice of "quacks" and "barbers", trained Muslim surgeons were performing a huge array of surgical procedures. Their success was mainly due to the use of fine sutures, the soporific sponge (the precursor of modern anaesthesia; a sponge soaked with aromatics and narcotics and held to the patient's nostrils) and the use of purified alcohol to wounds as an antiseptic agent. Remarkably, the first European use of antiseptics in surgery was some eight centuries later by the British surgeon Joseph Lister in 1865.

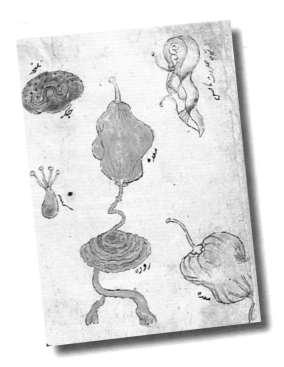

Above: Anatomical drawings appended to a Persian translation of an Arabic medical compendium.

Left: An image of the highly influential 12th century book on surgery called *al-Tasrif* by al-Zahrawi. The 30-volume work includes anatomical descriptions, classifications of diseases and information on nutrition and surgery. It was used by doctors and surgeons throughout Europe for over five hundred years, where it was known by the Latin title *Concessio*.

The treatise also contained detailed colour drawings of over two hundred surgical instruments designed by surgeons from the Islamic world. At the time, these types of surgical instruments were considered the most advanced in the world and revolutionised the practice of surgery. Amazingly, some of these instruments are indistinguishable from those used in modern surgery.

Islamic Crafts

The material culture of Islam has been and still remains, immensely rich and varied to this present day. The magnificently diverse arts of Islam range from huge architectural developments, miniature painting, book binding, beautiful Quranic calligraphy, lacquer, metalwork, unique pottery, ceramics, glass and rock crystal, arms and armour, lavish textiles and coins. Islamic art is characterized by Quranic calligraphy and geometric design and continues to enrich Islamic culture and influence many artists today. It is far beyond the scope of this book to discuss this subject in detail. A sample of the more unique exhibits from Exhibition Islam's collection are presented in the following pages.

Opposite: A beautiful 18th century Islamic Mosque Lamp made from blown enamelled glass (Exhibition Islam collection).

Artefacts from the Exhibition Islam collection.

Above: 19th Century Ottoman General's button made from silver and enamel.

Above and top right: A series of extensively decorated 18th century Middle Eastern metal ware pieces.

18th century brass Ottoman oil lamp in the shape of a shoe (Exhibition Islam collection).

A very rare 9th century oil lamp from Jerusalem. Traditional Islamic design and made from clay (Exhibition Islam collection).

18th century Ottoman scribes' inkwell made from brass (Exhibition Islam collection).

Islamic Coins

The coins of the Islamic world presented here are primarily religious, political and cultural documents which form a unique historical record. Classical Muslim coins usually proclaim faith in Allah, The Unique and Everlasting and also affirm the Prophethood of Muhammad (ﷺ), the Messenger of Allah. They also generally contain a statement of the place and date in which they were struck and, frequently the name of the ruler, his father, the future heir or political overlords. This enables the student to understand the interrelationships which bound each dynasty to the larger world of Islam.

If the complete series of coins issued by every Muslim dynasty were preserved and published, historians would be able to list with accuracy the names of each ruler and his principal vassals in every part of the world of Islam from the second century of Islam. They would also be able to determine with considerable accuracy the boundaries of each Islamic civilisation, at every point in its history.

Why have Muslim coins always been so important? In an age before newspapers, radio and television, the mosque and the coinage were the primary means of communication between a ruler and his people and, statements made through both mediums had the power of law behind them. The protection of Allah was invoked for the well-being of the sovereign whose name was proclaimed by the *Imam* from the *Minbar* (his seat of authority) to the congregation of the faithful during the Friday sermon (*Khutba*).

Furthermore, coins bearing the ruler's name and those of the cities under his rule, reminded his subjects of his power and responsibility for their economic needs. A change of ruler was made official when he was first mentioned publicly in the Friday sermon and when coins were issued in his name.

Above: The earliest Islamic coins in existence date back to around 652-664 during the rule of the Caliphs Uthman ibn Affan (رضي الله عنه) and Ali Ibn Abi Talib (رضي الله عنه). The above example is an Arab Sasanian coin from the old Persian empire and is one of the oldest coins in Exhibition Islam's prestigious Islamic coins collection. When Persian rule came to an end, the Muslim rulers carried on using the old coinage of the deposed Persian emperor so as not to cause unnecessary suffering in society especially to many of the poor and needy. However, coins were all marked with the Arabic inscription 'Bismillah' meaning 'In Name of Allah'.

Coins from the Exhibition Islam collection.

Silver coin minted by the Caliph Abd al -Rahman III during Spanish Muslim rule in the 10th century.

Arab Byzantine coin minted around 670-700 in Palestine

Coin minted around 750 during Umayyad Caliphate in Palestine/Syria.

11th century coin minted by Yayha al-Mamun the ruler of Toledo, Spain.

1/2 Quirate minted by Ibn Wazir in 12th century Islamic Portugal.

Arab Byzantine coin minted in 670-700 in Emissa, Syria.

Islamic Architecture

Islam influences every aspect of daily life for the follower. It is hardly surprising therefore, to see the way of life reflected in architecture, urban design and our natural environment. Islam is not a nomadic or a monastic tradition nor one that has a sub-culture based on prestige. Islamic civilisation did not see monasteries and nomadic retreats set up outside of the general populace. Islam teaches that all Muslims are equal before Allah and there are certain obligations on each and every Muslim not just on a few individuals. Enlightenment, prayer, reflection and worship is for everyone.

The focus on collective worship, the congregational prayer, cleanliness, attendance of the mosque on a daily and weekly basis, are obligations that involve the whole community. The mosque or *masjid* is at the very heart of every Islamic community. Throughout Islamic history, the *masjid* complex has always performed a variety of functions and is not just regarded as a place for prayer alone; it can act, for example, as a school, university, hospital and even a fort.

The Prophet Muhammad (ﷺ) wanted to ensure that ideas of nationalism, tribalism and racism played no part in Islamic communities. Thus, cities became cultural melting pots and in many places Islam emerged as a civilisation with different cultures and religions. Apart from Makkah and Madinah, there were not many cities in the Islamic world where the population was entirely Muslim. Muslims have always lived alongside Jewish and Christian communities. As Islam expanded and grew becoming the dominant political force within the Middle East,

the tolerance towards other religions did not disappear. To this day, communities of Jews and Christians can be found all over the Middle East.

Such was the success of the organisation and planning of early Islamic cities that many of the major cities that span from Algiers to Delhi and beyond can be traced back to an Islamic past. Although it is beyond the scope of this book to give a detailed review of Islamic architecture, this section has been included to briefly illustrate the rich history of Islamic civilisation. From the beautiful Ottoman arches of the Prophet Muhammad's (ﷺ) Mosque in Madinah and the majestic domes and slender minarets of the Grand Suleymaniye mosque in Istanbul, to the peaceful gardens of the al-Hambra in Granada and the geometric design of the Dome of the Rock in Jerusalem, all celebrate the Oneness of Allah in their own unique way.

Opposite page: 1. Mosque of 'Amr ibn al-'As, Cairo, was rebuilt and enlarged in 673 during the reign of Mu'awiya.

2. Citadel of Bukhara built around 705.

3. Courtyard of the Umayyad mosque in Damascus built in the 8th century.

4. Masjid al-Aqsa in Jerusalem was completed by Caliph Abd ul Malik in 647.

5. The 'Dome of the Rock' in Jerusalem was built by Abd ul Malik in 685.

6. Great Mosque of Guangzhou, built in 700, China.

1.

2.

3.

4.

5.

6.

1. Great Mosque of Shibam, Yemen, built around 753.

2. Entrance to the Mosque of Isfahan in Iran was built in 771.

3. Ibn Tulun Mosque completed around 876, Cairo.

4. The immense brick minaret of the Great Mosque of Samarra stands a staggering 55 metres high.

5. Aerial view of the Great Mosque of Samarra in Iraq, built between 847-861.

6. Al Azhar, University built in 969, Cairo, Egypt.

7. Multifoil arches inside the 10th century Great Mosque of Cordoba, Spain.

8. Rising like a rocket pointed to the sky the Tower of Qabus (Gunbad-i Qabus) was built in the 11 century, Iran.

9. 10th century Niujie Mosque, Beijing, China.

10. Al-Hambra built in the 11th century, Granada, Spain.

6.

7.

8.

9.

10.

Described in poetry as a 'pearl set in emeralds', the exquisite 11th century Islamic architecture of the Al-Hambra is reflected in its central pool. This ancient complex of buildings served as a mosque, palace and fortress of the Muslim rulers of Granada, in southern Spain (known as Al-Andalus when the fortress was constructed). Occupying a hilly terrace on the south-eastern border of the city of Granada, it was the residence of the Muslim rulers of Granada and their court. It is currently a museum exhibiting Islamic architecture. The situation of the Al-Hambra is one of rare natural beauty; the plateau commands a wide view of the city and plain of Granada, towards the west and north and, of the heights of the Sierra Nevada towards the east and south.

1.

2.

3.

1. Ichan-Kala mosque complex built in the 10th century in Khiva, Uzbekistan.

2. Minaret of the 12 th century Quwwatu'l Islam mosque in Delhi, India.

3. Great Mosque of Diyarbakir built in 1091, Turkey.

4. The 12th century Charbagh Mosque in Bukhara, Uzbekistan.

5. Evening shot of the Koutoubia Mosque, Marrakech, Morocco.

6. Completed in 1271 the Cifte Minaret Madrasa in Sivas, Turkey.

7. Salah al-Din (Saladin), best remembered as the Arab commander who recaptured Jerusalem (al-Quds) from the Crusaders in 1187, governed Egypt until his death in 1193. He began the fortifications we know as 'the Citadel' on a spur in the eastern Muqqatim hills in 1176 and took about four years to complete them. He also built hospitals, and *madrassas* (schools) and put into place a plan to provide for public education. The *madrassa* or teaching mosque, was introduced to Egypt by Salah al-Din.

4.

5.

6.

7.

1. Founded in the late 15th century, the city of Mostar in Bosnia was the chief administrative city for the Ottoman Empire. The city's symbol, The Old Bridge (Stari Most) is one of the most important constructions of the Ottoman Era.

2 & 3. Views of the sumptuous Al-Hambra palace, Granada, Spain.

4. 15th century Ulugh Beg Observatory, Samarkand, Uzbekistan.

5. View of the Old city of Baku in Azerbaijan.

6. Topkapi Palace built in 1718, Istanbul, Turkey.

4.

5.

6.

1. Highly decorated dome of the 16th century Selimiye Mosque, Edirne, Turkey.

2. Mosque in the city of Monastir, Tunisia.

3 & 4. The Great Mosque of Djenné is the largest mud brick or adobe building in the world and is considered by many architects to be the greatest achievement of the Sudano-Sahelian architectural style, albeit with definite Islamic influences. The mosque is located in the city of Djenné, Mali on the flood plain of the Bani River.

5. Great Mosque of Khotan, China 1870.

6. The Badshahi Mosque, or the 'Emperor's Mosque', was built in 1673 by the Mughal Emperor Aurangzeb in Lahore, Pakistan.

7. The old mosque of Yambol in Bulgaria was built in the 15th century.

5.

7.

6.

Above and opposite: A colossal architectural achievement, the cascading domes and four slender minarets of the magnificent Imperial Suleymaniye Mosque, dominate the skyline on the Golden Horn's west bank. Considered the most beautiful of all imperial mosques in Istanbul, it was built between 1550 and 1557 by Sinan, the renowned architect of the Ottoman Empire's golden age. Erected on the crest of a hill, the building is conspicuous for its great size, emphasized by the four minarets that rise from each corner of the courtyard. The prayer niche (*Mihrab*) showing the direction to Makkah and the pulpit (*Minbar*) are made of finely carved white marble. Exquisite stained-glass windows add to the grandeur by colouring the incoming streams of light. The mosque complex also includes four theological schools, a school of medicine, a caravanserai, a Turkish bath, a kitchen and a hospice for the poor.

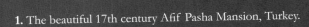

1. The beautiful 17th century Afif Pasha Mansion, Turkey.

2. 15-17th century Registan Square, Samarqand, Uzbekistan.

3. Completed in 1636, the Sher Dor Madrassa, Samarkand, Uzbekistan.

4. Built in 1622 (Bukhara, Central Asia), the Nadir Divanbigi mosque school creates a dramatic reflection.

Opposite page: An 18th century Ottoman kiosk in Turkey. The high proportion of glass used in the Sofa Kosku gives it a modern appearance.

The Mosque of Muhammad Ali in Cairo, was built over a period of 24 years, from 1824-48. It was modelled on the Blue Mosque in Istanbul.

Islamic Glossary

A:

Abbasids
The Abbasids were the second dynasty of Caliphs who reigned from 750 to 1258 CE. They helped to improve relations between Arab and non-Arab Muslims of all ethnic origins. In 762 CE, the Abbasid's built Baghdad now in Iraq and made it their capital city. The Abbasid Caliphate was finally abolished when Hulagu, the Mongol ruler, captured Baghdad in 1258, destroying much of the city including its unique libraries.

Adhaan
Adhaan is the Islamic way of calling Muslims to the five obligatory prayers. The Adhaan is announced from the mosques at every prayer time.

A.H.
Abbreviation of 'After Hijra' or 'Anno Hegirae' (Latin). Hijrah means emigration. The Islamic calendar is used in Muslim countries and by Muslims everywhere and starts from the year Prophet Muhammad (ﷺ) emigrated (made Hijrah) from the city of Makkah to Madinah, in 622 C.E. It is purely a lunar calendar having 12 lunar months in a year of about 354 days. The lunar year is about 11 days shorter than the solar year. Muslim holy days, although celebrated on fixed dates in their own calendar, usually occur 11 days earlier each successive solar year.

Ahl al-Dimmah (or Dhimmis)
Literally translated as 'The People of Protection.' The non-Muslim subjects of an Islamic State who have been guaranteed protection of their lives, property and practice of their religion.

Ahl al-Kitab
Literally translated as 'The People of the Book.' The term applies to the followers of monotheistic Abrahamic faiths who received revelation(s) (hence 'book') from Allah.

Ahmad
Another name of the Prophet Muhammad (ﷺ).

Al-Akhirah
The term encompasses the after-life, hereafter and the next world.

Al
Arabic for the word 'the'.

'Alim (pl. Ulemaa)
An Islamic religious scholar.

Allah
Allah - the greatest and most inclusive of the names of God. It is an Arabic word of rich meaning, denoting the one who is adored in worship, who creates all that exists, who has priority over all creation and who is lofty and hidden, who confounds all human understanding. The Arabic word 'Allah' has no gender associated with it.

Allahu Akbar
'Allah is the Greatest'.

Al-Haram ash-Shareef
Literally translated as 'The Sacred Sanctuary'. There are three Holy Sanctuaries: the first in Makkah, the second in Madinah and the third in Jerusalem around Masjid al-Aqsa.

Amirul Mumineen
Commander of the Faithful. Title of the leader of the Islamic dominion after the death of Prophet Muhammad (ﷺ).

Ansaar
Ansar means the 'helpers.' (singular: Ansari). In Islamic parlance the word refers to the Muslims of Madinah who helped the Muhajiroon (immigrants) of Makkah to adjust to their new environment.

Aqeedah
Comes from the Arabic word 'Aqd' which means 'bind' or 'knot'. It is used in reference to the six articles of Islamic faith that 'bind' Muslims together. The six articles of faith are:
1. Belief in Allah, the One God, 2. Belief in Allah's angels, 3. Belief in His revealed books, 4. Belief in His Messengers, 5. Belief in the Day of Judgment, 6. Belief in fate and the divine decree.

Arafat
Arafat is a pilgrimage site, about 25 kilometres east of Makkah. Standing on Arafat on the 9th day of Dhul-Hijjah and staying there from mid-day to sunset is the essence of the Hajj (the Pilgrimage).

'Asr
'Asr is the late afternoon prayer, the third compulsory prayer of the day. It can be prayed between mid-afternoon and a little before sunset. It is also the name of Chapter 103 of the Quran.

Assalamu 'Alaikum
Assalamu 'alaikum means 'Peace be on you.' It is the greeting of the Muslims. The response to this greeting is 'Wa 'Alaikum Assalam,' meaning 'And on you be peace.'

Ayah (pl. ayat)

Ayah means a sign (or 'token') which directs one to something important. In the Quran the word has been used in four different senses: (1) sign or indication; (2) the phenomena of the universe; (3) miracles performed by the Prophets; and (4) individual units (i.e. verses) of the Quran.

Ayyubids

Caliphate dynasty with Kurdish origins founded by Salah ad-Din b. Ayyub in 1171 to 1250, which ruled Egypt, Syria and northern Iraq.

B:

Badr

Badr is located to the south of Madinah and is the site of the first great battle between Prophet Muhammad (ﷺ) and the pagan Makkans in the year 624. The Muslim army consisted of 313 men and the Quraish had a total of about 1,000 soldiers, archers and horsemen. See Quran, Al-Anfal (8:5-19, 42-48) and Al-Imran (3:13).

Baitul Mal

An Islamic treasury intended for the benefit of the Muslims and the Islamic State and not for the leaders or the wealthy.

Baitul Maqdis

Al-Aqsa Mosque, the famous Masjid in Al-Quds (Jerusalem). It was the first Qiblah of Islam before Allah ordered Muslims to face the first House of Allah, the Kaaba in Makkah (Arabia). Baitul Maqdis is the third greatest Masjid in the Islamic world, the first being the Masjid Al-Haram in Makkah and the second being the Masjid al-Nabawi (the Mosque of the Prophet (ﷺ). It is from the surroundings of Baitul Maqdis that Prophet Muhammad (ﷺ) ascended to heaven. See Quran, Al-Isra (17:1).

Bakka

Another name for Makkah. See Quran, Al-Imran (3:96).

Barzakh

Literally means partition or barrier. In Islamic terminology it usually means the life in the grave, as the life in the grave is the bridge between life on earth and the life in the Hereafter. Life in the Barzakh is real but very different from life as we know it. Its exact nature is known only to Allah.

Bid'ah

Any innovated practice introduced in the religion of Islam. The Prophet Muhammad (ﷺ) said that every Bid'a is a deviation from the true path and every deviation leads to Hellfire.

Bismillah

'In the name of Allah'. This utterance is usually made by every Muslim who is about to embark on something lawful (Halal), regardless of the magnitude of the task.

D:

Dajjal

Anti-Christ. Also known as Maseeh ad-Dajjal. See hadith regarding 'the Final Hour' in both Saheeh books: Saheeh Bukhari, Hadith 649, 650, Vol. IV and Saheeh Muslim, Kitab al-Fitan wa Isharat as-Say'ah.

Dawah

Propagation of Islam through word and action, calling the people to follow the commandments of Allah and His messenger, the Prophet Muhammad (ﷺ).

Dhu'l-Hijjah

The twelfth month of the Islamic calendar. The month in which the great pilgrimage to Makkah takes place.

Dhu'l Qa'da

The eleventh month of the Islamic calendar.

Dhuhr

Noon. The second obligatory prayer (Salah) of the day. It can be prayed from the time when the sun begins to decline from its zenith until mid-afternoon.

Deen

As a Quranic technical term, *Deen* refers to the religion or way of life and the system of conduct based on recognizing Allah as one's sovereign and committing oneself to obey Him. According to Islam, true deen consists of living in total submission to Allah and the way to do so is to accept as binding the guidance communicated through Prophet Muhammad (ﷺ). See the following verses of the Quran for reference: 3:83, 12:76, 16:52 and 51:6.

Du'a

Supplication; invoking Allah for whatever one needs/ desires.

E:

Eemaan
Literally belief or faith. Imaan is the testification of the Islamic declaration of faith (the Shahadah) whilst believing in it and thereafter acting upon it.

Eid Al-'Adha
A four-day festival that completes the rites of pilgrimage and takes place on the 10th to 13th of Dhul Hijjah (the 10th is the day of Nahr and 11th to 13th are the days of Tashriq.) Literally means "the feast of the sacrifice." This commemorates Prophet Abrahams (عليه السلام) obedience to Allah by being prepared to sacrifice his only son Ishmael (عليه السلام). See Quran, as-Saffaat (37:100-103).

Eid Al-Fitr
A festival marking the end of Ramadan. It takes place on the 1st of Shawal, the tenth month of the Islamic calendar.

F:

Fajr
"The Dawn". The time of the first daily obligatory prayer (Salah). It can be prayed at any time between the first light of dawn and just before sunrise.

Faqeeh
An Islamic scholar who can give a legal opinion or judgment.

Fasad
Literally 'corruption', in Quranic terminology, means creating disorder and corruption on earth by following a path other than Allah's.

Fatwa
A legal verdict given on a religious basis.

Fidya
Compensation for missing or wrongly practising obligatory acts of worship. Fidya usually takes the form of donating money, foodstuffs, or sacrificing an animal.

Fiqh
Islamic jurisprudence.

Fi sabilillah
Fi sabilillah (in the way of Allah) is a frequently used expression in the Quran which emphasizes that good acts should be done exclusively to please Allah. The expression has been used in the Quran in connection with striving or spending for charitable purposes.

H:

Hadith (pl. ahadith)
Literally means communication or narration. In the Islamic context, it has come to denote the record of what the Prophet Muhammad (ﷺ) said, did, or tacitly approved. The whole body of traditions is termed Hadith and the Hadith collections are regarded as important tools for determining the Sunnah, or Muslim way of life, by all traditional schools of jurisprudence.

I:

'Ibadah
'Ibadah is used in three meanings: (1) worship and adoration; (2) obedience and submission; and (3) service and subjection. The fundamental message of Islam is that man, as Allah's creature, should direct his 'ibadah to Him in all the above-mentioned meanings and associate none in the rendering of it.

Iblis
Iblis literally means 'thoroughly disappointed; one in utter despair.' In Islamic terminology it denotes the jinn, who refused the command of Allah to prostrate before Prophet Adam (عليه السلام) out of vanity. He also asked Allah to allow him a term when he might mislead and tempt mankind to error. This term was granted to him by Allah whereafter, he became the chief promoter of evil and prompted Adam and Eve to disobey Allah's order. He is also called al-Shaytan (Satan).

'Iddah
'Iddah denotes the waiting period that a woman is required to observe before remarrying as a consequence of the nullification of her marriage with her husband or because of the husband's death. For details see the Quran, Al-Baqara (2:228-235), At-Talaq (65:4-7).

Iftar
Breaking of the fast immediately after sunset as soon as the call to prayer (Adhaan) is called.

Ihram
Ihram denotes the state of consecration which is essentially required for performing Hajj and 'Umrah. The outward garb which consists of, in the case of men, just two sheets of cloth instead of tailored clothes, is one of the conditions of ihram. One is also required to pronounce *talbiyah* - "Here I am at your service, Oh Lord, here I am - here I am. No partner do you have. Here I am. Truly, the praise and the

favour are yours and the dominion. You have no partner." In the state of ihram the pilgrim is required to observe many prohibitions e.g. they may not hunt, shed blood, use perfume, shave or trim their hair or indulge in sexual gratification.

Ihsan
Ihsan literally denotes doing something in a good manner. When used in the Islamic religious context, it signifies excellence of behaviour arising out of a strong love for Allah and a profound sense of close relationship with Him. According to a tradition, Prophet Muhammad (ﷺ) defined ihsan as worshipping Allah as though one sees Him.

Ijmaa
Ijmaa refers to scholarly consensus. Ijmaa comes next to the Quran and the Sunnah as a source of Islamic Law. Ijmaa is not restricted to eminent scholars (mujtahidun) of Islam in a given age. Ijmaa is more inclusive and can be of the ummah, the sahaaba, or the ulema.

Ijtihad
Is the judgment of a qualified scholar upon an issue, basing his judgment upon the Quran and Sunnah.

Injil
Injil signifies the inspired orations and utterances of Jesus (ﷺ) which he delivered during the last two or three years of his earthly life in his capacity as a Prophet. The Injil mentioned by the Quran however, should not be identified by the four Gospels of the New Testament which contain a great deal of material in addition to the inspired statements of the Prophet Jesus (ﷺ). Presumably, the statements explicitly attributed to Jesus (peace be upon him) constitute parts of the true, original Injil. It is significant, however, that the statements explicitly attributed to Jesus (ﷺ) in the Gospels contain similar teachings as those of the Quran.

Insha Allah
"If Allah wills."

Iqaamah
The call to prayer which announces to the congregation that obligatory prayers are about to begin.

Ishaa'
Ishaa' (Night) Prayer signifies the prescribed prayer which is performed after the night has well set in.

Islam
Literally means "submission to the will of Allah." The most important and pivotal concept in Islam is the oneness of Allah (See Allah for more on the concept of God). Islam teaches that all faiths have, in essence, one common message:

- the existence of a Supreme Being, the one and only God, whose sovereignty is to be acknowledged in worship and in the pledge
- to obey His teaching and commandments, conveyed through His messengers and Prophets who were sent at various times and in many places throughout history.

Islam demands a commitment to submit and surrender to Allah so that one can live in peace; peace (salam) is achieved through active obedience to the revealed Commandments of Allah, for Allah is the Source of all Peace. Commitment to Islam entails striving for peace through a struggle for justice, equality of opportunity, mutual caring and consideration for others' rights and continuous research and acquisition of knowledge for the better protection and utilization of the resources of the universe. The basic beliefs of Islam are:

- the Uniqueness of the one and only God who is Sovereign of the universes;
- the Revelation of the teaching and commandments of Allah through Angels in heaven to Prophets on earth and written in sacred writings which all have the same transcendent source; these contain the will of Allah which marks the way of peace for the whole universe and all mankind;
- the Day of Judgment which inaugurates the afterlife in which Allah rewards and punishes with respect to human obedience to His will.

Islam teaches that human diversity is a sign of the richness of Allah's mercy and that Allah wills human beings to compete with each other in goodness in order to test who is the finest in action, this is (according to Islam) the reason for the creation of the universe. A person who enters the fold of Islam is called a Muslim.

Isra
1. The 'Night Journey', refers to the journey of Prophet Muhammad (ﷺ) from Makkah to Masjid Al-Aqsa in Jerusalem.
2. Another name for Chapter Bani Israel (Chapter 17) of the Quran.

J:

Jahannam
Most commonly understood to mean Hell. In fact, it is one of the levels of Hell. There are seven levels of Hellfire.

Jahiliyah
Jahiliyah, literally 'ignorance', is a concise expression for the pagan practice of the days before the advent of the Prophet Muhammad (ﷺ). Jahiliyah denotes all those world-views and ways of life which are based on rejection or disregard of heavenly guidance communicated to mankind through the Prophets and messengers of Allah. It refers to the attitude of treating human life, either wholly or partly, as independent of the directives of Allah.

Jannah
Paradise. A created abode in the Hereafter containing unimaginable delights for those who believe in the Unity of Allah and in all His Prophets and Messengers and who follow the way of life of the Prophets. Jannah has eight gates around it and each of these eight gates has eleven doors.

Jihad
Jihad literally means 'to strive' or 'to exert to the utmost.' In Islamic terminology, it signifies all forms of striving including armed struggle.

Jinn
Jinn are an independent species of creation about which little is known. Unlike man, who was created out of earth, the jinn were created out of fire. But like man, a Divine Message has also been addressed to them and they too have been endowed with the capacity, again like man, to choose between good and evil, between obedience or disobedience to Allah. See Chapter 72 (Al-Jinn) of the Quran.

Jumada al-Awwal
The fifth month of the Islamic calendar.

Jumada al-Thani
The sixth month of the Islamic calendar.

K:

Kaaba
The cube-shaped stone building whose foundations were built by the angels and completed by Prophet Ibrahim (Abraham) and his son Prophet Ishmael (ﷺ) in Makkah. It was rebuilt with the help of Prophet Muhammad (ﷺ). It is the focal point towards which all Muslims face when praying.

Kabair (al)
Major sins such as Shirk (see Shirk), Qatl (murder), Zinah (fornication and adultery), the taking of Riba (usury), Sirq (theft).

Kawthar (al)
1. "The fountain of Kawthar." A sacred fountain in Jannah (Paradise). It is the source of all the four rivers of Jannah and feeds the Hawd (pool) of the Blessed Prophet Muhammad (ﷺ). The Hawd which is filled by Al-Kawthar is at the end of the Siratul Mustaqeem. It is a gift from Allah to the Prophet Muhammad (ﷺ). It is to quench the thirst of true believers (see Chapter 108, Al-Kawthar of the Quran).

Khalifah
Vicegerent. The Latinized equivalent is Caliph. Derived from the verb 'khalaf' meaning 'to succeed', the term Khalifah was used for the next leader and successor after the Blessed Prophet Muhammad (ﷺ) as a ruler over the Muslim Nation. The Khilafah was the domain of the rule.

Khutbah
Sermon. The greatest sermon in the history of mankind was called al-Khutbatul Wida' (the farewell address), given by the Prophet Muhammad (ﷺ), during his last Hajj in 10 A.H. There are various types of sermons, the most common one being the 'Friday Sermon' (Khutba ul-Jumaa).

Kufi
An Arabic writing style often used for early hand-written copies of the Quran.

L:

Lailatul-Qadr
'The Night of Power,' concealed in one of the odd nights in the last ten days of Ramadan; the night on which the Quran was first revealed by the angel Jibreel (Gabriel) to the Prophet Muhammad (ﷺ) and which the Quran itself describes as "better than a thousand months." See the Quran, Al-Qadr (97:3).

Lauh al-Mahfudh

A guarded tablet in the Seventh Heaven. The Quran was first written on the Lauh al-Mahfudh in its entirety before it was sent down to the Baitul 'Izza in the First Heaven.

M:

Maghrib

Sunset. The fourth obligatory prayer of the day. It consists of three Rakahs (units of prayer) and can be offered between just after sunset and before the stars appear in the sky.

Mahr

Mahr (bridal gift) signifies the amount of payment that is settled between the two spouses at the time of marriage and which the husband is required to give to his bride.

Mahram

A close male family member of a woman who can be in private with her (e.g. father, brother, uncle, son, etc.). Her husband is also her Mahram (See The Quran Al-Nur, 24:31).

Malaikah

Angels. Another name for Surah Fatir, Chapter 35 of the Quran.

Mamluks

The word 'mamluk' is an Arabic term for slave and was applied to soldiers used by the Muslim Caliphs and the Ottoman Empire. The Mamluks increased their power and by 1250 they deposed and appointed sultans, ruling until 1517. They were based on Roda island in the Nile delta and later in Cairo.

Mash'ar al-Haram

The boundary of Al-Masjid al-Haram in Makkah. It is prohibited to kill any game, or to damage any plant or tree, or to act in any manner that will violate the sanctity of the Holy Masjid.

Masjid

A place of worship and salah. The life of a Muslim revolves around the masjid, where for example meetings and discussions take place. It is called a 'mosque' in English.

Masjid al-Aqsa

The 'Farthest Mosque' built by the early Muslims in Jerusalem and the third greatest Masjid in Islam.

Masjid Al-Haram (al)

The Grand Masjid in Makkah. The Kaaba (the Qiblah of the Muslims) is situated within it.

Masjid al-Nabawi

Another name for the Masjid ar-Rasool or Prophet Muhammad's (ﷺ) mosque in Madinah. It is the second greatest Masjid in Islam, the first being the Masjid al-Haram in Makkah and the third being the Masjid al-Aqsa in Al-Quds (Jerusalem).

Mihraab

Prayer niche of a masjid where the Imam stands when leading the congregational prayers which, ascertains the direction of the Qibla.

Minbar

Steps on which the Imam stands to deliver the Khutba (sermon) on the day of Jumah (Friday).

Mina

A place five miles from Makkah and approximately ten miles from 'Arafat. An essential place to visit during the Hajj.

Mi'raj

Ascension of Prophet Muhammad (ﷺ) from Jerusalem to the realms of the seven heavens that took place in the year 620. See the Quran, Al-Isra (17:1), Bukhari Hadith 345, Vol. 1, 227, Vol. 5.

Mu'adhin

The man who calls the Adhaan loudly before each obligatory Salat, calling the people to prayer.

Muhadith (Plural: Muhaditheen)

An Islamic scholar of hadith.

Muhammad (ﷺ)

The last Prophet of Islam (570 to 632 C.E.), also called the 'Seal of the Prophets'. Allah revealed the Quran to the Last Prophet, Muhammad (ﷺ), starting in the year 610 CE. When Muslims write the Prophet's name, they usually include the statement 'Sallallahu 'Alayhi wa Sallam' or in Arabic ﷺ - this is often abbreviated to 'SAW'. The translation into English is 'May the peace and blessings of Allah be upon him'; or abbreviation 'pbuh'.

Muharram

The first month of the Islamic calendar.

Mujahideen
An Arabic term for those who engage in armed struggle (Jihad) against tyranny and oppression. The word is a plural form of mujahid, which literally translated from Arabic means 'struggler' but is often incorrectly translated in the West as 'holy warrior'.

Mumin
1. Believer.
2. Al-Mumin: Another name for Al-Ghafir, Chapter 40 of the Quran.

Muslim
A person who accepts Islam completely as his or her way of life.

Mustahab
An act in Islam that is recommended but not obligatory.

Muzdallifah
A site between 'Arafat and Mina where the pilgrims spend the night of the 9th of Dhul-Hijjah during Hajj.

N:

Nabi (Plural: Anbiyaa)
Prophet of Allah.

Nafl
A voluntary act of supererogatory devotion such as Nafl Prayer or Nafl Fast.

Naskh
A style of curved writing often used for early hand-written copies of the Quran and is still commonly used.

Nikah
Marriage contract requiring the consent of both man and women. Islam does allow divorce so this contract is revocable.

O:

Ottoman Empire
The Ottoman Empire was founded in the 13th century by Osman I from a tribe in Anatolia. The Ottomans ruled SE Europe, W Asia, & N Africa including to the greatest extent, Turkey, Syria, Mesopotamia, Palestine, Arabia, Egypt, Barbary States, Balkans, & parts of Russia and Hungary until the 20th century, superseding the Byzantine Empire.

The empire reached its greatest breadth across Asia and Europe under Sultan Suleiyman (1520-1566), called "The Lawmaker" in Islamic history and "The Magnificent" in Europe. Suleiyman controlled everything between Yemen to Vienna in Austria.

Q:

Qabr
Grave.

Qadr (al)
'The Power'. The night of Allah's power. Al-Qadr, Chapter 97 of the Quran.

Qiblah
Qiblah signifies the direction to which all Muslims are required to turn when offering their prescribed prayers namely, towards the Kaaba in Makkah, Arabia.

Quraish
The Prophet Muhammad (ﷺ) belonged to this Arab tribe.

Quran
The Holy book of the Muslims is the Quran that was revealed to the Prophet Muhammad (ﷺ) by the Angel Gabriel. It teaches human beings that they were created in order to worship Allah alone and that the basis of all true worship is being conscious of Allah. As such, worship in Islam is not limited to religious rituals but, any act done in seeking the pleasure of Allah becomes worship.

The existence of only one version of the Quran attests to the reverence in which Muslims hold it. For Muslims, the Quran, containing the word of Allah, provides irrefutable proof of His existence.

R:

Rabi ul-Awwal
The third month of the Islamic calendar.

Rahim
Rahim is from the root rhm (rahm) which denotes mercy. In the Quran, this attribute of Allah has been used side by side with Rahman (which is also from the same root rhm). As such Rahim signifies Allah's mercy and beneficence towards His creatures. Moreover, according to several scholars, the word Rahim signifies the dimension of permanence in Allah's mercy.

Rahman
Literally 'merciful' is one of the personal names of Allah. According to scholars of the Arabic language and some commentators of the Quran, the word has the nuance of intensity regarding Divine Mercy. Thus, the word does not just signify the One Who has mercy; it rather denotes the One Who is exceedingly merciful; the One Who is overflowing with mercy for all. Ar-Rahman: Chapter 55 of the Quran.

Rajab
The seventh month of the Islamic calendar.

Rak'ah (Plural: raka'at)
Represents a unit of the prayer and consists of bending the torso from an upright position followed by two prostrations.

Ramadan
The ninth month of the Islamic calendar.

Ruku'
Ruku' means to bend the body to bow. This bowing is one of the acts required in Islamic prayer. Additionally, the same word denotes a certain unit in the Quran. The whole Book, for the sake of the convenience of the reader is divided into thirty parts (ajza', sing. juz') and each juz' consists usually of sixteen ruku'.

Rasool
Messenger of Allah.

Riba
Literally means 'to grow; to increase.' Technically, it denotes the amount that a lender receives from a borrower at a fixed rate in excess of the principal. It is of two kinds: (1). Riba Nasi'a - taking interest on loaned money. (2). Riba Fadal - taking something of superior quality in exchange for giving less of the same kind of thing of poorer quality. In Islam interest is considered a sin and is forbidden.

Rooh al-Qudus
The Holy Spirit. Another name for the Angel Gabriel (Jibreel).

S:

Sabr
Sabr is a comprehensive term having various shades of meaning. It implies (1) patience in the sense of being thorough, dedicated and devoted; (2) constancy, perseverance, steadfastness and firmness of purpose; (3) disciplined and planned effort with confidence and belief in the mission itself; and (4) a cheerful attitude of acceptance and understanding under suffering and hardship and in times of strife and violence and thankfulness to Allah in happiness, success and achievement.

Sadaqah
Anything given away in charity for the pleasure of Allah.

Safar
The tenth month of the Islamic calendar.

Sahabi (Plural: Sahabiyeen)
The companions of the Prophet Muhammad (ﷺ). A Sahabi knew or saw the Prophet Muhammad (ﷺ), believed in his teachings and died as a Muslim.

Sahih Bukhari
A book of Ahadith (saying and actions of Prophet Muhammad (ﷺ) compiled by Imam Bukhari.

Sahih Muslim
A book of Ahadith compiled by Imam Muslim.

Sa'i
Going seven times between the small hills of Safa and Marwa; an essential rite of Hajj and Umrah.

Sajdah
1. Prostration. The act of prostration, particularly in the Salat. 2. As-Sajdah: Chapter 32 of the Quran.

Salah
Prayers. There are five daily obligatory prayers. These prayers and their time zones are:
(1) Fajr (morning prayer); After dawn but before sunrise;
(2) Dhuhr (early afternoon or noon prayer); early afternoon till late afternoon; (3) 'Asr (late afternoon prayer) late afternoon prayer till sunset; (4) Maghrib (sunset prayer); just after sunset; (5) Ishaa (late evening prayer); late evening till late at night. Each prayer consists of a fixed set of standings, bowings, prostrations and sittings in worship to Allah known as rakats.

Salat ul-Janazah
Funeral prayer. The prayer is performed in a standing position only.

Sallallahu 'Alayhi wa Sallam (S.A.W.)
Arabic transliteration meaning 'May the peace and blessings of Allah be upon him'. This is said whenever the name of Prophet Muhammad ﷺ is mentioned or read. Often written using Arabic calligraphy as ﷺ. The equivalent English phrase is usually abbreviated as S.A.W.

Sawm
Fasting. Plural: Siyam.

Sha'ban
The eighth month of the Islamic calendar.

Shaitan
Satan. Plural: Shayateen. See Iblis.

Shari'ah
Shari'ah (Islamic law) signifies the entire Islamic way of life.

Shawwal
The tenth month of the Islamic calendar.

Shirk
Shirk consists of associating anyone or anything with the Creator either in His being, or attributes, or in the exclusive rights (such as worship) that He has over His creatures.

Siratul-Mustaqeem
The straight path. This is the path that the Prophet Muhammad (ﷺ) demonstrated to mankind by way of the Quran. The path that leads to Paradise.

Siwak
A piece of branch or root of a tree called al-Araak used as a toothbrush.

Subhan Allah
"Glory be to Allah."

Subhana wa Ta'ala (SWT)
"May He be Glorified and Exalted."

Suhur
A meal taken before Fajr in the month of Ramadan before beginning the fast.

Sunnah
Ahadith and the way of Prophet Muhammad (ﷺ).

Sunnah Prayers
Sunnah Prayers are prayers which are considered recommended in view of the fact that the Prophet (ﷺ) either performed them often and/or made statements about their meritorious character.

Surah
A chapter of the Quran. Literally means "a form". There are 114 Surahs in the Quran. Plural: Suwar.

T:

Tafsir
A commentary, usually referring to the commentary of the Quran.

Taghut
Literally denotes the one who exceeds his/her legitimate limits. In Quranic terminology, it refers to anyone that exceeds his or her limit and adopts for themselves godhead and lordship. In the negative scale of values, the first stage of man's error is fisq (i.e. disobeying Allah without necessarily denying that one should obey Him). The second stage is that of kufr, (i.e. rejection of the very idea that one ought to obey Allah.) The last stage is that man not only rebels against Allah and transgresses Allah's rights, but also imposes his rebellious will on others. All those who reach this stage are taghut.

Tahajjud
Voluntary prayer that is done any time at night after Ishaa but before Fajr.

Tajweed
Recitation of the Quran with exact pronounciation.

Takbir
Saying "Allahu Akbar" ("Allah is the Greatest").

Talaq
The Arabic word for divorce which means 'freeing or undoing the knot'.

Talbiyah
The pronouncement pilgrims make to Allah during Hajj: "Labbaik, labbaik, Allahumma labbaik. La shareeka laka labbaik. Innal hamda wa n'imata laka walmulk. La shareeka lak." ("I am totally at Your service, I am totally at Your service, O Allah I am totally at Your service. You have no partner, I am totally at Your service. Truly, the praise and the blessing are Yours and the dominion. You have no partners.")

Taqwa
Fearing Allah as He should be feared. A major sign of being a faithful Muslim. See Quran, Al-Imran (3:102-103), Al-Hashr (59:18-19).

Taraweeh
Prayers conducted during Ramadan, the month of fasting.

Tashahhud
Literally 'testimony', a declaration of the Muslim faith recited towards the end of the prayers immediately after, the recitation of Tahiyah.

Tawaf
The circling of the Kabah. Tawaf is carried out in sets of seven circuits.

Tawbah
To come back; to turn towards someone.' Tawbah on the part of a Muslim signifies that they have given up disobedience and have returned to submission and obedience to Allah. The same word used in respect of Allah means that, He has mercifully turned to His repentant servant so that, the latter has once more become an object of His compassionate attention.

Tawheed
Oneness of Allah, The Divine Unity. Allah is One in His Essence and His Attributes and His Acts. This is the most important concept in Islam.

Tayammum
Literally means 'to intend to do a thing'. As an Islamic legal term, it refers to wiping one's hands and face with clean earth as a substitution for ablution when water cannot be obtained.

U:

Umayyad
One of the first dynasty of Caliphs after Prophet Muhammad (ﷺ) from the tribe of Quraish which reigned from 661 to 750 CE. During this time Damascus became the capital of an Islamic world which stretched from the western borders of China to southern France.

Ummah
Community, or nation; It particularly refers to Muslim brotherhood and unity. The Quran refers to Muslims as the best Ummah raised for the benefit of all mankind (3:110). At another place, (2:143), it calls them 'the middle nation' (Ummat ul-Wasat) a unique characteristic of the Islamic community which has been asked to maintain equitable balance between extremes: to pursue the path of moderation and establish the middle way. Such a community of Muslims will be a model for the whole world to emulate.

Ummul Mumineen
Mother of the Faithful. A title given to each of the wives of the Prophet Muhammad (ﷺ).

'Umrah
'Umrah (Minor Pilgrimage) is an Islamic rite and consists of pilgrimage to the Kaaba (See Kaaba). It consists essentially of ihram, tawaf (performing circuits) around the Kaaba (seven times) and sa'i (running) between Safa and Marwah (seven times). It is called minor Hajj since it need not be performed at a particular time of the year and its performance requires fewer ceremonies than the Hajj proper.

W:

Wa Alaikum Assalam
"And on you be peace." The reply to the Muslim greeting of 'assalamu alaikum'.

Wahy
Refers to revelation which consists of communicating Allah's Messages to a Prophet or Messenger of Allah. The highest form of revelation is the Quran.

Wali
Means guardian and more particularly refers to the legal guardian of a minor or representative of the bride at a Muslim wedding.

Walimah
A marriage banquet hosted and payed for by the groom.

Waqf
Endowment, a charitable trust in the name of Allah for the benefit of the general public.

Wudu
Refers to the ablution made before performing the prescribed Prayers.

Z:

Zaboor
The Holy Book revealed to Prophet Dawood (ﷺ).

Zakah
Literally means purification (purifying alms), whence it is used to express a portion of property bestowed in alms, as a means of purifying the person concerned and the remainder of their property. It is among the five pillars of Islam and refers to the mandatory amount that a

Muslim must pay out of his/her property. The detailed rules of Zakah have been laid down in books of Fiqh.

Zalim
A wrong-doer.

Zamzam
The sacred well inside Al-Haram ash-Shareef in Makkah, unearthed by the wife of Prophet Abraham (ﷺ), Hajira.

Index

A

List of abbreviations.

ﷺ: Arabic prayer 'may the peace and blessings of Allah be upon him' (transliteration - *salla Allahu alayhi wa sallam*). It is a religious recommendation for Muslims to repeat this phrase whenever the name of Prophet Muhammad (ﷺ) is mentioned or written.

عليه السلام: Arabic prayer 'peace be upon him' (transliteration - *alayhis salaam*). This statement is repeated whenever the names of any other Prophets (eg. Jesus, Moses, Abraham etc.) are mentioned or written.

رضى الله عنه: Arabic prayer 'may Allah be well pleased with him' (transliteration - *radia Allahu anhu*). This prayer is said whenever any of the male companions of Prophet Muhammad (ﷺ) are mentioned.

رضى الله عنها: Arabic prayer 'may Allah be well pleased with her' (transliteration - *radia Allahu anha*). This prayer is said whenever any of the female companions of Prophet Muhammad (ﷺ) are mentioned.

AH: After Hijra, Islamic dates are reckoned from the *Hijra* (the migration of the Prophet Muhammad (ﷺ) from Makkah to Madinah, in the year 622). They are usually written with the prefix AH or just H.

CE: The Common Era, sometimes known as the Current Era, begins with the year 1 on the Gregorian calendar. All dates throughout this book are Common Era dates unless stated otherwise.

BCE: Before Common Era.

Useful notes on this book.

i) Use of the words God and Allah.
In Islam, the proper name of God is the Arabic term 'Allah', hence the word 'Allah' has been used throughout this book. The reason for this is because, Allah is the personal name of 'The One and Only True Deity', who created the Universe and all that it contains. Moreover, the word 'Allah' expresses the uniqueness of 'Allah' more accurately than the word 'God', which can adopt a plural form, whereas the word 'Allah' has no plural. Furthermore, from an Islamic viewpoint, Allah is also the most precious name of God.

ii) Use of the word 'We' when referring to Allah.
Islam is based upon the central principle of the unity of Allah. So whenever Allah refers to Himself as 'We', this by no means denotes plurality of Godhead, rather it is what is termed the 'Royal We' or 'Majestic Plural'. When someone in authority, power, respect or high status uses the first person reference for themselves, the 'Royal We' is used to denote these very attributes.

iii) Quranic quotations.
These are referenced by giving the chapter name and number followed by the verse number in brackets. It is important to note that the English translation of the Quranic verses in this book by no means purport to be or to imitate the word of Allah Most High but only serve to give an understanding of the meaning.

iv) Hadith quotations.
Sayings and actions (in Arabic, *Sunnah*) of Prophet Muhammad (ﷺ) are taken from the authoritative collections of Saheeh Bukhari, Saheeh Muslim, Sunan Abu Dawud, Tirmidhi, an-Nasai, and Ibn Majah.

v) Use of italics.
Important Arabic names, places and terminology have been italicised and/or given in brackets.

'And All Praise is due to Allah, the Lord of the Worlds'